Behind Closed Doors

Behind Closed Doors

Why We Break Up Families –
and How to Mend Them

Polly Curtis

virago

VIRAGO

First published in Great Britain in 2022 by Virago

1 3 5 7 9 10 8 6 4 2

Typeset in Dante by M Rules
Printed and bound in Great Britain by
Clays Ltd, Elcograf S.p.A.

Papers used by Virago are from well-managed forests
and other responsible sources.

Virago
An imprint of
Little, Brown Book Group
Carmelite House
50 Victoria Embankment
London EC4Y 0DZ

An Hachette UK Company
www.hachette.co.uk

www.virago.co.uk

For everyone in this book,
because your stories matter

Do you cry out in your sleep?
All my failings exposed
Gets a taste in my mouth
As desperation takes hold
And it's something so good
Just can't function no more.
Love, love will tear us apart again

—JOY DIVISION

Open all doors.
Open all senses.
Open all defences.
Ask, what were these closed for?

—LEMN SISSAY

Contents

Preface   xi

PART ONE: How it works

Caitlin's story   'They didn't give me a chance'   3
The rise and rise of child removals

Alice's story   'It's a battle to stay in control'   28
Social workers, austerity and Baby P

Judge Wildblood's 'We've got to do something'   52
story   *Judges and their decisions*

PART TWO: What's really going on?

Francesca's story   'It's always the ones you don't suspect'   71
Class, privilege and poverty

Daniel's story   'Dad is not in the picture'   93
Invisible fathers

Kim's story   'You don't know what you're sending
them home to'   108
Schools, safety nets and the pandemic

Lucy's story   'The whole thing gets really toxic'   125
Lawyers and the trust gap

Gabrielle's story 'We could have done it – with support' 143
Race, ableism and the postcode lottery

Angela's story 'We are blaming mums who don't have anything' 168
The 'toxic trio' and loneliness

PART THREE: Consequences

My story 'What is good enough parenting?' 193
The judging of families

Nancy's story 'As normal as it can be' 208
Foster care and love

Emma and Sarah's story 'There are no fairy-tale endings' 224
Adoptions and afterwards

PART FOUR: Is there another way?

'To love is to act' 243
Relational activism and radical tenderness

A thought experiment 259

Author's note 281
Acknowledgements 287
Notes 291

Preface

In a country without the death penalty, separating a child from their parents is arguably the most draconian power the state has to intervene in our lives – in many ways as devastating as a life sentence, because the effect of that decision lasts for ever.

Family separation creates a trauma that is passed down, generation to generation, in a cycle that narrows people's chances of thriving at each step in a family tree. It's very hard to break that cycle.

The reality of separating a child from their parent, in the moment that it happens, is the stuff of nightmares. When my children were babies, I had a recurring nightmare that I couldn't find them. In the dream, their buggy would slip into a lake and they would be submerged in murky water. I couldn't see them. I would dive down again and again to try to find them. Sometimes I'd touch the buggy but couldn't drag it out. It was a physical, desperate, panicked feeling.

As a child I had felt something similar turning around in an open-air market to reach for my mum's hand and not being able to find it. I can still feel the hot rising terror, the tears welling up, feeling smaller and smaller the more I strained to see her through the crowds. I felt invisible without her. My eight-year-old described something similar to me. 'I get this feeling when I go round the corner and you can't see me,' he said. His worried eyes told me that the feeling he couldn't describe was terror.

The memory of those primal reactions returned when I watched footage from the US–Mexican border as the Trump administration enacted its policy of separating migrant parents from their children. Families split up by the authorities as punishment for their parents' efforts to get to America. The unspeakable cruelty of ignoring that most basic need – to be with your family – haunted the world; and it tested the limits of populist America. It had me waking in the night with the terrors again.

These nightmares, both real and imagined, are something I never thought I'd see anything close to in the England that I grew up in. But the authorities in England now separate more children from their families than at any point since current records began in the early 1990s. We're one of relatively few countries that practise 'non-consensual' adoption – or forced adoption, as critics call it. We do it far more than other Western countries.

Of course, we don't remove children from their families to punish anyone, or through any wilful cruelty. Rather, the authorities have a legal responsibility to protect children from abusive or neglectful parents. Social workers go into the profession with the very best intentions – they are, in many ways, the heroes of this story – but the system is stacked against them. The number of children being removed from their families has been steadily increasing to the current record highs. It wasn't planned and no one – including those working at the heart of the system, who spend their lives thinking about it – even really agrees why it has happened.

At the time of writing, there are 80,000 children in care in England. One of the most senior judges in the family courts, who led a working group to investigate the problem, told me that his group of experts estimated there are around 27,000 children in the care system who, with the right help, should never have even come to court and could have stayed with their parents. We are removing too many children from their parents. We are not giving families a chance to stay together. It's an open secret within the system.

A judge's decision to remove a child from their family involves a complex balancing of the state's responsibility to protect that child from harm against human rights laws that protect the right to family life free from state interference. But the dysfunctions within families aren't cured by separation: they are simply put on hold, while the trauma can make existing problems worse and entrench a profound distrust in the state that is then passed down through generations.

If we hold up the decision of when to remove a child as a prism through which to view society, it exposes some intolerable truths. This is a system riddled with class bias and prejudice against different ethnic groups and people of different abilities; it is a system that punishes isolation, focuses its powers on marginalised, vulnerable women and dismisses and ignores fathers. Communities who are subject to the system know this and it has eroded any trust that there was. There are parallels with the growing mistrust in other establishments and authorities that has been linked to the rise of populist governments across the world. But in this case it strikes at the heart of families. This book returns to the idea of that prism as we unpick the elements that have led to the removal of so many children from their parents and families and understand what it tells us about the kind of society we live in.

If the biggest test of a society is how it looks after its most vulnerable, then we are failing. The social contract between families and the state is now broken. The result is a battle of state v family. We need to talk about it. But we also need to stop the cycle of removal and find a way to help families stay together, safely.

Investigating and researching for this book took me across England, to Sunderland, Bradford, Leeds, Bristol, Birmingham, the West Midlands and London. I spent days in the family courts watching the ebb and flow of broken families. I sat in people's living rooms and heard their stories. I went to France to meet the British man who pays for women to flee social services; and I went to New York to learn how that city transformed a system facing similar problems to England. I held a series of eight public events, bringing people together from across the system to debate what's going wrong, and how it can be improved. This book tells the story of the systemic drift of our welfare state, through the dramatic and moving stories of the people who experience it. Each chapter introduces someone who has been involved – the mothers, a father, a social worker, a lawyer, a judge and more – and draws a portrait from their perspective. Taken together, I hope their stories build the deeper understanding I strive for.

Some of these stories might seem at times contradictory – I tell of dramatic interventions to whip a child out of their home; and of years of failure to intervene and support them to stay there safely. What underpins both these extremes is the eroding of the state's ability to make the hardest decisions well. As this book was going to press, the tragic news about Arthur Labinjo-Hughes's abuse and murder was reported, shocking the nation and instigating calls to remove children from their families faster. But we have a system that is both removing too many children, and failing to save some of those most at risk. Both these things are true because we are not equipping our children's social care system well. They are two symptoms of the same problem and a breathtaking double failure of our state.

In both these scenarios – the children separated too soon and those left behind – the prism reveals the worst failures of the state.

In recent years the focus has been on those left behind, minds focused by the appalling failures to intervene to save children like Peter Connelly – known as Baby P. This book looks at the other, more hidden end: the slide into removing more children and the damage that does. It doesn't deny that there are still children like Baby P left in unsafe homes, but shows the other kinds of damage we are doing when we remove children suddenly and without trying to support them to live safely with their parents.

The reality of removing a child can be as profound and violent as the family separations on the border in America. It is the horror of my nightmares. It involves unearthly screams, and parents' panicked, primal fights for their babies. But it can also involve the quiet wearing away of family ties, purely because we as a state failed to help that family to stay together.

This is a system designed to balance a child's safety with

their right to family life that has now drifted so far from its original purpose that some people are questioning whether it's possible to save it. I explore an alternative: a system built on a strong, supportive society and fuelled not by process and defence, but by love.

PART ONE

How it works

Caitlin's story

'They didn't give me a chance'

The rise and rise of child removals

Caitlin stands frozen, watching the scene unfold before her. She can't move. She can't breathe. She feels like she's in that dream when you open your mouth and you can't scream.

Her toddler Adam is trapped in her partner's grip, his face pushed up against a wall.[1] The sharp edge of a wooden panel is cutting into his cheek and splitting his lip. It is starting to bleed. Adam is screaming. Even with his cries in her ears, Caitlin doesn't react. His eyes say more to her than the sound he is making. His expression is pure fear.

Caitlin's mind moves too slowly to respond. She can't understand what she's seeing or how she arrived at this moment. She can't comprehend that the man she loves so much is hurting the little boy who is absolutely dependent on her for his safety. She can't fathom her own actions: why is she not tearing this attacker away from her baby? The only thought she can hold on to in her head is a question: How is this our life?

Over time his campaign of abuse mounts. Caitlin avoids the house more and more, she hangs around at mother and baby groups at a local children's centre after sessions finish, chatting and making friends, putting off going home. She tells herself stories about how the bruises appeared – Adam was always an active baby, he *did* sometimes headbutt hard surfaces accidentally. She sometimes convinces herself that maybe it wasn't her partner doing it. But her little boy's behaviour is changing and telling her the truth. He stops speaking and refuses to eat. He won't sleep at night. When her partner isn't around he has tantrums, screaming his name in terror.

How Caitlin ended up terrified in her own home, suffering emotional and physical abuse and now watching her son being hurt, was bewildering to her. She was nineteen and a very lonely single mother when she fell in love with this man. She had had Adam when she was just sixteen and his father was never involved. She met her new partner at a party. He bought her food and clothes and looked after her. Her son warmed to him immediately. As a young single parent without much support – her own mum was an alcoholic and had left the family some years before – she thought this man offered her love for the first time. It felt like he was taking over just when she was struggling to make her life work. She was grateful.

He did take over. In increments he invaded her head, undermined her confidence, and made her feel that whatever he did was her fault. At first it was relatively subtle. He developed an obsession that she was flirting with the local pet shop worker, flying off the handle every time she came back from buying dog food. Then one time he disappeared for two days and in the argument on his return he destroyed a room, punching through a glass window. He started to control her spending to the point where she was squeezing her son's feet into too-small trainers to avoid the expense of a new pair.

By this stage he was monitoring her wardrobe and her phone, policing who she could talk to. The aggression got worse; from punching walls, he began to punch her. But there was a colder menace to his abuse as well: he would refuse to talk to her or acknowledge her presence for days on end. This was almost the worst, the stony, threatening silence and withdrawal of the love that she had so craved. She chased harder, tried to please more and to make amends.

The slide from saviour to abuser was so gradual, yet so shocking, that she could hardly process what was happening. There was no moment when she realised she had lost control, just a steady campaign to take over her life. She made excuses. 'He's just being a man, a typical man,' she said of his jealousy. Blows landed on days that he was 'finding hard', she told herself. She began to question her own sanity and that it was even happening at all.

But it was happening, and it was happening on a daily basis – and Adam was seeing, or hearing, it all. His attention then turned to Adam, first by criticising her parenting and urging her to smack her son as punishment – something she refused to do. Then by taking on the 'discipline' himself, which began in that moment with Adam's face pressed up against the wall, but was quickly followed by bruises appearing on his small body.

The first time Caitlin saw her son being hit, a grown man's blow on his backside, it was punishment for having soiled himself and it was just before a support worker was due a visit. The worker arrived in the aftermath, called social services, and they ordered a medical observation, which identified thirty-three separate bruises or marks on his body.

An interim care order was made – a legal decision by a judge in the family courts that gives the social workers in the council powers to remove a child and place them with a foster carer. When they took Adam, Caitlin walked away in the same numb state of disbelief. The mind can play tricks in these traumatic moments, running parallel narratives. On one hand the teenager knew what her boyfriend was doing and was just relieved that her boy was safe; on the other hand her partner was so inside her head, controlling her thoughts, that she second guessed herself. Maybe she was going mad? Maybe they were all accidents? Maybe this was an injustice?

The result was that Caitlin covered for her boyfriend, explaining away the marks on her son's body. She kept covering for him until he turned on her and blamed her for the abuse. She ended up in the criminal courts with a suspended sentence for child neglect. And she was pregnant again.

She covered for her abusive partner so much that even after she managed to leave him, she couldn't tell the social workers that he was stalking her and turning up wherever she went, because seeing him would add to the case against her keeping her boy. While pregnant she was in the social workers' process of 'parallel planning': they plan for two scenarios where either a mother keeps her newborn or the baby is removed at birth. No decision can be made until the baby arrives, because there is no child to protect until after the birth. There was little support for her at that point because the system is focused on protecting children, and with Adam by then in care and her second son still in her womb, there was, the logic followed, no one who needed protecting at that point. The conditions were created for a slow, inevitable car crash.

After she gave birth, Caitlin moved to a mother and baby unit. That's where the social workers came for Jason, when he was just a few months old. 'We're going to take him now,' the social worker said. Two taxis were positioned outside the building, one containing her possessions, one full of baby stuff. The second car pulled away with her little boy inside. A silence enveloped her and with it that now-familiar sense of numbness, the dissociation from a trauma. She arrived at her new home to flowers, sent by a friend. She was trying to arrange them, but for some reason she couldn't hold on to anything or steady herself. She realised she had collapsed on the floor, rocking back and forth as she tried to stab flowers into the florist foam at the bottom of a vase. She couldn't feel anything other than the tilting of the room around her.

A little while later she met one of the other mums who had been at the mother and baby unit that day. She recalled a totally different version of events: not of silence but of Caitlin's screams, that tore through the building and terrified every other parent within earshot.

It's a sound Caitlin can't recall, but no one who heard it will ever forget it.

To get to grips with why we have become a society that removes more children than at any time since current records began, we can think of the child protection system as a prism into the wider problems of the society it serves. Changes in our collective economic fortunes, public health problems, social norms and political rhetoric all play out in the lives of families and the decisions made by social workers and the courts across the country every day.

Caitlin's case is just one of many thousands that have

been through the social services and courts system in the past decade, and at an accelerating rate. During the past ten years alone, the number of children in care in England has increased by a third to over 80,080 in 2020. We have quietly become one of the most interventionist states in the world. The number of children adopted from the care system annually has almost doubled from 2,000 to around 3,440 in the same time frame.[2]

Most people only hear about this when there is a catastrophic failure on the part of social services and a child dies in horrific circumstances. The deaths of Victoria Climbié and then Peter Connelly (better known as 'Baby P') were met by intense scrutiny, with the services that should have protected them taking much of the blame. It's well documented that interventions went up in the wake of those scandals.[3] One London social worker tells me that the fear of another scandal of this kind is now embedded in the thinking and decision-making of social work departments: 'Some managers worry about that more than anything.'

But the increase in children in the care system predates both these cases and has been almost steadily rising since the current records began in the early 1990s. Those harrowing, high-profile cases triggered significant spikes in the line graph that documents this rise, but the overall trend is more long-standing and less well understood. In fact, it illustrates many of the forces that have reshaped society over that time.

The biggest single risk factor in a child going into care is deprivation. Across the UK, children are ten times more likely to be in care if they live in the poorest 10% of areas, as opposed to the wealthiest 10%.[4] Social workers talk about a 'pincer effect' of deprivation and austerity since the Conservative/Lib Dem coalition government began its programme of spending cuts in 2010. Poverty has in fact flatlined in England over the period, levelling out after years of steady decline, according to research by the Joseph Rowntree Foundation,[5] while austerity has consumed local budgets and councils' capacity to support families effectively.

Manchester has one of the most hard-pressed social services systems in the country. A study in 2018 found that 48% of under-fives had been referred to council workers – the highest rate in the country.[6] One Manchester social worker told me: 'Poverty is the number one issue. If people had a bigger house, more money, they could be OK. But that poverty can trigger something bad to happen – or stop your ability to weather something bad happening.'

Social workers describe how austerity has worn away the tools they have to support families, to refer them for support services or spend the time with them that they need, leaving nothing but the nuclear option of taking them to court. Some of these services are now so rationed that parents fail to qualify for mental health support, or help to escape domestic violence – yet in a cruel irony that same mental health problem or abusive partner then becomes the reason their kids are taken into care.

A family lawyer I spoke to in Bradford described a client desperate for her daughter to return from the residential care she had been sent to because of her mother's abusive partner. The partner is gone, but the fifteen-year-old is stuck in care because while everyone agrees they need family therapy, none is available. The care costs £10,000 a month in social worker visits, foster care allowances and the supervision they require; the cost of therapy would be a fraction of that.

A 2018 study authored by the Chief Social Worker, Isabelle Trowler, warned that without services available to support families, 'social workers have few options but to initiate proceedings; the thin red line is crossed and families find themselves on a conveyor belt into court'.[7] And it's not just social workers saying this. Sir Andrew McFarlane, President of the Family Division of the High Court, in a speech ahead of taking up the position last year, warned that it was easier to take a child into care than to get them support. The language may be more legalistic, but the message is the same: 'It may properly be said that we have reached a stage where the threshold for obtaining a public law court order is noticeably low, whereas, no doubt as a result of the current financial climate, the threshold for a family being able to access specialist support services in the community is conversely very high.'

We are removing some children from their parents for want of timely mental health treatment. This alone is a monumental failure of the state and its relationship with its most vulnerable people.

Poverty plays out in people's lives in different ways. Social workers talk of the 'toxic trio' that leads to children going into care: substance abuse, domestic abuse and mental illness. All three can affect anyone but they are all more prevalent among poorer people – and, as we will examine later on, more strictly policed. Some add learning disabilities as a fourth category. For Caitlin, domestic abuse and her own poor mental health were the predominant issue in her family's life. Social workers focus on these obvious problems, despite the fact that they are, in part, symptoms of a poverty that in itself is just too big to contemplate, too seemingly unmanageable.

Meanwhile, different and more complex risks to children have emerged in local areas. Scandals in Rotherham and Rochdale exposed a hidden world of child sexual exploitation, and social services began to focus on their role in preventing it. Gang violence has drawn in younger and younger children, with the child protection system stepping in to remove young people from violent and dangerous situations. The number of unaccompanied asylum seekers has also risen, increasing social services' responsibilities in that remit, particularly in council areas where those children arrive.

Most people agree that poverty, austerity and increasingly complex social issues affect the rates of children in care. Thinking of the system as that prism into wider society, and considering those problems, you could begin to wonder why in fact our rates of intervention are not higher. But the extent of these effects is contested. The story is much more complicated.

As Chief Social Worker, Isabelle Trowler is based at the Department for Education in Westminster, where she advises ministers on the issues facing the sector. A quietly independent figure, her skills were honed reforming social work in the east London borough of Hackney. She urges me to examine the nuances of the debate and warns against simplistic narratives. Austerity might have affected the services available, but the increase in children going into care predated the beginning of the austerity cuts in 2010. 'You have to decide what's really going on. Everyone has a whole range of incentives to say and believe certain things. You hear lots of stories about increased poverty, reductions in public spending, complexity. I'm really sceptical that it's only those things.'

Trowler paints a picture of shifting societal norms and expectations. Smacking is no longer acceptable, parents are now expected to speak less sharply and listen more intently to their children. 'We have seen a shift in what society is prepared to accept as a standard of parenting they can tolerate,' she says. 'When that happens, that social shift, that ricochets into social work decision-making and court decision-making. If you look at history, abuse now was not considered abuse thirty years ago; every so often that shifts. There is a much lower level of tolerance for it.'

Trowler's argument plays out in the evidence. According to data published by the Education Policy Institute,[8] since 2010 the number of children taken into care because of physical and sexual abuse has remained steady. Meanwhile, the rise in overall cases is being fuelled by social workers increasingly recommending that children be put on a protection plan because of neglect or emotional abuse – and in many cases the risk that they might face such abuse in the future rather than evidence that it has actually happened.

The laws governing how the state can intervene in family life are set out in the Children Act 1989, which for three decades has remained unchanged as more and more children have come into the system.

The Children Act states that proceedings should be pursued when a child 'is suffering or is likely to suffer significant harm'. Two major things have changed in the thirty years since that law was enacted: first, the understanding of what constitutes harm; and second, a shift from interventions at the point of harm, to an anticipation of harm. This is why interventions on the basis of physical and sexual abuse have remained relatively consistent, while interventions for neglect and emotional abuse have risen. An accelerator to that was the 2015 law that introduced the concept of 'coercive and controlling' domestic abuse, shifting the understanding of what constitutes abuse from purely physical to psychological as well.

As we've seen, the number of children in care has been increasing almost steadily year on year since current records began twenty-five years ago. There are multiple layers of causes driving that trend: increased risk aversion driven by public scrutiny of decision-making in high-profile cases such as Peter Connelly, changes in how we recognise abuse and neglect, and a shift in attitudes to parenting. But the combination of this ideological shift with deprivation and decreasing budgets to support families has compounded those effects. Each element may be understood and justified in isolation, but in combination the impact has been an ever-increasing rise in numbers of children going into the care system.

This systematic shift in how we police parenting in England was not the result of any formal policy: it wasn't debated in public forums, listed in a party manifesto or communicated in any meaningful way to the people who would feel its impact for years to come. Rather, it was a cumulative process of unintended consequences and drift in a system which has resulted in a very different society.

We never intended to create one of the biggest systems of child removal in the world, one that costs the taxpayer £9bn a year.[9] We never set out to create a system that fuels mistrust in the authorities and then bakes that mistrust into the psyche of families for generations to come.

But we have.

*

The prism of the child protection system, and what it shows us about how society has changed, is the story of Caitlin's life.

In the end, her children weren't permanently removed because of the physical abuse Adam had suffered at the hands of her ex-partner – he was long gone by then. Caitlin knows she was making progress, but therapy wasn't available at that point to help her and looking back she is left wondering if she would still have her children if she could have been helped to make swifter progress.

Another factor that is likely to have counted against her is the hypothetical concern. There was also a 'future risk of emotional harm': that Caitlin might get into another abusive relationship and fail again to prioritise her children's needs. It's hard to compute this thinking – that a child could be removed from a loving parent to mitigate the risk of them getting into another abusive relationship with someone, one day. Imagine how it must feel to know you could be paying the greatest price for something you've not yet done – or that happening in any other area of the justice system.

But those are the thoughts Caitlin has to live with.

My experiences tell me that there may well have been another issue making it harder for the children to stay with her. Caitlin had become an expert at masking her problems and convincing people of her worthiness to parent, and inevitably that will have led to concerns that she might continue to see her abuser and hide it from everyone. That would lead to an impression that she couldn't be trusted to tell the truth about what was going on. She had initially covered for him, so gripped was she in his psychological control. But once she had escaped, even though she was being stalked by him, she could not go to her social workers for help.

Imagine being the social worker, faced with a history of abuse, terrible mental health problems and no resources to support Caitlin. Now imagine Caitlin is lying to you and you don't know what to believe – how would you assess the risk to the children?

Caitlin was still seeing the children four times a week in supervised contact sessions. The court decided they were to be adopted permanently.

In Caitlin's case, as she tells her story, you can picture the difficult process of balancing her needs against her children's. What the courts must decide is whether she has a chance to get to a point of parenting them well, within a timescale that doesn't cause too much suffering along the way. This is the heart of the debate about whether too many – or indeed not enough – children are being removed from their families. It is fiercely political.

At one end of the spectrum you have those who argue we are removing children with too much gusto, such has the faith in families withered away; at the other end you have those who argue we are still giving parents too many chances to change when the evidence shows that they rarely do. Should Caitlin have been given another chance to redeem her parenting, or was the best interest of her children served by finding them a new stable home, and fast?

Sir Martin Narey has spent a career navigating this debate and seeing its consequences up close.[10] He ran the prison service of England and Wales between 1998 and 2003, then went into child protection as Chief Executive of Barnardo's. In 2013 he was appointed a special adviser to the then secretary of state for education, Michael Gove. He has conducted reviews of the adoption process and into residential children's homes, and the reform of social work education. I interviewed him by phone at the beginning of my research. He argues that children should be removed more swiftly, without a delay in which permanent damage can be done.

'A good system would intervene much more quickly,' he says. He describes how the system could get locked into supporting 'poor sad' mothers, and trying to help them reunite with their child, but it all comes at a cost to that child. 'Of course we shouldn't be casual about taking children into care. The thought of someone taking your kids away is second only to death. But that doesn't mean it's not necessary. There's a general view we have too many children in care. We are quicker to intervene with families – and that's absolutely right and in the interest of the child.'

He pauses, then adds: 'The system is not perfect. I know. I sometimes help parents who have lost their children; they have been able to convince me that a mistake has been made. Of course the system gets it wrong. But you have to remember the hard evidence is that people who are left in harmful homes are profoundly damaged.'

Over the past twenty years, Narey has been an influential voice in an increasing political appetite for adoption. Tony Blair's Labour government began the work of advocating for faster intervention and swifter adoptions. Then in 2011 Gove, the then secretary of state responsible, introduced reforms to speed up the process of resolving childcare proceedings. His theory was fuelled by Narey's argument: children who are removed from abusive or neglectful homes, then quickly placed in permanent homes, do better. The evidence showed that children who bounce around in the care system fare badly compared to their classroom peers – they were more likely to fail their exams and leave school at sixteen; then they were much more likely to go to prison, end up homeless and, ultimately, their own children were more likely to be removed in the future.

Narey's thinking is backed up by the last twenty years of research into how early childhood experiences impact brain development and can dictate a child's future. The quality of care you receive, and on the flipside the levels of stress you experience, can hardwire your brain for life, and difficult, if not impossible, to reverse at a later stage.

On the positive side, brain development – and specifically the 'softer' skills of resilience, grit and confidence – are aided by the quality of interactions between a parent and a child from a very early age. One formative paper from Harvard University, 'The Science of Neglect', describes the 'serve and return' interactions between a child and their parent.[11] A baby smiles; the parent smiles back. Then a baby makes a sound and the parent returns it, building the foundations of conversation. One day they find themselves playing peekaboo. 'If the responses are unreliable, inappropriate, or simply absent, the developing architecture of the brain may be disrupted, and later learning, behavior, and health may be impaired,' the paper says. Much of the research that built this understanding was developed from studying the experiences of children who had been severely neglected in institutions in China and Romania.

As the science behind the quality of parenting was developing, so was the understanding of the impact of severe stress in childhood. The term Adverse Childhood Experiences (ACEs) was coined at the end of the 1990s, after studies which identified ten categories of neglect and abuse that can have profound, long-term impacts on a child's ability to thrive. They are:

1. Living with an adult who threatens or humiliates you
2. Being hit or slapped or injured by an adult you live with
3. Sexual abuse
4. A persistent feeling that no one is loving or supporting you
5. Parental separation or divorce
6. Lacking the basics of food or clothes
7. Domestic abuse within the family
8. Living with an alcoholic or drug user
9. Living with someone who is suffering mental illness
10. Having a household family member in prison

Children can experience one or two of these and still thrive, and they can survive more if they have received good parenting – through the serve and return interactions – that has helped instil in them an underlying confidence and grit to weather storms. But as the number and severity of these experiences increase, the greater the adversity that child is likely to face through their life. The American Nobel prize-winning economist James Heckman summed up the grim impact of this roll-call of experiences: 'Early adverse experiences correlate with poor adult health, high medical care costs, increased depression and suicide rates, alcoholism, drug use, poor job performance and social function, disability, and impaired performance in subsequent generations.'[12]

The debate around Adverse Childhood Experiences came on the back of the most famous research that underpins much of parenting theory now. John Bowlby, a British psychologist, developed the idea of Attachment Theory after growing up being cared for by nannies, who would abruptly leave, and only seeing his mother for an hour a day. Working in the 1960s alongside other notable psychologists, including Mary Ainsworth, Bowlby cemented the idea of the importance of close parent-baby contact in the early years for developing healthy relationships later in life.

In the UK, the Childhood Wellbeing Research paper further propelled this to the front of policy formation.[13] That study sets out the four states of parental attachment: secure; insecure and avoidant; insecure and ambivalent; and insecure and disorganised.

Hostile, rejecting and controlling parenting causes children to over-regulate their emotions, feeling unlovable and displaying anxious behaviour; these are the 23% with insecure, avoidant attachment. Children who are 'insecure and ambivalent' have parents who are inconsistent, unreliable or neglectful – the children work harder for parental attention but can mirror their parents' behaviour by switching tactics to get the attention they crave. Around 8% of children without a clinical diagnosis of any kind display these traits. Children who are cared for by people who are frightening or dangerous develop disorganised attachment. They struggle to remain in command of their own behaviour and reactions as a result. The same paper concluded that in the general population, about 15% of children fall into this category – but over 80% of children brought up in neglectful or abusive homes display these behaviours.

'A child's environment of relationships – particularly those with their caregivers – plays a critical role in shaping the development of their overall brain architecture,' the report said. 'Very early experiences need to be rich in touch, face to face contact and stimulation through conversation (or reciprocating baby babble). These stimuli encourage a deeply networked brain, particularly the regions which govern social aspects of life.'

Advances in the understanding of the impact of neglect and emotional abuse have informed the rise in children going into care. It is well reasoned that children should be given a permanent home quickly. The pendulum swung towards those swifter decisions, but it happened at a time that the alternative, supporting a family to stay together, was weakened by austerity.

It became in many cases the de facto choice. Stability has become the number-one priority in the courts' decision-making, and they are judged in turn by how rigorously they stick to the twenty-six-week target for resolving care proceedings. In the legal lexicon, this is known as the child's 'timescales'.

But no one ever added 'being separated from your parents by being taken into care' to the list of Adverse Childhood Experiences.

Ultimately, the choice between the known risk of their homes and the unknown risk of removing a child is made blind.

For Caitlin, who happens to be talking to me seven years to the day after her sons were permanently adopted, the word 'timescale' has a haunting resonance. She was told to write a letter to her children to apologise for not making the changes quickly enough. 'I absolutely hate the word "time-scales". I heard it so many times and repeatedly. But I didn't know how to make those changes without help. Once I had the right support, I could do it, but it was too late.'

Caitlin is now thriving but will always be angry that the system didn't have the same urgency to support her as it had for her children. If it did, she might have got the help she needed in time for them to stay together. The clock was against her from the start. Even if a parent wants to improve and become capable of looking after their own children, their fate lies in the hands of authorities that often lack the funding to provide the necessary help.

Throughout the two years of the court process Caitlin had access to some therapy, but mostly CBT (cognitive behaviour therapy), which did not prove to be helpful. The therapist who she met right after the adoption, who she says was central to her recovery, later said she would have improved in six months had she had access to the right therapy at the right time. By that interpretation, her children were removed because of an institutional scarcity of support for Caitlin to change.

The extent of people's capacity to change is disputed. There are those who argue that parents have historically been given too much benefit of the doubt, leading to their children bouncing around the system, in and out of care for years, until the instability and repeated failure to settle has left them scarred for life. In this analysis, putting the child first means less tolerance of parental shortcomings and a more sceptical approach to their capacity to change. That's why a parent's upbringing is so hardwired into the decision-making process.

As one judge noted in a published judgment, the risk of harm 'flows from the traumas which happened to the parents when they themselves were young. We are all the people we are because of what has happened to us throughout our lives, and these parents are no different'.[14]

Change is demanded to be linear: you're in a bad place, you get some support, you improve. But the reality is that the changes families need to make don't tend to happen in linear ways. Drug addicts relapse, domestic violence victims forgive their abusers, and mental health is not always something you simply recover from: it's more often something that, if you're lucky, you can learn to manage.

Studies expose the complexity of trying to assess a person's ability to change.[15] Academics highlight three factors that impact the ability to change in relation to child protection cases: first, a parent's own psychology – their ability to conceptualise what's going wrong and their responsibility for it; second, the external factors bearing down on them in terms of housing, employment or educational problems; and third, their relationship with the professionals involved in their case.

And then there's how these three factors interlock. In courts, emphasis is placed on the first of these, the parent's psychological dynamics. Evidence is made of their behaviour, their histories, their own experiences of the care system, of abandonment and of abuse. These behaviours are inherited and passed down, but for people who spend their lives trying to escape their past, to be forced to replay it can intensify their feelings of injustice.

Caitlin doesn't deny that she made huge mistakes in her parenting. We often look for the perfect victim to illustrate these stories. Caitlin wouldn't necessarily make the grade for that case study. She knows she made mistakes that she is judged for.

But she accepts that responsibility. In fact, at the time of her case she was so busy blaming herself for what had happened, she didn't even believe that she had the right to be a parent. Now – with time, therapy and a lot of reflection – she thinks there is responsibility to be shared. 'They needed to get me away from my ex. There's always more that could be done and sometimes you just need to hear the truth. If they had said to me, "If you do not split up with him you are going to lose the children for ever because they are not safe", I would have done it.'

Instead, Caitlin was punished.

'Why was no one helping me? Why wasn't he suffering the consequences? Now, it's about taking responsibility for all the mistakes I've made that has helped me heal. But I also need to be able to blame the right people for things. Blaming my ex for his part, social services for their part, and when I lied to cover up, I take responsibility for that. I know what I did was wrong, but I know that's not what posed the greatest threat to my babies. I know deep in my heart what has happened is unjustified. I wish I knew that then. I definitely would have fought. I just thought it was all my fault.'

Just entering the child protection system can become a self-fulfilling prophecy. Being watched changes your parenting. 'The moment when you give birth is the moment when you're supposed to bond with your child. I remember when I had Adam, I couldn't take my eyes off him. I'd stare at him for hours. But with my second I didn't because I felt like they could take him at any moment,' she says. 'The first twenty-four hours I could not look at him. I fed him, changed his nappy – I still took care of him but I felt like I wasn't allowed to love him.'

As we talk about Caitlin's own childhood, I mentally tick off the list of Adverse Childhood Experiences I hear about. Her mother was an alcoholic, who herself grew up in care. More than half of women who have had multiple children placed in care were in care themselves. Caitlin wasn't, but only because her dad picked up the pieces. But she sometimes wishes she had been, because despite his best efforts he just couldn't give her the protection she needed.

This is the cycle that the care system creates; and one that is so hard to break.

Social workers consider having been in care as a risk factor in suspected abuse or neglect. For Caitlin, even her mum saw it coming. When she, at sixteen, told her mum the news, the response she received was: 'I knew you would get pregnant.' Now she questions this. 'If she knew that, why didn't she do anything about it?'

Caitlin consciously tried to do things differently. When she was a little girl her mum threatened to slap her for blowing bubbles into her milk through a straw until it spilled on the table. When Adam did the same she set some boundaries: he could only blow when the milk was halfway down the glass, so it didn't make a mess. Abide by that rule and she would join in blowing her own straw and racing him to the top. 'It sounds stupid but those little things made me think I'd be different.' She was trying, in vain, to break the cycle.

Place Caitlin's story against the backdrop of wider changes in society that were driving the rising numbers of children in care, and you see where it fits. The removal of Caitlin's children happened just as the political dial was shifting towards more interventions, to being less tolerant of the mothers' experiences. It was at a time when austerity was biting into the budgets available to support Caitlin with her problems and help her become fit to parent. It also happened in the aftermath of the death of Peter Connelly, when social workers were under pressure to avoid risk. She vividly remembers one social worker saying to her: 'Why should I believe you? Peter Connelly's mum lied.'

After the adoption order was made, the months and years passed in a blur for Caitlin, and she credits a handful of close friends, and her clinical psychologist, for helping her climb out of the abyss. She now works with councils and families to try to reshape social services and put families back at the heart of their solutions when things are going wrong. As she recovered, Caitlin realised that she wanted to work to change the system. But she also realised that if she went in all guns blazing she would come across as another loud-mouthed disgruntled parent. 'I thought, If I'm going to do this I need to be smart. I need to make friends with these people; I need to be in their pockets. I need to be doing things differently,' she says.

Caitlin has brought together a group of parents, social workers, academics and psychologists to advocate for change in the system. They offer support to parents who are in the process of legal proceedings, they consult with organisations within the care and social work sectors to include parents' voices in their strategies and processes, and offer training on how to 'co-produce' services with families. The same councils that once labelled her not good enough invite her back in to help improve the system.

I watch Caitlin in action facilitating a training day in the swish King's Cross offices of Camden Council, with their panoramic views over the new Google HQ to the capital beyond. There are over a hundred people, but Caitlin has a presence that makes them all listen. You know when she is in the room. Her eyes dart from person to person, working out the dynamic and how to navigate it. Social workers from all over the country are gathered to hear about the pioneering work at the Central London authority. She hollers to get everyone's attention, chairs the panels and keeps everyone laughing along the way.

Ten years previously, a council recommended the permanent removal of her two children. She gets a sense of satisfaction from being able to walk into that building and command respect from the kind of authorities that once judged her.

Caitlin now lives across the city, near the banks of the River Thames. Her two-bedroom flat on the fifth floor is neat and homely. Her huge sofa swallows me up and the views stretch out across the capital. She lives with Freddy, her partner of three and a half years, who is training to be a social worker. He drifts in and out as we talk, checking in on her as she tells her story, appearing out of nowhere the first time she cries, as she recalls the day her son was removed.

Caitlin still sees her boys twice a year for a few hours. She's private about the time they spend together. It's important to her and sometimes very difficult, affecting her mood for long stretches either side of their meetings. She knows that at some point they will turn eighteen and have the option to dictate the relationship they want with her.

Her main complaint is that the social workers and courts

didn't do everything within their powers to keep her family together. They reached for the nuclear button, despite the fact that there was help that could have kept them together. But she also argues that adoption is considered a magic bullet that erases all the problems that came before – and she contests that.

'So much happens within the moment of the decision to separate a family,' Caitlin says. 'Everything is done quickly so children aren't affected too much, but the children are affected regardless.'

Caitlin pauses and then says something that reverberates around my mind for months afterwards: 'The system is not set up for people like me. "People like me" meaning people who have been through oppression, poverty, people who have been discriminated against because of the way you look, the way you sound, the way you dress, because you're young, because you're black, because you're Asian, because of whatever you are.

'I always had social services involved in my life and every time they failed me, from when I was a little kid. When I really needed them they failed me again by sweeping everything under the carpet and saying, "You've done this, you must suffer the consequences." And I thought, Yes, I might suffer. Because that's what I've always done: suffer the consequences, put a face on and got on with it.'

Alice's story

'It's a battle to stay in control'

Social workers, austerity and Baby P

Alice looks at the stack of files in her hands. There are three, each five inches thick, and together they weigh as much as her own arm. The pages document the life of a thirteen-year-old child that her supervisor is charging her with safeguarding. 'This mother is going to be one of the most difficult people you ever work with and you will learn more from this than any other case I could give you,' her supervisor says. It's Alice's first case in child protection. She's only twenty-five. Her more experienced colleagues choke on their tea when they hear the name of the girl her superior is tasking her with: Jemima.[1]

Jemima has been known to this social work department since before she was born, and her case predates everyone working there now. Her two younger siblings are also part of the case. Her mother has a complex personality disorder and has, for thirteen years, danced circles around this team.

The family dynamics are so complicated and difficult to manage that her last two social workers moved to different jobs to escape the case.

Alice looks down at the file, hears the sharp intakes of breath from her colleagues, and decides two things: one, she's not going to read the whole file and fill her head with more than a decade of other people's opinions; she'll make her own mind up. Two, she's going to find a way to help this family.

It's in Alice's nature to be bloody-minded; her determination to make a difference brought her into social work in the first place.

Jemima and her siblings are 'children in need', meaning social services are involved and providing support to the family on a voluntary basis. They are not at the point of child protection where social workers have more powers to compel a parent to comply with what they think is best for the child. Once a month the children spend a weekend with foster carers to give their mother a break.

Alice arranges the first meeting at the council buildings with the mother, who is loath to let social workers into her house. Alice is surprised when instead of a grown woman, she's met by the thirteen-year-old Jemima. She wears an immaculate, preppy uniform. Her hair is beautifully braided. Her trainers are brand new. Her school record shows huge academic promise. It's not the image of a neglected child Alice had been taught to expect. Jemima is confident, assertive and she knows what she needs: 'Mum says we need foster care this weekend instead of next. You'll sort that, right?' she asks.

Alice sorts it – and some vouchers to help with the

shopping. The next time, the mother turns up for the meeting with a shopping list of things she says she needs. When Alice can't deliver she goes into a screaming rage. Her demeanour is unpredictable: sometimes charming and open, other times irrational and furious. Sometimes she can be all of these things in the same day with different people. When she is at her most ill, in the midst of an episode, she can't look Alice in the eye. Her gestures change and she rocks back and forth. When her moods switch violently and dramatically, Jemima's follow. Alice tries to understand the roots of the mother's problems – there are hints of her own abuse, and sexual abuse, but she can't really tell her own story. Sometimes she claims things have happened to Jemima, and then it becomes clear she's talking about herself. The boundaries between mother and daughter are disintegrating.

Yet she simultaneously manages to advocate for her children to get them into the best state schools in London and to get the highest level of support – including respite care. It's the mid-2000s, just as the spending on such services is peaking under the Blair government. Her moods are so unpredictable, her manipulations so extreme, the dependency between mother and children so warped, that sometimes Alice feels like she's being drawn into a collective insanity. The drama is escalating so quickly that one day the mother makes a passing reference to Jemima having been sexually abused, and the next day the family has gone AWOL and refuses all contact. One crisis supersedes the next and Alice just can't keep up.

The complex personality disorder that Jemima's mother is suffering from is a common diagnosis for parents who are accused of emotional abuse and neglect. It's tightly associated with trauma and neglect in the parent's own childhood, often corrupting their sense of love and parental duty despite the very real love they feel. The symptoms interfere both with a parent's ability to show their love for a child, and their ability to work with social workers. Personality disorders are widely diagnosed but poorly understood, and the best treatments exist at the cutting edge of therapeutic processes and are not readily available on the NHS. In her book *Understanding the Borderline Mother*, the psychologist Christine Ann Lawson quotes a six-year-old she worked with whose mother had a personality disorder. 'Mummy only loves me with part of her heart,' he says.

Alice never finds any evidence of physical abuse or sexual abuse, but there is the sustained emotional abuse – or neglect, it's hard to say which – of living with someone so deeply unstable you don't know where you'll be from one hour to the next. Jemima's school is complaining that her case isn't being escalated to child protection. There are two things stopping Alice pushing that button: first, she knows that the minute she does she will destroy the relationship she has built up with the family, that it would by all intents and purposes be a declaration of war.

There's also pressure within the authority to not get the decision 'wrong'. The council's success is, in part, measured on how few children are 're-registered', meaning they've been escalated, then de-escalated, then come back on to the child protection books. It's a bad look that suggests nothing has been done for that family and things have got worse. So Alice stumbles on, trying to find the solution to an impossible situation.

As the months pass her desperation mounts. Jemima is displaying more of her mother's behaviours. She mimics her rages, her moods flip. Confrontations consist of the two of them against Alice. Jemima is so enmeshed in her mother's behaviours that it becomes harder and harder to separate them, especially as they appear to launch a campaign to sabotage everything, including the foster care placements that were the one bit of respite they had from one another. Alice lives, sleeps and breathes the case. Her heart stops every time she sees their names pop up on her phone; she feels equally sick when silence descends and they cut contact with her.

Then a colleague suggests a new tactic: a plan for the council to pay for Jemima to attend a private boarding school. The mother, who is passionate about her kids going to the best school, agrees to possibly the only course of voluntary action that will put some space between her and her child. Alice takes Jemima to visit. The school is part Hogwarts, part gleaming new buildings, with immaculate gardens and a sports hall bigger than either of them have ever seen. She can ride ponies there. All Jemima can say, in a small and disbelieving voice, is: 'The uniform is red.' The vulnerability in her voice melts Alice's heart again.

Jemima lasts three terms at the school. At first she appears to thrive. Alice is even happy for her that she's somewhere where she can lie about her family and get away with it. She tells her classmates her mother's a nurse, painting a picture of her stable family life. Then her mother turns up at the school, ranting and demanding to see her, and things swiftly deteriorate. At the last-ditch conference where Alice thought she might rescue the placement, mother and daughter shout at her while the house mistress wrings her hands and apologises that she just doesn't think it's going to work.

Jemima is approaching her sixteenth birthday. Soon it will be too late for social services to do anything for her. Alice is pragmatic at this point – she feels almost proud to have stuck it out for over two years – but she is also sad, because she now believes that Jemima should have been taken into care a long, long time ago. Her 'bleeding heart' social worker act hasn't helped the family, only enabled its dysfunction. She's just getting to the point of thinking that it's too late for Jemima, and she needs to focus instead on Jemima's younger siblings, when she goes on holiday.

On her return the social worker who covered her case is looking sheepish. There's been an escalation while she's been away. Jemima's mum has convinced the social worker covering for Alice that she needs a holiday and, extraordinarily, persuaded her to pay for a trip abroad, which she promises to take at the next school holiday. She gets on a plane the next day, in the middle of term, taking Jemima and abandoning her son at school. She leaves a message telling the foster carer to pick him up. He didn't even know they were going away.

Alice, emboldened by a new manager who pushes her to take tougher decisions, immediately starts care proceedings to remove him. He's younger, he still has a chance.

Alice goes on maternity leave soon after and the case is reassigned. She goes to a new job when she returns and it's only years later that she hears anything about the family, when her curiosity gets the better of her and she breaks the rules to search the databases for the little boy who was removed. She nearly cries when she hears that he's at university now, overseas, and on a scholarship. She knows nothing of Jemima, but suspects it's very different for her.

Years later Jemima is still the case that sticks in Alice's mind, the one she looks back on with regret. It's the case that taught her how damaging mental illness can be and what emotional abuse looks like. 'It wouldn't happen now,' she says. 'It wouldn't have happened then, in other authorities. We all got it wrong. They shouldn't have been there.'

Alice is forty-three now, and lives with her husband and three kids in a rambling house full of noise and play. Her youngest, a daughter, tells me when I visit that she wants to be an actress, or perhaps go to the moon. At nine she can explain the job of a social worker: 'You chat to kids all day. Then you go to court in a suit and say "your honour".' Alice's two older boys are wrestling on the sofa. A cockapoo is bouncing at their feet. Her husband John, an academic, is on his knees scooping handfuls of Lego from the floor.

'Social worker' can be a heavy label to wear; it can also be a badge of honour. Alice knows the poisonous reputation of her profession in some of the communities she serves. But at weekend dinner parties in her middle-class urban enclave, she's proud. Friends consider hers to be a real job. People want to know all the gory details. Alice lives this double life, experiencing some of the grimmest stories of families' struggles during the day; returning home to cook kale and spray her pillows with lavender scent at night to relax. As she describes it, she laughs at the clichés of the privileged life she lives.

Most people become social workers to help people; for Alice there was also a need within herself to do something really interesting, dark even, that meant she would never be bored. She never has been.

Social worker is a label that encompasses several different roles, and each council operates in slightly different ways. Alice has worked in the voluntary sector, with child cancer patients at the Royal Marsden, then as a frontline social worker in child protection and working with 'children in need' – whereby they receive support from social services but are not under the force of law. She has been a chair of child protection panels for one local authority – a more senior role that convenes decision-making panels and makes recommendations. And she's been a social worker based in both a children's centre and a school, working with multidisciplinary teams. She loved those roles most because children sought her out for help. She now works as an independent guardian for Cafcass (The Children and Family Court Advisory and Support Service). Cafcass manages social workers who represent children in court proceedings, appointed to ensure that there is a representative in the room who is truly independent and making the case for the child.

Alice is one of just over 100,000 social workers in England. Each has an average of seventeen children on their books. But the caseload varies widely across the country: it's lowest in Kingston upon Thames, at just twelve per social worker, and highest in North East Lincolnshire, where one social worker has responsibility for about twenty-seven children.

In the past ten years something curious has happened. According to a 2018 National Audit Office report, referrals to social workers, made by teachers, doctors or people in the community have gone up by 7% – very close to the 5%

increase in the child-age population.[2] Nothing abnormal there. But while referrals have gone up by just 7%, the number of investigations resulting from those referrals has leapt by 77%. However, no one agrees whether this is because the threshold for investigating has been lowered, or because the cases themselves have got worse. Of those investigations, the proportion considered to have been experiencing or at risk of experiencing harm is 26%.

More of those cases then end up in court. Over the same period there was a 54% increase in new court applications to remove children. But there's another striking difference. One in three of the cases that go all the way to court are then sent back to the local authority with the judge insisting on a supervision order instead. This can mean the family having to abide by certain conditions to keep the children safe, or risk a return to court and their children being removed; or it can mean the council being forced to provide greater support. It adds up to a picture of relative stability in rates of initial concerns, but a system that is more likely to reach for the courts to remove children.

The report that highlighted this was authored by the Chief Social Worker, Isabelle Trowler, and subtitled (rather poetically for the social work lexicon) 'The case for clear blue water'.[3] In it, Trowler urged councils to provide more support for families before resorting to the courts, warning that otherwise children are placed on a 'conveyor belt to care'. She highlighted the 'pre-proceedings' phase – the flurry of activity just before a case goes to court. This is supposed to be the moment when everything is attempted to avoid the legal process that ultimately leads to families being separated. Instead, it has warped into a preparation process, getting the case documented to then present to the court, with social workers and councils too nervous to make drastic changes that could later be seen as weakening their case. The clear blue water, Trowler argued, should be between the cases that do and don't end up in court.

A young, newly qualified social worker I meet describes this impulse to rush towards a court process. 'Before a case goes to court you are sitting with the risks, with limited amounts you can help that family. It feels scary and chaotic,' he says. 'Once in court there are steps you can take, a process you can follow. It feels safer.'

Alice is shocked to hear this – but then she recalls another case she worked on. In this family, the children were well cared for and were looked after meticulously, but the parents lived in a paranoid state where they were convinced the whole system was conspiring against them – a belief they were inculcating their children with, and one that would set them up against the world. Alice had no idea whether or not that would be classified as 'good enough parenting'. In the end, she and a colleague agreed to go to court to trigger an official assessment.

If children's social care is a prism on the shifts in society, it quickly reveals how resourcing of its services has impacted people's lives. The past ten years of austerity has eroded social workers' capacity to help families.

Kirsty, thirty-four, is a London social worker who has also worked in different parts of the system. She agrees that austerity is a major factor in the snowballing of cases going to court. 'The main driver is the complete lack of resources to do any social work or interventions, so the only recourse you have is going to court ... The protocols for court are black and white. If you are not able to work with the family, that becomes the go-to route.'

In the period since the austerity cuts began in 2010, there has been a shift in spending that reflects this pattern of reduced support for families before the court processes start. Spending on children in the social care system is divided into statutory and preventative. The statutory part is what the state legally has to do to safeguard children – the money spent on social workers intervening in family life, on taking the case to court, on lawyers and then on the care system. The preventative side is everything that comes before that point to support families. Since austerity began, spending has shifted from preventative to statutory.[4] It's a stark illustration of what we see again and again across the system – the safety net of support is frayed and eroded, leaving families without back-up as they approach crisis point.

This is further illustrated in another set of statistics. The number of 'children in need' – those for whom there has been no investigation or evidence of harm, but who require services from the council to stay safe, healthy and reasonably happy – has gone up by only 2% compared with the 5% increase in the population since 2010.

It's another indication that there has been a shift away from early intervention and care towards court procedures. We're missing chances to prevent fires and so there are more fires to put out later.

Kirsty tells me about one case she's struggling with: a family of five children who are often left alone by a vulnerable mother who is in relationships with violent men. The house is in a mess and an older sibling is bearing the burden of trying to keep the children fed and safe. The children are eventually removed and put up for adoption. The middle two are adopted together and the youngest, twins, are adopted by a second family. The oldest, the responsible one who kept the show on the road for all that time, can't settle with any foster family and is too old for adoption. The neglect is too ingrained, but the process also inflicted the cruellest blow. 'It's not just neglect he experienced,' says Kirsty. 'But the whole system separated him from the only purpose he had: to protect his siblings. They told him he had failed. It destroyed him.'

When social work fails, the victims are the children who have been trying to hold things together.

'Most social workers would say neglect is the hardest type of harm to deal with because it is so difficult to quantify and the impacts are slow burning. It's more like waiting until something terrible happens.' But rather than bruises and breaks that can be examined, photographed and put before a court, neglect has to be interpreted, understood and disentangled from a social worker's own expectations of what parenting should look like.

'I've worked in local authorities where things needed to be seen to be done rather than actually working. I've worked in another where you feel it's absolutely hopeless from the very beginning – it's such a mess. Then there are those where you think: They get it, I can help here. Some managers are more risk averse, setting expectations insanely high; it didn't matter if social workers were burning out at their desks.'

In the conversation around social work, the word 'risk' rings out loudest. Families are 'risky'. Social workers are 'risk averse'. Managers are fearful of 'carrying risk'. Some talk about 'sitting with the risk'; others 'eliminating risk'. The word is baked into the system. After all, the fundamental judgement social workers have to make is about how risky the situation is for a child.

But the escalation in risk awareness did not come from nowhere. It can be traced back to the story of one little boy, whose death hangs like a shadow over the daily work of every social worker in the country: Peter Connelly.

On 3 August 2007, Peter's lifeless seventeen-month-old body was taken by ambulance to hospital and he was declared dead. He was covered in bruises, had a missing tooth and a torn frenum – the piece of skin that connects the upper lip between the two front teeth. The post-mortem three days later revealed a tooth lodged in his colon, eight fractured ribs and a broken back.

A full investigation later documented over fifty injuries Peter had suffered in the eight months leading up to his death: a ripped ear, a missing fingernail, torn skin, chronic skin infections and lice infestations. It also identified more than sixty times he had been seen by doctors, health visitors, the police and social workers. Chocolate was smeared on his face to hide the bruises. The report concluded: '[Peter's] horrifying death could and should have been prevented.'[5]

In November 2008, the boy's mother, her boyfriend and his brother were convicted over his death. But that did not appease a mounting sense of outrage. It was revealed that the day before his death Peter's mother had been told she was no longer being investigated for child abuse. (Elated, she said she was off to enjoy the summer holidays with her son and other children. She was reported to have remarked that they might do some baking.[6]) The tabloid press launched a campaign against the social workers involved, while politicians broke with the convention of not commenting on such cases and thrashed it out in Parliament at Prime Minister's Questions.

Sharon Shoesmith and Ed Balls have both had over a decade to reflect on the case of Peter Connelly.[7] Shoesmith was Director for Children's Services in Haringey, the north London borough where he died. Balls was the secretary of state for children at the time. The two have never met. But the lives of the former Labour politician – known for his pugnacious political career, his appetite for policy detail, and more recently for appearing on *Strictly Come Dancing* – and the former teacher, who he sacked after Ofsted said her department had failed in the Peter Connelly case, are now forever linked. I interviewed them both.

Ed Balls insists that his mission throughout that crisis, and the guiding principle behind his every decision, was to protect the care system. 'The question in my mind was whether this was a Haringey issue or a system-wide crisis. We didn't know which it was going to be.'

This corner of north-east London was already synonymous with the failure of the state to protect children. Another child, Victoria Climbié, had died there eight years previously, leading to a review of the entire child protection system. Peter Connelly risked becoming a test of the Labour government's delivery of their promise that 'Every Child Matters'. Balls' fear at the time was that a second public scandal would be a symptom of a wider failure, bringing the entire system into the frame. Meanwhile, the opposition had their claws out for Labour.

'David Cameron went for it in a much more political way than we ever thought he would,' he says. 'It fed into this David Cameron/the *Sun* "broken society" narrative.

'The crisis was building and building. Suddenly every police force, every GP, every school thinks: There but for the grace of God go I. The swamping of social services with referrals begins that day.'

He resisted the pressure building around him for weeks and only removed Shoesmith from her role when an emergency Ofsted inspection was published damning the council (despite having given it a bill of clean health before the story broke). When he finally fired her, he did it on live TV.

Shoesmith still suffers from her experience of being in the eye of that political storm. Her post-traumatic obsession over what happened, and why, resulted in a Ph.D. and then a book documenting her side of the story. She won a court case for unfair dismissal, but still has nightmares about finding dead babies in her handbag or applying lipstick only to realise that it was, in fact, human excrement.

Her sacking on live TV sent a shiver of fear through the social work system. 'It wasn't about "is this a Haringey problem or a national problem?"' she says. 'It was "is this a Haringey problem or a political problem for Ed Balls?"'

Her argument is that social workers can do all the right things, with every best intention and to the best of their ability, and sometimes bad people still harm their children. That eliminating all risk is impossible. 'Doctors are not blamed when they can't cure cancer,' she says.

Across the country in the weeks and months afterwards, there was a huge spike in children being taken into care. The year after the court verdict saw a 36% increase in applications to the courts to remove children from their homes. It became known as the 'Baby P effect'.

But the impact of the Peter Connelly case was not uniform;

it was the poorest families who bore the brunt. One study published in the *British Journal of Social Work* found that in the two years after Peter Connelly died, there was a 42% increase in rates of children entering care in the most deprived neighbourhoods, while rates in the least deprived neighbourhoods fell or remained the same.[8]

It was in the aftermath of that moment that Caitlin, from the previous chapter, first came into contact with social services.

Josh MacAlister was Chief Executive of Frontline, which brings high-achieving people into the frontline of social work, before he was asked by the government in 2021 to lead an independent inquiry into the child protection system. Frontline was launched to shake up social work, but it's treated with suspicion by swathes of the sector, which saw its very creation as an implicit criticism. He describes how 'defensive practice' and risk aversion sets in. 'A mistake is made. Through good intentions, managers say, "To stop this happening, let's put in place these rules." There is a belief that writing down how people should respond will make us safe in the future. The more that happens and the bigger the rulebook gets, the more we're telling professionals, "You're not adults, you can't be trusted." The more we tell professionals how to behave, the less responsibility they take. There's a doom loop in this. Where people don't have agency, the job becomes less attractive. It deters good people from coming into the profession. That leaves bigger gaps in talent, so you need more rules.'

In the years since Peter Connelly died, the structure of the social work force has changed markedly. A survey by the British Association of Social Work suggests that social workers now only spend 20% of their working lives actually with families.[9] Meanwhile, new data in the past couple of years shows that only half of social workers actually see families at all, with the rest in managerial and administrative roles.

In 2011, Eileen Munro, now Emeritus Professor of Social Policy at the London School of Economics, delivered a report urging the government to strip away some of the bureaucracy that was calcifying social work.

Munro describes those months after the 'Baby P' story broke.[10] 'It encouraged process as a defence. People thought: I did the right thing, it's just the child died,' she says. 'The move away from judgement and creative work was part of that fear. You presented up-to-date data and forms that were ticked off without looking at things that are valuable. We moved into a pseudo-world of bureaucracy as a way of understanding uncertainty and anxiety.'

But did that defensive practice actually do any good? Were lives saved as the system moved towards taking children more readily into care? There is no clear correlation between the numbers of children going into care and the numbers of children dying. And of course even if a pattern were clear, that correlation would not prove a cause.

Shoesmith has reflected on the whole situation in the years since and now speaks to social workers about what she has learnt. 'The challenge for social workers is to educate the public on what we can and can't achieve for them. We need to stand up for social work,' she says.

And just as Shoesmith has tried to find ways to overcome the trauma of the whole experience, so has the system. Munro says that social work practice is starting to improve in some areas. 'There are examples of really good work happening, but now it's about getting enough of it to have the momentum for it to become the norm. We're still very fragile. Another Peter Connelly would knock the whole system back.'

Alice returned from maternity leave in 2009 in the aftermath of the Peter Connelly scandal. When she met with other councils it was clear how deeply some had been affected. 'I went to one training course with people from across London where we examined the data since Baby P. In our area the number of court applications was stable. But others had really shot up,' she recalls. 'It made a huge difference. There was a lot of fear and defensive practice. The idea was that "we can't afford not to escalate in case we've missed something". It was on everyone's mind.'

These high-profile scandals over child abuse failures also have an impact on the market in social workers between councils. A scandal breaks, the reputation of the council is trashed and then social workers leave, making it even harder to recruit. But there is another stage to that cycle. To improve and attract better social workers, councils then look to compete for better pay and conditions for social workers, meaning that they then recruit from neighbouring councils. Layered on top of this is a market created by agencies.

Alice doesn't understand why social workers would want to work for an agency rather than a council directly. 'It feels like less of a commitment to a community, like you're happy to be removed at any point,' she says. But there's one obvious reason: agency workers are paid up to £45 an hour, compared with around £25 for regular social workers. Alice started on £27,000 and, fifteen years later, earns £48,000 a year. Would paying social workers more help raise the status and standards of the profession? 'Yes please,' says Alice. But then she pauses. 'The truth is that people don't leave because of the money, they leave because of the culture within a local authority. It's the culture that matters.'

A toxic culture might play out in tensions between teams: as a case passes from one to the other there are recriminations over the work that was previously done. It's as if they have internalised the scrutiny that is exerted on their profession from every direction, replicating the same dynamic within their own teams.

The pressures of the job also mean burnout is a major problem. 'Good people come. But they don't stay. Shit people hang around,' Alice says, with startling honesty. One study of UK social workers found alarming levels of burnout. In it, researchers at Queen's University Belfast and *Community Care* magazine used a technique called the Maslach Burnout Inventory.[11] The MBI tests people's psychological responses in relation to their work in three areas: emotional exhaustion, depersonalisation and personal accomplishment.

The study found that social workers are emotionally exhausted, with a score of 33.6 compared with a national average of 21. 'High' emotional exhaustion is considered anything above 27.

The depersonalisation scale measures an 'unfeeling and impersonal response toward recipients of one's service, care, treatment, or instruction'. Social workers are slightly higher than the norm (9.22 as opposed to 8.73), which is considered within the normal range. But they score much better than the general population on personal accomplishment. Within the results you can see the struggle social workers face: emotionally they are burning out more than anyone else, but they keep going because of their belief in the role and the fulfilment it brings.

Alice recognises this. 'Social work breaks some people. They just can't go on,' she says. 'I can't carry the emotional load all day, every day. I have to go home and enjoy the privileges I have. I can't feel guilty for it, I couldn't do it if I did.' Sometimes she feels that when people ask her how she can cope with the awful scenes she sees in families there is an implicit criticism, that somehow she shouldn't be able to cope because it's so awful. But she approaches it with pragmatism. She questions herself during our conversation: has she depersonalised too much? She believes not. But there is a degree to which she has to, or she couldn't carry on.

The one point where she felt like giving up wasn't because of the low pay or the caseload getting worse; it was because the council she was working in was so dysfunctional. As an independent reviewing officer she questioned systems, tried to make them better. After one meeting where she had raised concerns she received an email telling the team there should be no more 'moaning' about managers or social workers in team meetings. The same day, she started looking for a new job.

She recalls some of the worst practices she has seen: social workers lying to cover up where they have missed signs of neglect, even claiming to have seen parents when they haven't. There was another case where a teenager told a social worker he was being beaten by his father but asked her not to tell anyone – the one thing a social worker can't promise. She agreed and kept her promise. In both of these isolated cases, when the problems were uncovered the social workers in question were simply moved out of the job and into other roles. Or they left the area, only to pop up in another council. Alice describes one social worker she knows who has worked at thirty different councils in thirty years.

Many of the systems and structures that are set up around social work to regulate and hold it to account are masking a fundamental problem: there are just not enough good social workers. As Josh MacAlister, who is leading the independent review of social work, puts it, the 'doom loop' tries to control social workers, but unintentionally disincentivises the good ones. Indeed, the job is so demanding, requiring skills that are so nuanced and varied, that it's incredibly hard to find enough people to do it – particularly on relatively low pay. It's another example of caring professions being devalued by society.

Various efforts have been made to address this – campaigns for better training and accreditation of social workers, and the Frontline scheme to attract highly educated people into the profession. This has had an impact in major cities, which are attractive to new graduates, but in other corners of England it has proved harder.

Frontline worked with the think tank the Centre for Public Impact to produce a paper titled 'Putting Relationships First', a new blueprint for social work based on an Amsterdam model for nursing called the Buurtzorg system. The diagnosis of the problem was simple: 'Too many things get in the way of social workers' ability to do their best work with families. They work in a bureaucratic environment, with excessive layers of management and oversight, built on a culture of mistrust.'

They propose a different way of working: to take the layers of management away, the accountability models, and devolve the decision-making to social workers. Give them the time back to build relationships with families, rather than service a bureaucracy, and use that time in group decision-making. Instead of there being a hierarchy of sign-off procedures, groups of social workers debate each case to provide rigour and challenge. Process and box-ticking are replaced by building relationships; peer learning replaces high-stakes auditing; instead of social work being something that is done *to* a family, social workers work *with* them.

The blueprint appeals for this 'brave new approach' to social work, arguing that the status quo can't remain. 'A transition to this model will be highly challenging, and a significant mindset shift will be needed to put it into practice,' the report concludes. 'However, the benefits will secure better outcomes for children and families, while also addressing longer-term morale and staff retention issues.'

Other approaches to trying to improve social work have included new frameworks designed to change workforces' approach to the job. The most common of these, Signs of Safety, encourages social workers to look at the strengths of the families they work with, not just the risks, and to question their own prejudices and assumptions around what they are encountering. Social workers are encouraged to reflect on their understanding of the circumstances of their families, rather than digging into an entrenched view and collecting only the evidence that reinforces that idea.

An official evaluation of Signs of Safety, conducted by the government-commissioned What Works in Children's Social Care centre, however, gave it a mixed review: it has been evaluated in the UK, Australia, Denmark, the Netherlands, New Zealand, Canada and the USA, but there is no evidence that it reduces the need for children to go into care.[12] The theory is all there, but the practice is often hampered by high staff turnover, poor training and distant, unengaged leaders who fail to make cultural change a priority.

The relationship between a social worker and a family is critical to the final decision to remove a child. Parents' 'inability to work with professionals' can often be the final straw that tips towards a removal. Where the relationship and trust break down, where parents are deemed to be untruthful, uncooperative or aggressive towards their social workers, it can be the undoing of a family. But this means that any serious objections to decisions social workers make can count against parents.

I interview one mother who is accused of being unsupportive of decisions social workers and a foster carer are making for her child. The decision in question was whether the child should attend school during the pandemic. The mother objected, as many, many parents have throughout the country, but that was deemed to be obstructive and was presented as evidence to the court of her inability to work with the authorities. It's Kafkaesque. The power imbalance means that parents risk alienating the social workers they work with simply by questioning the decisions being made for the children.

Parents are held to account for how they manage their relationships with social workers, but social workers are not so directly accountable for how they help establish those relationships. The Chief Social Worker for England, Isabelle Trowler, in her report highlighting the problem of the 'conveyor belt to care', says that part of the problem was the collapse in trust between social workers and families.[13] She writes:

'One of the most striking findings of the study was the extent to which families were expected to have open and honest relationships with social workers, and that an absence of this trust was taken as an indicator of increased risk to the child.'

But without that trust and confidence, Trowler argues, the social worker has little choice but to consider care proceedings as the best way of protecting a child. For the system to be a fair one, she concludes, the social workers need the skills to build the relationships with trust and confidence, as well as the parents having to demonstrate it.

High-quality social work is about overcoming distrust and the blighted reputation of the profession and building relationships with families.

I ask Alice to tell me about the standard of social workers. 'Variable,' is her answer. She talks about the various personas you see in social work: the hero, the understanding friend, the charismatic encourager. But she says there's no single personality trait that makes a good social worker. 'I think it's about intellectual rigour and thoughtfulness. People who are willing to really think about the children and their circumstances. There's this idea of the charismatic hero social worker who people love. That feels old-fashioned to me. You can't do it on the cult of personality. Much more important is to do it fairly – and fairness takes deep thinking.'

And the worst? 'Someone who can't think, who is going through the motions. You meet people and they are dead behind the eyes. It's like they've lost their humanity.'

Judge Wildblood's story

'We've got to do something'

Judges and their decisions

Judge Wildblood jogs through the corridors of the Bristol Family Court, joking with the clerks he squeezes past in the narrow corridor. He waits impatiently for the lift he uses to navigate the private routes between their chambers and the courtrooms. His foot taps and his mind races. He's just reread the last of thirty-odd lever arch files containing the intimate details of the life of the family on whom he's about to deliver a final verdict. Unlike the emergency hearing that landed on his desk for that afternoon, in which he will have to make a decision today about removing a child who he knows nothing about, he knows this family's case well. It has been through a long, arduous process in his courtroom. There have been fact-finding hearings and case-management hearings; he's heard the view of every professional and every member of the family. They've tried many tactics to support them; now, there is nowhere else to go.

Now he has to deliver the decision that will change the course of this family's life.

He arrives at the private entrance that takes him to the bench of courtroom 17. He stands behind the door and steadies his mind, focusing on what lies ahead. He takes several deep breaths, checking in with his body, a technique he's cultivated through the practice of mindfulness meditation. It's time. He taps the door twice to announce his arrival. As he enters there is a quiet whoosh and the scraping of chairs, the sound of the dozen people rising to their feet.

But that's as much as I can witness and share with you. To tell this story of what actually happens in court when a decision is reached I walked with Judge Wildblood to the courtroom door as he talked me through the process. I experienced the atmosphere in the courtroom, the tension and the desolation. I saw this not only in Judge Wildblood's courtroom in Bristol but in several courtrooms around the country.

But I can't report the details of what actually happens in court. At the time of writing, it is illegal to report what happens in the family courts – only published judgments and cases where a journalist has applied successfully to lift the reporting restrictions can be reported. There are good reasons for that: to protect the children's anonymity. But it also means the process is clouded in secrecy, hidden behind closed doors, beyond scrutiny and transparency.

There's another way I can show you what happens behind those closed doors. The description of the judgment delivered below, and the families' reactions to it, are from a dramatised version that Judge Wildblood produced for a theatre production. None of the characters, save from his own, are real. Instead, they are built on the reality of the thousands of cases that he has heard in his courtroom. This is the truest way, within current laws, to show you inside the courts and the moment of this seismic decision, without censure. And this is what it looks and feels like:

The atmosphere is thick in the full, windowless court-room. It's quiet but for the rattling of an old air-conditioning system. It's like the court is holding its breath in anticipation. Judge Wildblood scans the room, reading the mood into which he will deliver his findings. His eyes meet the young mum's impassive gaze at the back of the room. She appears emotionless, hiding the hope and dread she is feeling. He is impassive in turn, hiding a crushing weight of responsibility.

He takes another breath, then slowly and clearly begins to read the words he's prepared.

'Overall and very sadly, it is evident that this mother is simply not able to meet the needs of this baby boy, despite her heartfelt wish that she should do so. There is no doubt that she loves Kye and, over the past three months, appears to have coped with his basic care when fully supported within the mother and baby foster placement.

'However, her recent engagement in drug rehabilitation has to be set against her lengthy history of street work, addiction and previous parenting history. Those difficulties are such entrenched parts of her background that I have profound doubts about her ability to derive, in the long term, any sustained benefit from the support and rehabili-tative measures that are available to her. To that must also be added her learning disability which, I consider, serves as a further barrier to effective and sustained intervention. I agree with the psychologist that her own childhood has left her with such disadvantages that any benefit that might come from untested therapeutic input is now outwith the timescales of this child.

'If he is adopted, Kye will have all the advantages of a stable, secure and loving new family. Kye is of an age where he cannot wait longer. He would suffer harm through neglect in the mother's care and it would be emotionally harmful to him if these proceedings were further delayed. No amount of professional support would now surmount this mother's difficulties and her continued but concealed contact with the father signals how ineffective supervision is likely to be.'

The mother sits blinking, but the atmosphere in the room has changed. He rapidly rules out the teenage father as a potential full-time parent on the basis of his 'chaotic lifestyle', largely the result of brain damage from an injury when he was fifteen. He's struggled even to attend the hearings.

The teenage boy is present today and pulls his hoodie over his head, lays his head on his forearms and cries quietly.

Judge Wildblood then rules out the grandparents as special guardians – they have too much on their hands with another adopted daughter, strains in their relationship and mental health difficulties themselves. The grandmother's sobs break the fragile authority in the room.

She interrupts the judge: 'Please don't do this. I'll do anything if you let us look after him. Please don't take him away from us. He's our grandson.'

The judge's grip on the room is draining away, protocols punctured by emotion. He calmly asks her to sit quietly. Now the grandfather joins in. 'We don't deserve this,' he tells the judge.

'Look, you just need to listen to what I'm saying,' Judge Wildblood insists. 'If you really don't understand, I'm sure your solicitor will explain it all to you afterwards. OK? Now, you must not interrupt again please. Otherwise I will order you to leave court.'

Their interruptions stop for long enough for Judge Wildblood to continue his judgment. But he speeds up, rushing through the words, knowing that they won't hear anything else now that they know they have, in their minds, lost. 'I am therefore driven to the conclusion that it is necessary and proportionate for care and placement orders to be made,' he says.

Judge Wildblood clears up the final details. The mother's contact will diminish over the next two months, then all direct contact will end and the boy will be adopted. Both the mother and the father will be allowed to send one letter a year via social workers. He leaves it to the council to finesse the detail.

The mother is still sitting quietly. The judge can hear her question the social worker sitting nearby. 'What does it all mean?'

Judge Wildblood starts to clear the papers from his desk. His job is done.

He stands, bows his head briefly to the court in a show of humility and service, and leaves. As he closes the door he hears two things – a chair being kicked over, by the grandfather, he later finds out, and the mother's increasingly urgent question of 'what's happening?' turning into a rising, raw cry.

Judge Wildblood wrote the play, which has been performed in theatres around the country, to try to show people behind the closed doors of the courtroom. He is the Designated Family Judge for Avon, North Somerset and Gloucestershire. His courthouse is a giant municipal building with security on the door and a sandwich shop opposite where the judge, lawyers and families all go for their lunch.

There are three distinct parts to the building: the public side – the waiting rooms and courtrooms the families, councils and their lawyers are invited into; the judges' chambers, with a separate warren of corridors around the back that give the judges their own doors by which to enter the courtrooms; and a cavernous office where the court clerks coordinate the elements of each case. It's like a vast factory that processes the most intimate, painstaking decisions about humans that can be made.

How the state intervenes in family life to remove a child is a lesson in how we are governed. The state is made up of the legislature, the executive and the judiciary, each with its role to play: the elected legislature, parliament, sets the rules; the executive, in this case local government, implements them; and the judiciary plays a critical role in deciding when the law is met.

In practice this means social workers investigate children's lives, and make recommendations based on the law agreed in parliament. These are represented to a judge in a family court, who makes the final decision to remove a child. The weight of these decisions, the sum of the quality of the laws and the work that is done to enact them lands on the judge. Judges are the office holder, applying the law according to the facts. It's not their opinions or personality that bears down on those decisions. Their prime responsibility is to dispassionately and fairly apply the law.

Family courts hear two kinds of cases: private law, when the state isn't involved, and public law, where it is. Private law cases are brought by individuals and largely concern divorce hearings and resolving custody disputes. They also resolve financial settlements after divorces. Public law involves care orders, which give local authorities parental responsibility; supervision orders, which set stipulations for either the parents, carers or the council to follow; and emergency protection orders, to remove a child quickly in order to keep them safe. The family courts also make the adoption orders that end a parent's or parents' responsibilities, and make that child the legal child of the adopters.

A judge in a family court makes his or her decisions differently to those in criminal courts. There is never a jury; the judge makes the call alone. The standard of proof is different. In criminal cases a judge or jury (depending on whether it's in the magistrates' or a crown court) has to decide 'beyond reasonable doubt'. In the family court, like in civil claims, the standard of proof is on a balance of probabilities. Crudely put – and judicial minds hate this analogy – criminal cases have to be as close to 100% sure of guilt as it is possible to get; family judges simply need to be more sure than not, to make their decision. This lower standard of proof is seen as an injustice in itself by many families for whom the severity of the decision, to remove their child, is as life-changing as the sentences handed out in the criminal courts.

The decision to remove a child can happen over a protracted period of court sessions and 'fact finding' hearings, during which a judge will get to know the intimate details of a family's life and the personalities involved. But other times, an emergency hearing lands on their desk and they will have to make a decision with just a few hours' notice on the basis of the notes before them.

Judge Wildblood's chambers are lined with bookshelves, with a spare desk for a clerk in the corner and a larger table for hosting visitors in the middle. Mementoes line the bookshelves. 'Badly behaved children will be made into pies,' reads one sign.

I spend some time in Judge Wildblood's courtroom. On the first day I sit next to him on his bench, raised above the wider courtroom, from where you can read the dynamics in the room; the frostiness between estranged parents fighting for their child, the fluster of a social worker who can't find the right papers, the tempered steeliness of the lawyers as they cross-examine. You feel the deference in the room through the language of 'your honour' and 'may I just assist the judge by . . . ' Judge Wildblood wears his authority lightly, putting people at ease and humanising the process with concern and care.

A second day I sit at the back of the court – the perspective that parents generally have – positioned behind their lawyers. I can't see anyone's faces. It's hard to keep up. That air-conditioning unit buzzes behind me. Then, after coronavirus hits the UK, I watch a remote hearing, conducted on Microsoft Teams, and the effect is somehow democratising: everyone in the courtroom is an equal-sized box, side by side, magnified only when speaking. But the backgrounds add a new element: the grandness of a judge's bookshelf, the comfort of the lawyers' home offices; the bustle of the social workers' office; the plainness of the mother's wall and the knocking on her door of a neighbour's child who wants to play.

Sitting in his chambers, generous with his time, Judge Wildblood describes his process for arriving at a decision. When he's heard all the evidence, when he's considered every allegation, mitigating factor and the characters of the people before him, how does he actually decide? 'The only valid way of doing that is to have an open mind to start off with. If you've got a closed mind you're not going to get it right. You don't make the decision until all of the jigsaw is complete. Don't rely on what any one person says or the impression in the witness box. If you stand back and let the pieces come together then at the end almost invariably the picture emerges and you can see it. That's judging.'

The judgments Judge Wildblood and his colleagues make in decisions to remove children come in stages. First he has to decide whether the threshold set out in the Children Act 1989 has been met. Is the child 'suffering, or likely to suffer, significant harm'? This is often relatively straightforward.

The next stage gets more complicated. This is the welfare stage, in which the judge must consider whether the harm of removing the children will outweigh the harm of them remaining, and what mitigating factors there are that could improve their circumstances now.

He must consider Article 8 in the Human Rights Act 1998, the right to respect for privacy and family life, which states: 'There shall be no interference by a public authority with the exercise of this right except such as is in accordance with the law and is necessary in a democratic society in the interests of national security, public safety or the economic well-being of the country, for the prevention of disorder or crime, for the protection of health or morals, or for the protection of the rights and freedoms of others.' Then he must work out how likely a parent is to change to better care for their child, what support they have to do so and, to a lesser extent, the local authority's capacity to provide a better alternative.

The course of a case is a worrying time when Judge Wildblood often genuinely does not know what the right thing to do is until the last moment. 'You always feel the pressure of "I've got to make jolly sure I get this right". It's sometimes obvious only at the very last moment. I don't want to be walking down the steps and questioning whether I had thought of a particular point enough.'

When, in the moment, it becomes obvious, Judge Wildblood feels a flood of relief. But that doesn't always happen and he has to rely on the principles and probabilities of the law.

Judge Wildblood speaks slowly and deliberately. He tests each statement in his mind before speaking. He wrings his hands as he emphasises his point. He searches my face to make sure I understand what he's saying, the nuance of the job he does.

He has a humility in recognition of the power he holds. He reflects on his decisions after he makes them, sometimes for long periods. He sits in judgement of his own performance as much as of the families before him.

'It's an immensely privileged job. What gives me the right as an individual to make a huge decision about other people's lives? Imagine if you had to decide whether someone could keep their kids or put them up for permanent adoption. It's an immense power. So of course you think, Am I fit for purpose?'

Judge Wildblood has a reputation for being outspoken in the conservative world in which he operates. He encourages transparency in a process that's often closed. Through his plays, he's trying to show people how the courts work, something that also informs his thinking about how things could be improved.

In Bristol there has been a 9% increase in court proceedings in care cases in the year before I visit alone. His court serves different local authorities and he sees the different patterns of child removals between those areas. 'In some areas there is much more focus on trying to intervene earlier outside of court proceedings rather than investing in the legal part.' It's a glimpse of the postcode lottery in child removal that we will explore further, later in this book.

Judge Wildblood has in mind a prescription for what needs to be done: more education for young people in their late teens and early twenties to understand what happens in these cases; more general information for the public to explain the family courts, which he has taken on himself with his plays and talks; more support for families at the pre-proceedings stage to prevent cases coming to court; support for families in the court process; and support for parents after a decision is made, especially if they lose their children.

'If we made more effort within those five stages it would have an impact on the amount of care proceedings,' he says.

Judge Wildblood is in a pensive mood when we meet, reflecting on the sense of mission in his role. It's his default position and he has coping mechanisms to stop it all getting too much: every day he runs six miles listening to Puerto Rican dance music. It's a boost of endorphins and musical sunshine that helps him process the weight he carries each day, giving him respite and a chance to breathe.

*

Sir Andrew McFarlane is the President of the Family Division of the High Court, which makes him the most senior family court judge in the country. He makes occasional proclamations on the system and in one of his first, in December 2019, he issued this stark warning: 'Despite the best efforts of everyone in the system, often working at well beyond capacity, we are not keeping pace with the volume of cases that are coming in and the backlog continues to increase.' He went on: 'We are, in effect, running flat out up a down escalator which is outpacing us.'

He set up a working group to investigate what could be done to both parts of the system he is responsible for: public law (care proceedings and adoption) and private law (mostly divorce and custody battles). For the public law working group, he appointed a colleague, Mr Justice Keehan, to lead the work. His group concluded that it doesn't matter why so many families are being taken to court to remove their children, the fact is that it is too many.[1] Many more cases could be safely dealt with before they ever reach court proceedings, through intensive social work.

Mr Justice Keehan works from his wood-panelled chambers in the modern wing of the Royal Courts of Justice. His shelves are lined with thank-you cards from families and relatives of children who have passed through his court. His working group made nineteen recommendations designed to tackle a central problem: that too many cases were coming to court too late in the process, unprepared, and setting up families – and the system intended to support them – to fail. They recommended a series of measures – including additional funding – to focus more on the social work to support families and avoid them ever having to come to court at all. Intervene earlier, provide more support, build the relationships between social workers and the families, and in many cases you might never need to even think about removing children.

When I visit Mr Justice Keehan in his chambers I am surprised at his candour. I expect someone as senior as him to have a degree of defensiveness of the status quo. But he wants to expose the problems and is willing even to estimate the extent to which the social work and family justice system is getting it wrong.

'We are of the view that if our recommendations are implemented in full, something like a third of all cases could be safely diverted away from the court and dealt with by local authorities working with families. It would avoid the need for proceedings altogether.'

There are currently nearly 80,000 children in the care system in England. A third of them need never have come to court at all if social services was resourced to focus on this 'pre-proceedings' stage. That's more than 26,000 children who needn't be in the care system.

Quantifying the problem makes it feel shockingly real. Before Keehan estimates this there is a mixed picture – some children being removed unnecessarily, before everything is done to help them stay with their parents. Others being left in appalling conditions. But this is real: 26,000 children, in any one year, whose lives the state has fundamentally changed. Think how that number accumulates over time. Hundreds of thousands of children and young adults scarred by a period separated from their parents. This is the number that should be on all of our consciences.

Keehan is keen to stress that this is an estimate, but it's

one made by a group of people at the heart of the system. If anyone knows, they should.

It's from the judges' benches that you should, have you been there long enough, be able to explain why the rates of children going into care have increased so much. It's judges who see a shift in reasons for child care proceedings, changes in social work and the impact of political interventions.

But the truth is that not even they can define the problem with evidence. I go to see the former President of the Family Division of the High Court, Sir James Munby. He's McFarlane's predecessor. I ask him why so many more children are entering care proceedings. His answer stops me in my tracks. 'We simply don't know. We are very much operating in the dark.'

Munby served as President of the Family Division of the High Court of England and Wales from 2013 until 2018. A thoughtful and fiercely independent reformer, he made judgments that challenged political doctrines right up to the limit of what is appropriate for a judge,[2] and planned changes to improve the transparency of the famously secretive courts without jeopardising children's anonymity.[3]

The problem is, Munby suggests, the entire system is acting in an evidence-deprived vacuum. It's not about a lack of evidence in the individual cases, the documentation of bruising or social workers' accounts. The first problem is that social work and the legal system are out of touch with the latest research on things as basic as bruising in babies, or the theory around how children form attachments at different ages. The evidence is changing but the system isn't keeping up. Munby is candid: 'In all the time I sat as a judge

I was only ever twice in the whole of that time pointed to any specific piece of research.'

The second is that, despite all the care that judges take over their decisions, they never know what happens next, so they never learn about what works best. The system-level data that is available to explain who is going into care, where and why, is patchy and inaccessible.

Considering the magnitude of the decisions that are being made and their impact upon children and families, this evidence vacuum is startling. Munby says that instead of evidence, there are assumptions that get passed on unchallenged through generations of lawyers. 'There are lots of what might be called articles of hope within the court system,' he says.

Now retired, Munby can confront things more than his colleagues who still operate within the system. He queries the rate of non-consensual adoption that takes place in England. 'For the first time over the last two or three years there are people beginning to question, in the mainstream, whether we've got it right on non-consensual adoption,' he says, pointing out that few other countries do it to the extent that the courts in England and Wales do. 'I think we need to look into it. We've just tended to assume that it's the right thing. That assumption is based on elderly research. It's something we've all grown up to believe. It's simply part of our mental furniture.'

Munby is now chairing the new Family Justice Observatory, funded by the independent think tank the Nuffield Foundation, trying to gather the evidence that is needed to improve the system. They plan to draw together the evidence and make it accessible to the courts, then to identify the gaps and commission research to improve the system's overall understanding.

We meet in Munby's Wiltshire home of thirty years, hidden in a wood and full of a jumble of books on political history and the law alongside his grandchildren's toys. It's like a fairy-tale cottage from another era. He talks for two and a half hours about the lack of evidence, the 'postcode lottery' in the rates of family separation in the UK, which the existing data has revealed, and how the middle classes are all but absent in the story.

Does he believe that the system is fair? 'It's by and large fair and just – within its own assumptions,' he says. 'Everyone in the system is desperately striving, on the day and in a particular case, to be as fair and just as they can be . . . I suspect on a micro level people are doing their level best, but that's within the parameters of the system as they believe it to be. People desperately trying to do individual cases fairly don't have time to sit back and think about these things.'

We talk about Caitlin's experience of the paucity of mental health treatment she needed to help her parent well. He puts it in stark words: 'Deeper and more profound is that taking the child away may be cheaper in the long run than supporting the family. When it's asked what is needed to support the family with therapy and support, the answer is: We can't afford it.

'I suspect that's not a conscious driver. People in the system are desperately short of resources and they know that support costs a lot of money. Human nature being what it is, these pressures are quite subtle and it's quite easy to persuade yourself to do the thing that costs less money.'

It is horrifying that some children are being removed

from their families, however unconsciously, because it might save money in the short term. Councils and social workers would certainly deny that, but Munby has looked into the eyes of the people making these decisions and is voicing his suspicions.

The pressures within the family courts are at unprecedented levels, with more cases being heard than ever before – and the pandemic added to this by forcing the whole system to shift overnight to digital processes. But add to that Munby's concerns, and it becomes clear that the system is perilously unfair. Without the evidence on outcomes and impacts on parenting, the judgments come down to individuals making huge decisions and, no matter how fair-minded they are, that lack of context and evidence gives more space for personal prejudices to play out.

For judges such as Judge Wildblood, the pressure makes for a hard, lonely existence carrying the weight of the decisions on his own. It comes at a personal cost: 'You can't ever sit back or have a down day because the consequences for people are too big. It's like being on stage every single day and always performing to the same standard.

'We've got to do something. We can't carry on working at this ever-increasing rate,' he says. 'I'm one person in a courtroom full of lawyers and parties; it's an enormous responsibility to place on one person. If work keeps increasing either we will need more judges, more courts, or we will just not cope.'

PART TWO

What's really going on?

Francesca's story

'It's always the ones you don't suspect'

Class, privilege and poverty

Francesca checks the route on her phone. Her eleven-month-old baby, Jacob,[1] is snuffling loudly in his sleep in the car seat behind her. She can hear him wheezing. The summer heatwave has left the car stuffy and humid. The nurse on the 111 NHS phone line said to get him to a doctor as soon as possible and the map is giving her two options: turn right to the GP in the local village or turn left to the A&E department in the nearest town. She turns left.

She doesn't know the area well. She's on holiday and this is the first leg of their month-long tour around her children's godparents across the country. The weather is glorious and they should be on the beach. But the damp in the holiday home has aggravated her baby's wheezy chest, so instead they spend a couple of hours waiting in A&E, then a couple more waiting for the steroids and puffer to work on a ward. When that doesn't improve things, they go for a two-minute X-ray that triggers a four-month nightmare.

Fifteen minutes after the X-ray, the curtain surrounding Jacob's bed on the ward whips open and a doctor steps in. Without stopping to say hello, she looks at Francesca and says: 'Have you ever harmed your baby?' The questions keep coming. Does she ever hit her child? Is her husband an alcoholic? Is she? Francesca and the doctor had got off on the wrong foot when they first met. The doctor wore plain clothes, with no white coat or stethoscope, and Francesca had asked whether she was a locum, and received a frosty response. Now, Francesca is being questioned about potential child abuse in her home.

The X-ray had revealed a thickening of one posterior rib next to Jacob's spine. It suggested a possible fracture. Francesca racks her brains. Five months previously Jacob had choked, paramedics had been called, and he had been repeatedly slapped on the back to dislodge the food he had swallowed. Could that have been the cause?

Francesca is told they cannot leave the hospital. Jacob is on the mend, his wheezy chest easing, but they are being kept there while the hospital seeks more medical opinions about the X-ray. Social services in their home borough have been informed. Jacob spends two hours having a full skeletal survey X-ray and CT scan, then his blood is taken to check for any other problems. Francesca is increasingly stressed – but not because she thinks this is a serious situation. She hates that Jacob is trapped in the hospital while all the other kids carry on their holiday. It doesn't for a second occur to her that it could escalate any further.

Five consultants see the survey and all agree there is

nothing of concern. Francesca is told there is no concern and the family can leave. With some relief they load the family back in the car and head for their next stop halfway across the country.

But the social workers from their home borough call again, checking on their whereabouts. And they keep calling. Francesca suspects the fact that they've moved authorities again might be raising concerns. But the matter is closed as far as she is concerned. Then a strange thing happens: the original X-ray is sent to a final, sixth consultant, who responds with an ambiguous judgement that could be read either way.

The mood of the social workers immediately flips. They demand the family return to London. Francesca is pressing them to clarify this ambiguous statement. She stays up late that night with her husband thrashing out what to do. They have nowhere to stay in London, having let out their house for the duration of their holiday. It feels unreasonable that the council is pursuing them. They ask the social workers to come to them instead. 'If they had said "this won't go away until you come back" it would have been a lot simpler. We would have gone,' says Francesca now. 'We had complied and complied and complied.'

The next day social workers from the council local to where they are staying come and observe the family and leave saying they have no concerns. The family move on to their next stop, another 200 miles away, so another switch in local authority. Francesca calls the social workers to let them know exactly their movements – fearing they suspect the family is on the run rather than on a long-planned holiday with friends. When they have arrived and settled in, they are told to go to a children's centre for a meeting. On the phone it sounds unthreatening and friendly. Once they arrive at the council facility it feels very different.

They want to interview the children on their own. Francesca feels uncomfortable putting them through interviews which last an hour, and later ashamed that she lets them go. She has no idea what happened in the room but later pieces together that her second son, the most confident of her children, described how Francesca had thrown water at him that morning (during a game while loading the dishwasher) and claimed she threatens to lock them in the bathroom. Francesca knows how this sounds, tries desperately to give it context: the bathroom is for timeout, it doesn't even have a lock on it, and she has never actually done it; her kids know she is too soft. As the evidence is assembled, Francesca feels her family life being twisted out of recognition.

The family are told to attend the local hospital for further assessments. Leaving the children's centre, her oldest boy is in floods of tears. 'Are you going to go to prison, Mummy?' he asks. Francesca says no, of course she isn't, it will all be OK. Then one of the social workers leans down to him and, as Francesca recalls it, says: 'No matter what happens to Mummy, we will look after you.'

The same social worker told Francesca's friend: 'It's always the ones you don't expect.'

At the hospital, her older children, who are all under ten, are given full body surveys under strip lighting. Every remotely unusual detail is noted down, from the fact that they are circumcised to a scratch from the blackberrying expedition the day before. Francesca pleads with the medics doing the body surveys to note down that the scratches were caused by the brambles, now fearful that every single detail is being used to build a case against her.

The next day two new social workers arrive out of the blue. They inform the family that their home council wants to issue an EPO – an emergency protection order – removing the children from the family and putting them into foster care while the council works out what is going on. At that point the London council social workers had not met Francesca or the children, nor had they talked to their school or teachers. The social workers where they are staying put their own jobs on the line and advise them to get back to London, otherwise the order will be made there and then and the kids will be taken into care 140 miles from home.

Francesca and her husband scramble their stuff into the car and hurtle down the M1 towards London.

On the drive back, the London social workers call again. They are informed they are being followed by a police car. Police will be waiting at their home to remove the children. A foster care match has been found but they can't take all the children together. So the children will be separated, and more than likely sent out of London and will certainly be going to a different school in the new term.

By luck all the children were asleep in the car by that point. Francesca is trying to hold down her hysterical sobs. Then she has a moment of clarity and gets on the phone. She's not giving up without a fight. She rings her neighbours, the children's headteacher and her vicar and asks them to meet her at the house. She also rings her lawyers again, who are seeking to overturn the removal order. She phones over thirty friends and compiles a list of local families who are willing to take the children to avoid foster care.

The car pulls up outside their home and she falls into the arms of her vicar and community. It's seven o'clock, approaching the kids' bedtime. The house is full of people distracting the kids and feeding them pizzas when the police arrive ahead of the social workers. Francesca later remembers them looking perplexed at the task ahead of them. Every time the doorbell rings her heart lurches.

Then the call comes: an emergency judge her lawyers have applied to has overturned the order due to the ambiguity of the medical report.

Francesca's home is an explosion of Cath Kidston florals, bunting and bright pastels. A kettle steams on the gas stove and the walls are covered with children's paintings of their family adventures. Photos show them in neat matching sailor outfits. It feels like they live in a happy bubble from another, more innocent, age. It also feels completely at odds with the story of the woman who ended up speeding down a motorway, with police ready to remove her children and put them in care.

The house sits proud on a back street in London. The local high street is rundown, decked with kebab shops and off-licences. But the homes behind are models of middle-class life. It's a familiar social map of London, rich and poor, side by side, street by street.

Francesca calls the street, the route to the church where she is a warden, and the school her children attend, her 'nook'. You'll find her there on any given day, doing the school run, walking back with a neighbour. She's well known in the area. It's not a surprise that Francesca works in the arts. She uses dramatic flair and gilded language to paint a vivid picture of their lives. Each friend she mentions, she gives their full name, like they are someone I should have heard of – because on the stage that is her world, they are famous.

Her family's experience of social services in 2018 has left her traumatised and angry. She's telling her story because she believes the only reason her children are with her now is because she had the resources – social as well as financial – to fight the system. She's angry on the behalf of parents with less ability to challenge such decisions. She knows that there are times when the state should intervene; hers is not a libertarian anti-state argument. But her experience of the sharp end of the state has left her with no faith in it to make the right call as to when it exercises its most extreme of powers.

It didn't end for Francesca's family when the EPO was overturned. They kept the children at home, but had to agree to twenty-four-hour approved supervision, including through the nights when Francesca was still breastfeeding Jacob. They had to pay for her sister-in-law to come from America, then a teacher from the school who had recently left moved in for six weeks. It cost the family thousands of pounds – money another family might not be able to find – but helped them avoid their children going into foster care.

The action involved five return visits to court, before the council abruptly withdrew the case. They signed a document accepting that even if this was a fracture, it was caused by an accident in the home. They came again, four times in January, to give advice on safety in the home to prevent any other accidents. Then it was over.

'That was it. They are out of our lives. We've not heard or seen them again.'

*

'It's always the ones you don't expect,' the social worker had told Francesca's friend.

The truth is actually rather the opposite. The story of family separation in the UK is usually straight out of central casting, with roles determined by class. The families who have their children removed nearly always fit into prejudices about poverty. If the rise of children going into care is a prism through which to assess society, you find it riven with bias about class, disadvantage and wealth.

The process of the state intervening in a family's life can be the result of a slow, sometimes futile, attempt to help. Or it can be a snap intervention triggered by a specific event, such as Francesca's near miss.

Here is how the state makes the decision to remove children from their families. First, a family comes to the attention of social services. In the best-case scenario that happens when troubles are first brewing. Perhaps a parent even asks for help. Social services can step in to coach and support. They work out the root of the problem and make referrals to services that might support that family: with mental health care, drugs and alcohol services, housing or benefits advice. In the ideal world we're imagining, that might quite often be a source of support that parents seek from the state, just as they might push for a diagnosis of a special educational need: in order to get the help they require to deal with it.

The reality is often different. A teacher might notice their pupil is looking less well cared for, with no clean clothes, arriving at school unable to concentrate because they are so hungry. Or perhaps a teenage girl has no money for menstrual products and is soiled at school. In other cases the child might have changed their demeanour and become withdrawn, or the opposite: become suddenly angry and physically aggressive. The parents can't be reached. Then the pupil acknowledges something is going wrong. Or it might be the GP, worried by a pattern of illnesses and infections. Less common is the 'blue lights scenario', when police are called because children have been left home alone, abused or neglected. Or because they have an injury and the doctors at the hospital are suspicious.

Social services are called. The call comes in the 'front door' of social services, to the referrals team. Increasingly these are being replaced by Multi-Agency Safeguarding Hubs that bring together social services with police, schools and health services to pool information about the children being referred and decide the best route to take. Within social services the case might be referred to the family support team; the Child In Need team, which provides a more intensive form of support; or the child protection team, which is stitched into the legal process.

They begin to investigate. They spend time with the family and the children. They might test the children and, if physical abuse is suspected, doctors will do a full-body inspection marking down anything unusual. This can involve full-body X-rays to look for historic fractures, for example. Assessments are made. The social workers make their recommendations – they might place the child back on a 'Child In Need' plan. This happens when they agree with the parents what support is needed to improve their family life. If it's more serious and there is, as the law puts it, a 'risk of serious harm', the case may go to the family court to seek either the removal of the child or a supervision order, which compels the parents to comply with strict conditions.

But social workers only make recommendations; it is up to a judge in the family court to make the final decision to remove a child.

A family court is the most striking demonstration of the British class system I have witnessed in one room. In these stark municipal venues, the structures that bind our society are laid bare. At the back of the court sits the family. They rarely speak, except when being cross-examined, and at times they barely know what is happening. They are almost invariably poor and less educated. They struggle with the impenetrable language of the law, often looking like they've tried to dress appropriately for the formal surroundings, but without the resources to do so. I watch a young mum who has cobbled together a suit, but her scuffed trainers don't match. It's cold outside and she has no overcoat.

They are surrounded by social workers. There is one from the council – the friendly face who turned up to help the family and who is now making the case to separate them. There is already a sometimes long and complex relationship between the family and social worker. Another social worker, known as the child's guardian, is there to represent the child's best interest. They look harassed and stressed. Some wear the weight of the decisions they've had to make heavily and look physically pained by the point they've arrived at. Others go through the motions – one way of dealing with the horror they are met with, and the decisions they have to make, is to shut down their empathy. It's too raw to feel every time. They've worn their court clothes: M&S suits that have seen better days.

The front of the courtroom is a wall of lawyers: there are a surprisingly large number. One for the council, one for the parents, one for the child. Sometimes there are more if the parents are estranged, or grandparents and other relatives are involved too. They are articulate and efficient to the point of speaking a different language to the rest of the room. They all know each other, and there is a gallows humour to the way that they chat in the hall. Like war reporters, they exchange stories. They wear Jigsaw and Hobbs – more expensive, another rung up the social ladder.

On the bench at the front of the room perches the judge, looking down on proceedings. The heart of the legal establishment, the judge is the powerful elite and bears ultimate decision-making power, and with it responsibility. They are so powerful in this world and wealthy compared to the rest of society that it doesn't matter where their suit is from. You know where the power is. They enter the court from their own door, knocking to announce their arrival. Everyone stands.

The scene in the family court is not a loose illustration of the British class system. It shows the structural grip of class on power in people's lives and it follows a tight script. In the family courts, these are largely decisions made by privileged people about some of the least powerful in the country. The correlation between class and children in care is obvious but unquantified. As Sir James Munby explained, there is little good data collected on who is going through this system. But if you map the postcodes of the country with the highest rates of child removal, they are also the poorest.

When middle-class families such as Francesca's do come to the attention of social services, the truth of what other families face comes as a shock. In some ways these cases also prove the rule that powerlessness and poverty go hand in hand, because being middle class also gives you advantages to escape the system.

Class bias is an injustice that runs through the decisions to remove children and the structures of support for families. Francesca's middle-class family is an outlier in a system that largely affects lower income families. But class as we talk about it isn't nuanced enough to help us understand. The families I see going through the court systems and that social workers talk to me about are not working class. Outdated terminology struggles to show the challenges these families face. They lack education, they are the latest in generations of people who have been controlled by the state. They are families who are either small and isolated or tight and marginalised.

This is who goes into care: of the 80,000 children in care in England, over half (56%) are male. The largest age group (39%) are aged ten to fifteen years; 23% are aged sixteen years and over, 19% are aged five to nine, 13% are one to four years, and 6% are under one year.[2]

Paul Bywaters, professor of social work at the University of Huddersfield, has done most to painstakingly dig beyond these statistics to find out who in society is most likely to be in care. The Child Welfare Inequalities Report found that black and minority ethnic children are more likely to be in care than white children overall.[3] But white children in the poorest areas are the most likely to be in care – 120 out of every 10,000 white children in those postcodes. Overall, children in the most deprived 10% of UK neighbourhoods are over ten times more likely to be in care than children in the 10% least deprived localities. We will look at the patterns of ethnicity of children in care in the next chapter and the intersectional discrimination at play, but it's worth bearing in mind that the strongest indicator of whether a child ends up in care is poverty.

Bywaters' research goes further: it finds that poor people in relatively wealthy areas, with high levels of inequality, are more likely to be subject to child protection investigations. Partly this is down to supply: in more uniformly deprived areas there are fewer resources to go around; but there also seems to be a more significant reason. Poor people are more policed in relatively wealthy areas than in more homogenous poor places.

This isn't about working-class families, it's about poor families with multiple odds stacked against them. Some economists talk of an underclass of workless families, but underclass is a loaded, negative term that can further alienate already disenfranchised families. I'm uncomfortable using it. Darren McGarvey, the Scottish rapper and social commentator known as Loki, describes the problem with labelling the underclass in his epic book *Poverty Safari*:

> As social inequality widens and the chasms in our relative experiences become more pronounced, we make assumptions about the people on the other side of the divide, their lifestyle and beliefs, their intentions towards us. These projections don't account for the complexity and richness of people's lives. This is what makes talking about class so difficult.

Labels, in general, are itchy; they scratch at our sense of self. The British economist Guy Standing coined the concept of the precariat, an emerging class of insecure households. This idea was expanded on in a project in 2013 to redefine the class system led by the BBC and conducted by a group of leading universities.[4] It arranged the class system into seven strata, with the precariat at the bottom, low on economic or social capital, isolated at the edge of society, earning extremely low wages in precarious jobs.

I asked Caitlin (from the opening chapter) if she considers herself working class. 'My parents never worked, so no, less than that,' she says, looking frustrated by the labels, and further judged. I ask Caitlin what part class played in her experience of social services. 'They look at you differently,' is all she says.

In Caitlin's chapter we examined myriad reasons why the numbers of children going into care have increased and the shift in rationale for removing children, away from physical and sexual abuse and towards neglect and emotional abuse. Examine the reasons for neglect and it's sometimes hard to understand the difference between neglect and poverty. If you're too poor to have stable housing, or if you can't make your benefits last the week, or if you're too ill to keep your house in a good condition, or if you're working two jobs and forced to leave your children alone for periods of time, that might ultimately be judged as neglectful parenting. Social workers have relatively little power over the material problems in their clients' lives: they struggle to fix housing shortages or employment problems. But parents can still be blamed for these issues that are, to a large extent, beyond their control.

Some of the major factors that lead to child removal – domestic violence, poor mental health and substance misuse – are also more present in marginalised families' lives. Degree holders are significantly less likely to experience domestic abuse than those who finished their education after GCSEs. Women in the lowest earning households, taking home less than £10,000 a year, are three times more likely to experience domestic abuse than those in households earning more than £50,000 a year, according to government statistics.[5]

Meanwhile, higher earning households can pay for therapy. Parents from poor homes who do drugs and neglect their children are on social services' radars, but middle-class parents too hungover to get up in the morning, or microdosing on acid to perk themselves up, are not. And when middle-class families such as Francesca's do come into contact with social services, they have the resources to help themselves more readily.

Spend any time talking to families, social workers and lawyers, and the stark class divisions, or perhaps more accurately the poverty traps, become impossible to ignore. Cathy Ashley is Chief Executive of the Family Rights Group charity, which campaigns for reform. She says that while actual physical abuse is one thing that can be measured and proven, assessing the *potential* of abuse, and neglect, is much more subjective. Prejudices start to creep in about what constitutes good or acceptable parenting.

'Neglect needs much more exploring,' Ashley says. 'We are blaming individuals for their failure to deal with situations which may be, at least in part, a result of society's actions and economic situations.' Factors that play into that decision-making might often include answering questions like: 'Are the family willing to work with social services?' But sometimes that

presents families with impossible choices. Ashley describes circumstances where parents have to choose between attending
a meeting with social services and going to a job interview – in
that situation, which choice would demonstrate that you were
prioritising your child and not neglecting them?

In dozens of extensive interviews with social workers,
Paul Bywaters identifies a common theme: 'The notion of
an underclass that social work must regulate and persuade
into respectability'.

Bywaters' research also reveals the bizarre hoops that
social workers unconsciously jump through to disregard the
impact of poverty on family's lives:

> 'On the one hand social workers can articulate the rela-
> tionship between poverty and harm, but on the other
> hand their practice takes little if any account of this anal-
> ysis. In concert with this convoluted position (or maybe
> as a result) social workers have adopted a number of tech-
> niques and frameworks for disengaging with poverty, and
> justify this approach by using notions of equitable and
> non-stigmatising practice.'[6]

That idea of an underclass – the 'broken Britain' portrayal
of the undeserving poor – has been internalised in the social
work profession, Bywaters says. Where you'd think social
workers would be trained to see past class prejudice, many
have adopted the narrative wholesale.

'There is an absence of processes, systems or resources
to support social workers in this task of understanding and
addressing the consequences of poverty,' Bywaters concludes. The statistics that document the reasons for child

removal have a category for poverty, but social workers rarely record cases as attributable to this, instead choosing the 'abuse or neglect' label for the majority of cases.

The retired judge James Munby is troubled by the class grip on the family courts he served in. His suggestion is that neglect and emotional abuse may simply go below the radar in middle-class homes because they aren't examined as closely. 'The question that has gravely troubled me for years and years is how often do you see a middle-class family in a care case where there isn't sexual or physical abuse? The honest answer is virtually never.

'One of my suspicions is that if you are wealthy, middle class with private doctors and private schools, those referral mechanisms don't work in quite the same way as they do with the local state school. They get below the radar.'

In other words, schools and doctors in wealthy areas are not as vigilant about children showing signs of abuse or neglect. They are not policed in the same way.

'Partly there is an assumption these things don't happen in the middle classes – which is nonsense, of course they do. And partly I think people are less attuned to it. A lot of emotional harm and neglect cases start as a kid arriving at school dirty, unwashed and hungry. You only have to add on to that Mum turning up smelling of drink. Well, there are plenty of alcoholic parents who probably turn up at a public-school sports day or regatta stinking of drink. Nobody would think of ringing up social services.'

I'm reminded of Darren McGarvey's even more blunt description in his book *Poverty Safari*: 'It all begins with social deprivation. When it comes to child abuse, poverty is the factory floor.'

This is a system that pretends to be class blind, and that it treats everyone the same regardless of their circumstances or where they come from. Social workers I meet insist that they investigate middle-class families too. But the evidence is clear: the inequality that runs through our society is omnipresent in this story, igniting and fuelling the injustices that families face. Bywaters describes the poverty that pervades the lives of people in the child protection system as 'the wallpaper of [social work] practice; too big to tackle and too familiar to notice'. This system isn't class blind; it's poverty blind.

'Broken Britain' was the Conservative mantra going into the 2010 election. If that idea could be encapsulated in one case, it would be the death of Peter Connelly in 2007. The brutal tragedy became a symbol of a broken state. David Cameron talked of a 'social recession'. He cited cases such as Fiona Pilkington, the mother who killed herself and her disabled daughter because she was unable to tolerate constant bullying from neighbours – a case that represented a 'breakdown of community', Cameron said, a 'breakdown of morality'.

After a decade of living with 'broken Britain', the question remains: who judges what good enough parenting is? And whose standards are we applying? What I have seen in the child protection system, again and again, are processes enacted by middle-class powerbrokers – in politics, in the courts and in social work – on a precariat, for want of better language.

There are cultural aspects to this dynamic too. We live in bubbles defined by our social class that increasingly don't even share a common language. Lucy Reed, a family lawyer who works in the south-west of England, gives an example: 'Quite often we've seen parents criticised for calling a baby "sexy".

Most of us would think that's a bit weird. But then there are hysterical responses. But I've met so many who don't see it as sexualising. They mean "cute" and "gorgeous". It's a mismatch of what acceptable parenting is. There are some families that need their children taking away because things aren't right. But we also need to get underneath people and build them up.'

Where I live and parent, in middle-class north London, the idea of 'good parenting' is built on attention and responsiveness, positive reinforcement and modelling the behaviour you want to see in your children. At its most extreme it's the 'helicopter parenting' trend identified in Western countries that have grown more wealthy – and more unequal. As parents have had more time for parenting, the potential downfalls of their kids not being successful has grown in divided and unequal societies, economists argue.[7] So parents have swooped in at every opportunity to support and nurture – or, like me, felt a bit inadequate for not doing so. In Scandinavia they call it 'snowplough parenting' – the mums and dads who clear the path of all difficulties before the kids can work through it themselves.

One study I read makes me reflect on parenting styles, and the class bias in them.[8] The researchers observed parents and assessed their attachment with their children and realised that you didn't need to respond to every cry of your baby for them to secure an attachment. Indeed, those who did excessively had less confident children, less willing to try new things and make mistakes, as a result. They drew a picture of what 'good enough' parenting actually looks like, which rather than being automatically responsive, is being responsive as little as 50% of the time.

The same study pointed out this was particularly

important for parents in lower socio-economic homes. 'Because low socio-economic-status parents juggle multiple challenges associated with low socio-economic status, it may be helpful for them to know that holding a crying infant until fully soothed, even 50% of the time, promotes security,' the researchers said. 'Such a message could help parents increase positive caregiving without raising anxiety regarding "perfect parenting" or setting the bar so high as to make change unattainable in families that face multiple stressors.'

The researchers talk about the formation of a 'secure base' rather than a constant responsiveness, pointing out that looking at it in this way avoids emphasising a monocultural view of parenting practices that are 'often associated with white, middle-class populations, such as moment-to-moment attunement, prompt responses, sweet tone of voice and affectionate verbal comments'.

We return to the theme of 'good enough' parenting later in the book, but like Lucy's comments on the language we use, and how it is interpreted, the cultural assumptions around what a happy, healthy home looks like can build prejudice into the judgement of families. Especially when the majority of the social workers and legal teams are middle class.

Class brings advantages and disadvantages at every stage in the child protection world. Once they are in the social services system, things can be different for middle-class families. Like with Francesca's case, where she was able to draft in a powerful community network for support, the more social capital a person has the more they are likely to have resources to help them. The labyrinthine care system takes a lawyer to navigate, and then you need the connections – the teachers and other figures of authority that will vouch for your family. Being educated and accustomed to being asked for your opinion also gives you the confidence that you can question the authorities.

Francesca's fury at the system and determination to talk about it is in part a recognition of that privilege. She has the network – the Church, school and wider community – that could and did vouch for her. Social workers say that sometimes the difference between removing a child or leaving them with their family can be the network of support systems around the family. Just as Caitlin emphasised, isolation is deemed to be a greater risk to the children under investigation.

'I knew how to get a headteacher, a vicar and an MP to hear my story and even some of those to come to court with me. I could access money to pay for people to stay in my home when we weren't allowed unsupervised contact,' Francesca says. 'What about people who can't? What happens to them?'

She describes how within a week of the initial court appearance, they had collected 200 personal letters from community and friends. Character references were provided by vicars, high court judges, lawyers and an MP. 'My point being: without being well connected, would we have been separated from our children?' she asks.

A year on, Francesca's family is together, has no contact with social services – something she was told was unprecedented after such a big investigation – and is getting on with life. But the emotional scars remain.

Francesca believes that the younger two boys were too small to have any lasting effects, but she saw signs of trauma in her two older children. Both began to wet the bed every night. They would cling to her at the school gates and were unsettled at home. It took her and her husband months to feel anything like normal; Francesca couldn't stop crying in the aftermath.

She worries about her second son's feelings of guilt over what happened. 'Once, after it had all long ended, he was having an altercation in the playground with another child and I said, "It's not your fault." Out of the blue he said: "But I told them about the water." He was talking about the social workers, even though we hadn't spoken about it for months.'

I sit with Francesca in her kitchen. The bigger three children are at school and nursery. Jacob is wandering around playing with a handheld hoover, clearing up the mess he makes as he goes. Francesca makes him scrambled eggs on toast and he demands jam.

Francesca is haunted by the whole experience. She doesn't understand why the first solution the social workers reached for was to remove her children, despite there being not even a hint of a problem before. None of her children had so much as broken a bone, and their GP had no concerns. She hates the fact that her children were put through multiple interviews, asked what she thinks were 'leading questions' sowing ideas in their minds. The only evidence they had was one contested doctor's report, yet the more they failed to back it up, the more it felt like they tried to construct a case. It's like they dug their heels in. In the end, she was desperate for the court and the 'sanity of the judges', she recalls.

She's still confused by her experience and horrified that this could be happening to other families. 'I don't understand why the first resort was removal. We should be doing everything to keep parents and children together. Of course, sometimes it will require intervention. But why have removal as the first choice?'

Daniel's story

'Dad is not in the picture'

Invisible fathers

Daniel is just a few weeks shy of his eighteenth birthday when he receives the text message that changes his life forever.[1] The problem is, he doesn't understand what it means. He looks at his phone, rereading it over and over again. The message tells him his girlfriend has gone into labour. But he doesn't know what 'labour' means. It's definitely connected to the fact that their baby is coming, he reasons. But he doesn't know what to do. Is the baby minutes or days away? How can she be texting if she's giving birth? he wonders.

He texts back to his girlfriend's phone – he later learns that her aunt has been using it – and asks how urgent it is. Should he come straight away or later that day? 'Just make your way to the hospital,' comes the reply. In a daze, he debates this with his brother and cousin, who are gaming on the PlayStation with him, then he and his cousin decide to walk the two miles to the hospital. By the time he arrives, his son has been in the world for forty minutes.

He holds his baby, heart bursting with pride and freezing with fear. He has no idea how to do this. It's a panic that has gripped him in a depression for the five months since his girlfriend took a pregnancy test.

When the test result came back positive his world shrank. He stopped talking to his friends, who couldn't relate to his experience, either because they were nowhere near becoming parents or because they had no contact with their babies. The one thing he was sure of was that he wanted to be a father, to provide for his girlfriend and baby and make sure they had everything they could want for in life. He just didn't know how he was going to do it.

His college work suffered and he turned inward, plagued by the worries running round and round his head. How was he going to be a parent? Who was going to teach him what to do? How was he going to provide for them? And what if the baby wasn't even his? No one talked to him about it; no one asked him how he was feeling, as if it were already assumed that he would not have a significant role in his son's life.

And now he's standing by a hospital bed, surrounded by his girlfriend's family, holding a baby. The room is hot and noisy, the child is snatched away from him and passed around the room. He craves a moment with his girlfriend and son to mark their new family. But the bustle continues as though he's invisible. The midwives talk to his girlfriend and her aunties. He's just a shadow in this scene.

The first interest a professional shows in him is a call from a social worker. Social workers had got involved because his partner was still a teenager and not long out of the care system herself. The only thing the social worker at the end of the phone line asked was whether or not he had a criminal record. They intended to run police checks on him. He didn't. He wondered why that was the only question that might be asked of him, given the responsibility he hoped to take on for his son.

At this point he understands three things about social services. One: they take kids. Two: people hate them and you shouldn't open your door to them. And three: they might pay for you to go on trips with your family.

His girlfriend moves to a hostel with the baby where he visits them regularly – and where social workers come to observe them too. Throughout his son's infanthood, his girlfriend is put under the microscope and her ability to parent constantly assessed. There are regular child protection meetings, which he attends. Their case is de-escalated from child protection to the 'Child In Need' category, meaning that there is no statutory force behind the social workers' demands, because they are deemed to be handling their parenting sufficiently well. It means a lower level of monitoring. In those early meetings Daniel takes a back seat, observing the conversation that focuses on his girlfriend's parenting and rarely turns to him. He describes himself as 'laid back and phlegmatic' and will only speak when he feels confident. They explain to his girlfriend all the ways she needs to comply; she meets the milestones and he watches on, supporting where he can but still unsure of his place in this foreign process.

Everything changes after the Halloween party. He wanted just a few friends over to the supported-living hostel where she lives. More turn up, including a group of boys associated with a rival gang who set out to make trouble. When he bars them from the flat, they trash the communal areas, resulting in everyone in the building receiving warnings from the housing authorities, including his girlfriend. The police are also called, and between the police and the housing officers, social services are asked to inspect his son's situation again. His son is two now and wasn't in the flat during the party, but staying with relatives.

As the child protection investigation drags on and on, the strain on the young couple's relationship is mounting. Eventually it is too much and they split up. By his third birthday, the little boy is in care.

What happened after that is not unheard of, but it is still unusual. It was Daniel's lawyer who first suggested he seek full parental responsibility after hearing about the wide family network he had – including eight aunties who all lived nearby and were willing to support him. He had a steady job at a corporate gym where he was a personal trainer. The social workers explained he could fight in court for custody alongside his now estranged partner from whom the baby was being removed – or go it alone. When his partner became more troubled, facing police investigations on separate matters, Daniel decided that he would ask for full parental responsibility. He was still only twenty years old.

That's also when he met a social worker named James who changed how he worked with the authorities.

James was the senior social worker sent to assess Daniel's ability to parent. Despite Daniel having been present in his son's life, he says that it was only when he applied to become the lead carer that anyone ever assessed him personally. When his boy was still a baby, assessments were made, but when he later saw those documents in court it was like he hadn't been in the room. He was a ghost in his son's paperwork, despite his real role as a father.

James came from a developing school of social work that over the past ten years has been pushing to build better relationships between people and their social workers. Instead of turning up with a checklist to inspect and standards to dictate, he asked Daniel how he wanted to be observed and they did the school run together instead of a formal inspection. They negotiated how James would interact with his son, rather than pretending to be invisible and observing them. He won Daniel's trust.

Daniel booked off the five days he was told it would take for the final court case. They settled the case in the first four hours and he was given full parental responsibility. He didn't know whether to laugh or cry. 'It's done,' his lawyer told him. He spent the next few days running from the GP surgery to their dental practice to the school with the documents to show that he was legally responsible for his son. He wanted everyone to know. His son was his, and no one could argue with it.

From a lifetime of being a shadow in his son's story, that day he felt like a real dad for the first time.

Today Daniel's son is aged nine. They have a tight bond and Daniel works thoughtfully and tirelessly to be the best dad he can be. His little boy is carefree and comfortable in his skin. They've lived together for five years and Daniel has given up personal training and works with a homelessness charity helping people get into work. He has also worked as a consultant to local authorities, teaching social workers to include fathers more in their practice.

He says he was discriminated against as a father, but that there were intersections to the discrimination he faced. 'They probably didn't listen to me because one, I was young. Second, I am a man and raising a child is a woman's job in so many people's eyes. Then third, if it was because I was black I'd struggle to say – I grew up in a multicultural world so I wouldn't recognise racism.'

But he was consistently surprised at the low expecta-tion people had of him as a parent. 'One social worker was amazed that I cooked fresh food for my son. She was shocked. She wanted me to write a statement about it. She said it was unusual for a man to do all these things,' he recalls. 'I iron his clothes, I taught him to go to the toilet, I cook and clean. We don't live in McDonald's or restaurants. I put it down as discrimination. Why as a man do I have to put that out there?'

James remembers the first time he met Daniel. 'He was so sweet and charming, but very young. He was just making sense of his identity,' he recalls. 'He was trying to be a personal trainer and a parent, but at the same time hanging out with his friends and doing what young men in London do.' The council he works at – which was managing Daniel's family's case – is a progressive one that prioritises relationship-building at the beginning of the social care process. James arrived at the stressful height of the court process, when the family was already in court facing the removal of the child from his mother.

'Social workers sometimes fall into the trap of prescribing too much rather than getting to know each other. We built a relationship. I shared things about my life – I had small children too. I recognised that as a white middle-class man from the north-east I wouldn't understand everything about a younger working-class boy who grew up in Congo. So we got to know each other.'

For some in social work, sharing personal experiences and information is anathema and even risky. Increasingly there's a school of thought championing a more human approach. James says: 'We got through that crisis period together. Through those difficult moments our relationship was strengthened.'

Six months after his case was settled and Daniel had transferred to another authority, James received an email from Daniel. They started to exchange information that they were learning about different support services for families and James invited him on to a parent board for his council's children's services. They keep in touch, appear at events together and are still learning from one another even now.

It's rare that it ends up this way for fathers.

There's a cover-up going on in the story of family separation. Every law, every service, every website that forms the infrastructure that exists to keep children safe uses the generic term: parents. The Children Act 1989, the legal underpinning of everything I'm reporting on in this book, does not mention mothers or fathers, but parents. On paper, in the eyes of the system, parents are equal; no assumption is made. But the truth is that this is an organisation that focuses on mothers and dismisses fathers as the problem, or irrelevant. Academics describe fathers as the 'ghosts' and the 'shadows' in the child protection system.[2]

I watch a court case where a lawyer patiently presents five days of evidence on behalf of a father, who doesn't once turn up for court. More often than not fathers are perpetrators and abusers in the lives of the mothers I meet. Men move in and out of the stories I hear, their attachment to their children seemingly disposable.

At best the system is blind to dads; at worst it's an institutionalised bias that not only writes men out of their children's stories but heaps more pressure on women to fix complex problems and holds them responsible for the shortcomings of men. But it's a bias born of the fact that, routinely, men are a problem in the dynamics of the families in care. When so often men are the violent parties in abusive families, should they even be considered part of the solution? There's a tension around even questioning the role of men in child protection cases.

Men are as much a part of this story as women. Around 82% of care proceedings cases involve a father. While more and more fathers become primary carers in wider society, in the court system it's slipping backwards; the number of men involved is declining slightly relative to mothers.

Fatherhood seems to be an ignored factor in children's lives – and academic research provides further evidence to back it up. In the case of Peter Connelly, the social workers' focus on the mother, and disregard of her partner and his brother (who are thought to have inflicted the most harm), blinded them to the abuse. One study identified six roles that fathers can play in child protection cases: they are 'marked men', with histories of abuse or violence that label them as high risk; 'in the frame' meaning suspected of abuse or neglect; 'on trial' where the concerns are less but their parenting needs testing; 'good enough' meaning they are deemed acceptable but in need of monitoring; a 'safe pair of hands' when they are trusted; and finally 'on the fringe' when they are peripheral and not considered relevant.

The same study, by the respected professor of social work Marian Brandon, concluded: 'Engaging fathers should be part of everyday practice in child protection and not an unmanageable task. Most men in child protection pose both a risk and a resource for their child. The actual and potential benefits they bring to their child should be discerned as well as any risks.'

Gary Clapton is a lecturer in social work at the University of Edinburgh but spent most of his career practising in London as a social worker. He wrote the book on the subject, *Social Work with Fathers*. He says that ignoring fathers can have different results. 'Dads are usually not included. Or they are the bad guys. They are ignored as a potential resource to help make the family work. And they are ignored as a threat, like the Peter Connelly case. Women are then held solely responsible for children. That is ingrained across the social work literature and percolates across the professionals,' he says. 'The common phrase is "Dad's not in the picture" – that allows professionals to move on and discuss what is in the picture. Usually there's a guy around the corner who they haven't looked for.

'I advise two things: One, get to them earlier. Whoever takes referrals needs to ask, Where is Dad? That's not done as a matter of routine. Two, register dads at primary schools. The nearest relative is often Mum's mum. Make it Dad and you set the ball rolling in the right direction.'

The situation is compounded by the fact that fathers can

struggle to engage in what seems a female-only space. The overwhelming majority of children and family social workers are female (86%), compared to male (14%). It's not only alienating, it presents pragmatic challenges.[3] Social workers have to find the dads if they aren't living with their children, and mothers are often the gatekeepers to those relationships. A busy social worker with twenty cases might not have time to do the detective work to find a father, or the legwork to gain their trust. Meanwhile, it's important to remember that men are very often the problem, particularly when it comes to domestic violence.

Georgia Philip, a researcher at the University of East Anglia, describes how social workers can struggle to understand this apparent contradiction: that a father can be both the problem and part of the solution. 'There is a tendency to see only the risks rather than recognising that most are a combination of the two, and unless you can hold the tension and understand they can be both, the child will miss out,' she says.

But she warns that the politics around even debating the role of fathers is fraught: 'This is really emotive stuff. The model of parenting where the mother is the primary parent runs so deep. We're still stuck with a model where fathers are optional to the process. For as long as they are seen as optional they get to opt out.'

Women whose children are removed are left with the blame of a 'failed parent', whereas men can escape that label more easily. Meanwhile, while men are ignored more pressure and responsibility is piled on the women to carry the load. It's another way that sexism finds its way through this system to punish women.

Philip adds: 'What I find troubling is the zero-sum game: if you are seen to be advocating on behalf of fathers the response is that we are undermining the gains achieved for women. That's part of what's difficult for social workers. It's binary, pick a side. But it's not a zero-sum game. The patriarchy is bad for women, but also for men in different ways.'

Georgia's most recent research, not yet published, challenges some of the tropes that single women are the most likely to have children repeatedly removed. Actually, many more couples resurface in the system with subsequent children. Yet all services are aimed at individual parents, usually mothers, rather than at couples and family dynamics. It's a glaring error that writes men out of their own responsibilities – and needs. It betrays an enormous cover-up in the system over the role of men in their families that does no one any good.

In a community centre in central Glasgow, a fathers' support group shares videos of themselves playing with their kids. The leader tells me, 'Three seconds into one of them, another dad said, "Stop. I know you are struggling but I can tell how much your son loves you just by the way he's looking at you."'

Twenty years ago, the Mellow Parenting programme was built around two insights: first, that it was children's behaviour that triggered support and there was very little that focused on the parents themselves. Second, that support programmes kicked in only when kids reached school age, but by then damage had been done. Parents need support from before their children are born. It was designed to help all parents, but the dads weren't turning up.

Since then it's had a visionary rethink, developing a father-focused programme which invited a group of dads to come together weekly with their children over fourteen weeks. There is a therapeutic element, discussing and reflecting on their own parenting experiences (while the kids are supervised separately in a play area); there is a play element, learning to do fun activities with their kids; and there is an educational element, learning about their children's milestones. But it's the fact that it's a space for fathers to reflect and share their experiences that makes it so power-ful. Raquib Ibrahim is a psychologist and the Research & Development Officer at Mellow Parenting; he developed the dads' programme seven years ago.

It's Raquib who describes the father with the video. He wasn't allowed unsupervised access to his kids; it was clear he felt like a failure. 'The father cried when the others com-mented on his son's love for him. He was so emotional. He thought he was a terrible dad. Everyone said, "You are work-ing on it." I was in tears watching the group coming together for him. There was a huge change in his attitude. Contact changed to unsupervised by the end of the programme.

'Parenting by default means mothering. Dads are assumed to be a problem or absent. Everything is geared around the mums. Having something specific is very much needed.

'I delivered a group in prison. Dads say, "My dad used to slap me and I turned out OK." We're sitting in a prison and they think they turned out OK. Another dad said, "I'm in here with my dad having father-to-son bonding time." Maybe bond somewhere other than prison? We want men to realise there are alternatives to what they grew up with.'

He says that the branding – Mellow Dads – is important.

It's a safe space which gives them something to aspire to. 'Dads often feel like they don't justify help – they want the mum to get help first. We're justifying their feelings as valid and genuine too.'

The dads who come on the courses he runs have incredibly damaged views of social workers. 'The discussion is around how they've been deceived or let down. There is a sense that social workers are out to get them and they just want to remove the child. We've had to negotiate with social workers to get the support to the dads. But you're getting deep into human relationships. The female partners are often the gatekeepers and Mum doesn't allow the dad access to bring the child to the group. We have to work together to bring them all into the groups.'

When you ask social workers why they don't work more with dads, they say they think the dads aren't interested, or they are dangerous, he says. The flip side is that dads say it feels like social workers don't want them there. 'There is a communication gap, an assumption on both parts that's wrong,' he says.

This is a story I hear about dads throughout the system. Kim, the Child Welfare Manager at a school in Tipton, whose story I'll explore in the next chapter, says: 'I always ask social workers, "Have you tried to make contact with the dad? Are they even aware their children are on a child protection plan?" It's a rule that both parents should be aware. Sometimes they try and can't, sometimes they don't see the point or are too strapped for time. If you've got a domestic abuse situation the mother doesn't want the father being brought back into the fold, but the child might still need that relationship in the long term.'

Lucy Reed, a family lawyer in Bristol who we will also meet later in this book, tells me that gender prejudices can work both ways: 'There are a lot of mums who feel the courts are too pro-dad and dismiss domestic violence. There are dads who feel they aren't given the same chances as the mothers.'

James, Daniel's social worker, experiences the issues differently as a man. 'As a father I think I have always seen it as incredibly important to bring both parents into the mix, even if the father is not involved on a day-to-day basis. I was always very interested in why the father was not involved. Sometimes I was told that he had been violent to Mum once – I would challenge that as a reason. If he didn't pose a risk now why wasn't he involved for the child? We owe it to fathers and children to make sure they have the opportunity to be involved where it's safe.

'That child needs to know we gave both of the parents the same opportunity to be involved in their life. As a male social worker it was easier for me to reach out to a father. But sadly when you are working in a crisis it is harder to reach out. We are pretty good at it where I work. It's considered essential. That doesn't happen everywhere.'

Daniel describes how throughout his experience all the social work assessments of his child's parenting focused on the mother of his child. They didn't see that he was capable of parenting. Or that he was surrounded in the area where he lives by eight aunties, all willing to support him with his son. Now he's learnt his vocation as a father. Now he describes his son as his number one focus; nothing is more important.

It's taken the lifespan of his parenting for him to mature

from the eighteen-year-old who panicked at the thought of having a baby so young. 'I've learnt to trust my instincts and speak what I know,' he says. He often describes parenting as a fight to get the best for his son, from the school, from the council's services, to be heard as his son's advocate.

Daniel spent his first years in Congo, and sought asylum in England at the age of nine. He was always a voracious learner, first trying to understand the rules of the new country he arrived in, then the education his parents wanted for him and finally the child protection system that policed his life for so long. His insights into social work are thoughtful and reflective.

He says that all he ever wanted was for social workers to really hear him, to move him out of the shadows of his child's life. He's noticed three styles of listening social workers adopt: the first is when they listen but are really thinking about what they are going to say next; the second is when they listen to make judgements; but the best is listening with an open mind to hear the reality of that family's life and to help them achieve what they want for their children. He describes it as 'open listening'.

Daniel quotes a Congolese saying his grandmother often used – and writes it down for me: '*Muana a beti bumda.*' He drums the table as he says it. It roughly translates as when a child drums, the elders must listen. It's about children's ability to be profound, just like the saying 'out of the mouths of babes'. It's also about that 'serve and return' grounding in the parent-child relationship. And it also urges those with power and responsibility to listen to the voices of those children. That's what Daniel really wants from the social work system: for people to listen.

Kim's story

*'You don't know what you're
sending them home to'*

Schools, safety nets and the pandemic

The roads around Tipton are eerily quiet. The kids are at home in lockdown. The terraces are rundown, to varying degrees. Some gardens are unloved and in most of the windows the curtains are drawn. A few of the families round here keep horses in their back gardens, a nod to their traveller roots. The teachers at the nearby school say that when they make home visits it is not unusual for a horse to pop its head through the living-room window.

Kim Maynard tours the Tibbington Estate, known locally as the 'Tibbey', in her mint-green Ford Fiesta. There are two main areas that feed the Q3 Academy in Tipton where she works: the Tibbey and the 'Lost City', as the kids call the second collection of streets. The drive around Tipton's roads, ten miles outside Birmingham in the Black Country, reveals a geography of deprivation.

Kim has driven these streets a thousand times. She's from the local area, she knows the families. She works as a welfare manager at the school and her number-one job is trying to get parents who have had low levels of education, and themselves had bad experiences at school, to support their children's schooling. But today, driving around the Tibbey, she has a more pressing concern. She just wants to make sure the kids are OK.

As it dawned on Kim and her colleagues that the school would have to close in the first nationwide lockdown of the pandemic, their initial thoughts were with the most vulnerable children. She was less worried about those with social workers – the council would find ways to look out for them. It was a wider group of children, who don't qualify for support at home but have difficult lives and no one looking out for them. For them, school is their safety net.

Kim and her colleagues at Q3 quickly cook up a plan to check in once a week on all children they consider vulnerable. They phone the parents and talk to the kids if they can. They try to work out from the sound of their voices whether they are OK. Every kid on free school meals is getting food vouchers, however there are many more households that don't qualify but are struggling with the extra cost. The school develops a tag team with the council, whereby they identify who is going hungry and the council drops off food parcels.

But there are parents who won't pick up their calls from private numbers, and children they can't see, behind these closed doors. So that's when Kim and her colleagues get in her little green car and go door-to-door, looking families in the eye to make sure everything is OK. Over the course of four months, they knock on 256 doors. At first, they find hungry children. Then they start receiving more notifications of domestic abuse cases in their kids' homes. After the initial confusion over what social workers can do, the number of referrals for inquiries starts to increase. 'It's not a happy time,' Kim says.

The school serves a particularly diverse area: 41% of children are non-white, compared with 21% in the country as a whole. Those who are white are exclusively from poorer and working-class homes. Some 30% of children living in Sandwell, the district that contains Tipton, are in poverty; 21% receive free school meals compared with a national average of 14%. The largest minority ethnic groups in the area are Indian and Pakistani. I wondered why Tipton rang bells for me, and Kim reminds me of the 'Tipton three' who ended up on terror charges in Guantanamo Bay in the early 2000s.

Out of 174 councils in the country, Sandwell comes seventeenth highest for rates of kids in care; 109 children per 10,000 are in care compared with a national average for England of 65. To put it mildly, the school is a challenging place in which to teach.

When we judge a school, we look at the wrong things. A parent walks into the building and looks at the artwork on the walls, the welcome they receive and the way kids behave in the classroom. But education is actually the result of two things that are much harder to see: the first is the quality of teaching in each individual classroom. It's possible to have a terrible education in a brilliant school, and a brilliant one in a terrible school, depending on your teacher. The second is the geography of the area, which districts the school serves, what options those kids have and the make-up of the student body – itself the result of a complex movement of pupils around the area.

The rest of what makes up an education system – the curriculum, the buildings, the leadership and whether the school is an academy or a church school or a regular comprehensive – are just about trying to shore up teaching, and calibrate an education to fit the needs of a particular student body.

Kim is employed by the school to help ensure that kids are safe and looked after well enough so they can learn. Her job exists on the cusp of education and social services. As such, hers are the first eyes and ears of the welfare state, watching for kids who aren't safe at home. In an area such as Tipton this gives her a very different perspective on social services. Kim sits in on the meetings at the council where decisions are made to escalate or de-escalate social services involvement in families. There are times where she believes they are being heavy-handed, but there are more times when she is pushing them to intervene earlier, to provide more help and support to families that are struggling.

Kim's is an ongoing fight to get help for children. She worries less about those who are registered as a 'Child In Need', are on a protection plan or are already in care. They have been prioritised for help and support. It's the ones who don't quite meet the council thresholds for these interventions that she worries about. These are the kids being left in neglectful homes, witnessing abusive relationships and drug-taking. They are being set up for educational failure through a thinner version of neglect. In Tipton, it's largely the white families in this category, she says, and boys in particular.

Over the five years Kim has been in the job she's watched more and more children pour into this 'bad but not bad enough' category. The changes have not necessarily been in the community, but in the council's measure for what qualifies for help. The thresholds for intervention have gone up. Every council has a thresholds document that guides social workers in their decisions about struggling families. Every so often it is reissued with updates. Sometimes that involves whole categories of needs that could qualify you for help being shifted down a level. What once would have been a red alert becomes amber as shrinking resources are more thinly spread.

This has changed Kim's role into a de facto social worker. 'The thresholds are so high now we're having to pick it up. The schools that don't pick it up are failing because the kids are too troubled to focus on learning,' she says. 'It's not the kind of child protection that proper social workers do, but it's a higher level than what we would usually manage in schools.'

Kim talks at a hundred miles an hour. She grew up nearby in Smethwick and still lives just a twenty-minute drive away. She describes the delicate role her colleagues play as cases escalate with social services. When they don't meet the thresholds to be on a child protection plan the main problem she faces is that they have no authority to compel parents to address the things that are holding the kids back, affecting their mental health and preventing them succeeding at school. But these are the same cases she wouldn't want to escalate to a court stage, because she knows the damage removing them from their families would cause – and doesn't trust the council to do better as corporate parents.

Engaging parents is an uphill battle. 'It's a generational thing, especially in Tipton,' she says. 'It's one of the main areas for domestic abuse. One of the main areas for poverty and neglect. You've got generations who haven't taken education seriously, or who haven't got anything from it, so they don't value it. Then they feed that to their children. The attitude is: what's the point?

'But when you go to child protection plans, and parents don't engage, that will only lead into a legal spiral and they end up being removed. What we need is to support them on a voluntary basis.'

Kim and a colleague start talking about the children they worry about most at the school, using initials to protect their anonymity. Parents who are recently out of prison, alcoholic, who never live in one place. But they also talk about the strong bonds the same children have with those parents and the damage that removing them would cause; it's a Catch-22 situation. Referring to one child in the school, she says: 'The only way she can excel is to have a different home life but there are huge dangers in that as well. The ones that go into care, our local authority isn't stable enough to provide really good care. We've got some brilliant foster carers but the job is tough.'

We're having the conversation in the school dining room and the key worker kids, plus the vulnerable kids who are in care or have special needs, are still in school. A small Year Seven boy strides across the room singing and calling out to the teachers as he passes. Two teachers follow him. He's en route to get his medication to calm his symptoms of ADHD. Once he's had them, he might be ready to learn.

Kim works closely with her colleagues in the council

and insists that while there are social workers who do good jobs, there is too much turnover in staff, which means kids have no continuity. She draws a picture of the conferences to make decisions about a child's level of intervention from social workers. The meetings are independently chaired, including all the professionals working with the child in one room. The sticking points around escalation are routinely about the parents' involvement. 'If parents understand the concerns, are willing, sometimes that can tip it into a "Child In Need" process back from the brink of child protection.'

But, with up to half a dozen professionals seated in a U-shape around a whiteboard, those conferences can feel like a courtroom. She found it intimidating when she first started going to them and worries about how it must feel for the parents who aren't used to it. 'They must feel so judged. It can be a very vulnerable experience. When it gets to court that's a whole new level.'

After having her daughter at eighteen, Kim trained in theatre and singing. She thinks this helps her to be confident in these situations. Then, when she was pregnant with her second child, she switched to train as a counsellor. That led to a counselling role with a charity, working with teenage victims of domestic violence. She was drawn to the role of school welfare manager by the stability (charity contracts are short and unstable) and the school hours, which fit with parenting her children.

The worst moments are when the removals occur at school. 'We've had maybe four incidences where a child has come to school to be told they are being removed. Some have gone willingly. Others have tried to run away and jump over the fence. Once we had to restrain the kid. Another time we had to take them to the foster carers because the boy wouldn't go with the social workers and would only stay with the teachers.

'We don't want to see that. It's traumatic. But you've got the other side: kids being neglected on a daily basis and nothing being done about it, and that costs us too. It's equally traumatic to send kids home to neglectful places every night. That costs us emotionally every day. We know that kid is going home to somewhere that's just not good enough. We often say we just want to take a kid home, give them a good bath, feed them up. You can't.

'In our communities this neglect is normalised. They don't understand that their environment is not good enough, the home is not good enough, the way you dress your kids isn't good enough, the way you speak to your children isn't good enough. Who is to say that it's not good enough? These parents are just doing what their parents did. With neglect it's very difficult to say. Is it neglect or is it poverty? What is the government doing about poverty? You can't just remove children because of poverty.'

For Kim, a lot of this is personal. She knows this area, she knows the lives the kids lead. She's come from a life on benefits with small children to having a good job. 'When I didn't have any money I was taking handouts from charity and buying really cheap furniture. My home didn't look great,' she says. 'Some of these families never leave Tipton. Even going to West Bromwich is a big move. They are trapped here. Poverty traps them here. Family tradition traps them here. They don't see a life outside. For children that's OK, but for adults as you grow up you realise you are trapped.'

*

There's a complicated dance between social workers, schools and the police. After Victoria Climbié died aged nine in Haringey, London, and an inquiry pinpointed mistakes made between the authorities, a bureaucratic mountain was scaled to make sure they were communicating with one another to protect children. But in the scarce years of austerity, dwindling resources have hamstrung some of these relationships. For Q3 Academy in Tipton that has meant the removal of their designated police liaison officer, so that when they suspect a child is carrying drugs or a weapon, they have to call 999 instead of a local officer who knows them. It's also meant that the support the council would otherwise have been able to provide under the guise of social services is falling to them.

Scarcity creates tensions: between school and social workers when they disagree on actions; between secondary schools and their feeder primary schools, who are blamed if they haven't identified the kids' problems early enough, which costs the secondary in assessments and more intensive teaching. And there are tensions between the secondary schools themselves, who vie for places at alternative schools known as Pupil Referral Units. Q3 could fill several of these, but is focused on supporting kids in mainstream school for as long as possible.

That's why headteacher Keziah Featherstone spends around £1m of the £9m budget on welfare rather than education, employing Kim as part of a team that includes heads of year and family liaison officers to try to solve the problems at home, so the children are better equipped to thrive at school. It's social work transferred into the school. That has even happened in a very real sense: in lower-level cases,

Kim and her colleagues who work as family support officers employed by the school are now the lead safeguarding adults for kids, coordinating a team from the council to meet their needs – a role once ring-fenced for social workers.

Featherstone is starting to see the fruits of her labour: the first sign is a reduction in exclusions. She has only been in place for two years, and the school was taken over by a new academy chain eighteen months previously. Before that it had been labelled inadequate by Ofsted inspectors, who described a school that was struggling to control its pupils, let alone teach them. Corridors were strewn with rubbish and there were no effective behaviour policies. Just prior to Featherstone's appointment, local newspapers reported a lockdown at the school after reports (never substantiated) of children coming to school with a gun.

Featherstone was the fifth headteacher in eight years and, two years in, is now the longest-standing in that period. Things were slowly and steadily starting to come together and improve. The team I met at Q3 believe that after a long haul, the pupils were finally beginning to settle down.

But when Covid-19 hit and the school, along with every other in the country, closed its doors to the majority of their children, the line of sight between the school and its pupils was broken. That's when Kim got in her little green car and started knocking on doors.

Across the country, other schools were squaring up to the same challenge. As the pandemic took hold and lockdown started, the narrative initially homed in on exams, and then on the frantic efforts to set up home learning and socially distanced teaching for kids of key workers as well as those classed as 'vulnerable'. But on the ground, schools knew their role was about more than just education. They couldn't abandon their less visible duty of keeping kids safe in an extraordinary situation. One assistant headteacher I met in Grimsby personally delivered over 7,000 meals to vulnerable children, by foot, over the long, hot summer term of lockdown. My son's primary school in north London opened up its playgrounds for families who didn't have gardens. Deliveroo trained some of its drivers to spot signs of abuse, knowing that they were the only people regularly going to the doors of people's houses. It was a moment of innovation, but it barely scratched the surface.

Nationally, when schools closed, referrals to social services fell off a cliff. There was an eerie quiet in the offices across the country that receive the calls reporting allegations of abuse or neglect. But everyone in the system knew how worrying that silence was. As the weeks of lockdown passed they feared the pressures that were heaping on to families, cooped up at home together for hours on end and with increasing insecurity around jobs and money. Social workers were painfully aware that all the things that keep their families safe were being stripped away: victims were locked up with their abusers with no excuse to leave the house; drug addicts were struggling to get the fixes that keep them going; the universal anxiety about the virus was bearing down on the nation's mental health. Things were getting worse inside people's homes, but referrals to social services were declining. Those who work in child protection lay awake at night worrying.

Coronavirus shut down society, which forms the bulk of a vulnerable child's safety net. Social workers are rarely the first to spot abuse; that tends to be friends, family, teachers, GPs or neighbours. The isolation that can make families so vulnerable was enforced, necessarily, by the government in the form of social distancing. It pushed all the problems in family life firmly behind closed doors, and locked them in.

While schools were valiantly scrabbling to set up systems to check in on their pupils, social work departments were desperately trying to figure out how their work – based on face-to-face interactions, relationships and judgements – could continue in a socially distanced world. Across the country the differences in services were dramatically exacerbated. Some councils initially cancelled all face-to-face meetings, then thresholds were set about what amounted to critical work that necessitated human contact and the risk that involved. Like the rest of the world, much of social work – child protection conferences, talking to families and exchanging information with colleagues – migrated to video conferences.

Working behind a mask is especially hard when you're trying to gain the trust of vulnerable families. For the first time, social work departments had to source the PPE (personal protective equipment) needed for safe meetings. Many were also shielding at home because of their own health conditions, or trying to juggle work with home educating their own children. One social worker described how inappropriate it felt to have their own kids walking in and out of the room as they spoke via video conference to clients. And all the time children's services directors feared that an outbreak of the virus in their teams could cause a complete breakdown of their services.

A further curve-ball came from the government in the

form of the temporary replacement of a slew of regulations around vulnerable children. In recognition of the unprecedented situation and challenges in local authorities, the Department for Education relaxed rules governing how much contact social workers should have with children in the care system, as well as some elements of scrutiny and time spans for temporary placements. The Children's Commissioner, Anne Longfield, stepped in: 'I appreciate that Local Authority children's services are likely to be experiencing challenging working conditions during the pandemic, and there are many inspiring examples of front-line workers going above and beyond the call of duty to keep children safe,' she said. 'Nevertheless, I do not believe that the changes made in these regulations are necessary – except perhaps for some clarifications (in guidance) about contact with children taking place remotely during the lockdown.'

Meanwhile, difficult decisions were being made about how contact could be maintained between birth families and those in care through the pandemic. Babies removed at birth couldn't receive their mothers' breast milk and their mothers were being offered contact with their newborn via video link. Siblings were no longer able to see one another. Children facing a final removal lost their chance to say goodbye. Some contact moved to video conferences, and happily, some families – teenagers, in particular – found speaking via screen was more rewarding than in a council contact centre with a social worker observing. But the rules across the country diverged sharply: some councils banned all contact, others bought in the gowns, masks and gloves to make it happen.

Problems ricocheted through the system. From schools

to social work to the family courts, the entire network that protects children was disrupted.

Councils rapidly reviewed every case on their books to prioritise the ones that still needed court intervention. The courts, once indivisible from their official courtrooms and defined by a physical space, reinvented themselves digitally, amid huge anxieties emerging about unfairness. The Family Justice Observatory (FJO), which gathers evidence on the process, conducted a rapid review of how courts were functioning in this new world. It revealed deep concerns – and hopes that modernisation might lead to better reforms once the crisis was over.[1]

Concerns ranged from the practical – some families couldn't afford the data to dial in and had to be provided with devices – to the deeply personal – parents left alone at home after hearing difficult decisions. Children were sometimes present during virtual hearings. Judges worried about the boundaries that are broken when everyone can see into one another's homes.

There were particular concerns around the removal of babies in lockdown. One barrister described: 'I found it profoundly inappropriate not to be speaking to the mother I represented in person but on a telephone when she had never met me before and had given birth to her baby only the previous day. The court decided, almost inevitably, that the child should be removed, but for that mother to be listening to the hearing in a side room in hospital and to be told of the court's decision by telephone (she missed the judgment because she had been called away to feed the baby by a midwife) without me being there to put an arm round her seemed horribly cruel to me.' One judge described conducting a hearing to remove a child with the parents sitting in a car outside the hospital watching proceedings on their phone.

The President of the Family Division of the High Court, Sir Andrew McFarlane, stepped in on one case to rule that a decision couldn't proceed on the basis of remote justice: 'The judge who undertakes such a [remote] hearing may well be able to cope with the cross-examination and the assimilation of the detailed evidence from the e-bundle and from the process of witnesses appearing over Skype, but that is only part of the judicial function. The more important part, as I have indicated, is for the judge to see all the parties in the case when they are in the courtroom, in particular the mother, and although it is possible over Skype to keep the postage-stamp image of any particular attendee at the hearing, up to five in all, live on the judge's screen at any one time, it is a very poor substitute to seeing that person fully present before the court.'

In the first part of lockdown, referrals to social services declined rapidly, a symptom of the invisibility of the families once schools closed. The courts were only deciding very easy or very pressing cases, little that required serious cross-examination. But with all the extra burdens on vulnerable families, the cases that weren't being heard were not disappearing. They were just creating a huge backlog behind the scenes. Reports of domestic violence – one of the biggest factors in child protection cases – were going off the scale in the pressure cooker of lockdown. New legal cases arriving in courts dipped sharply in April, to levels usually only seen during the Christmas season, then started climbing sharply from May onwards as the backlog overflowed.

But like so many aspects to this story, there were wildly varying effects happening across the country: some councils rushed to get kids into care where they were more confident they would be safe; others put everything on hold. Some judges accepted only the most serious cases, while others stalled the same cases, not trusting to decide.

The results of all of this will not be known for some time, as the statistics are collated and impact assessed. But one thing is known: the number of serious cases of child abuse and neglect resulting in a child's death or serious injury rose sharply in the first lockdown. Some 285 'serious incident notifications' were made in April to September 2020, up 27% on the previous year. Children were less safe behind the closed doors of lockdown.

The lockdown exposed schools as a central part of the welfare state designed to rescue kids who are in trouble. It exposed the weakness in a national system with no common standards, exacerbating the postcode lottery. Everyone did something different at the moment of crisis; no one collected the lessons to apply what worked best.

Back in Tipton, Kim continues to work over the hot summer during the first wave of Covid-19. She is on call through the holidays for meetings between social workers and the kids they are most concerned about. When the school returns in September there is a flood of new referrals at a rate she's not seen before. Cases are escalating to the next level, and every other phone call is a social worker with new information. Her head spins, she can't keep up with the details and has to meticulously record every conversation to keep track. The stories are similar: domestic violence and mental health problems, both aggravated by the lockdown and its after-effects. Parents are being sectioned; other cases that were on hold during lockdown – when parents refused to let social workers in the house under the social distancing guidelines – have got worse.

Despite the challenges she's confronting, Kim is more at ease now that children are back in school. But she can see the rollercoaster coming around again: Q3 is in a high infection area with additional local lockdown procedures. The school hasn't had a confirmed case of Covid-19 yet in the autumn term. But it will – many of its neighbouring schools have. 'It's just a matter of time,' she says.

She didn't know then that the lockdowns would roll on for many months, moving the children who are keeping her up at night in and out of the school routine, and making them invisible again.

Lucy's story

'The whole thing gets really toxic'

Lawyers and the trust gap

The private side room in the Bristol family court where Lucy Reed first meets Mia has no windows, just four chairs and a table. Lucy flicks the sign on the door to 'in use' for privacy and sits down next to her new client.

'Hello, Mia,' she says. Mia won't meet her eyes and is monosyllabic. Lucy knows three things about the woman in front of her: her name; the fact that she is in court today because the council are seeking an emergency removal of her baby; and that she has a drug problem.

She learnt these details that morning when the clerk rang to ask her to take on the case. On Friday mornings she eyes her phone nervously. Tricky emergency removals often come at the end of the week as social workers make sure they have all the legal work in place before the courts close for the weekend, spiking the adrenalin levels just as she's limping towards the weekend.

Sometimes Lucy has time to get to know her client, to cultivate a relationship and understand what's happening in their world – and to help explain to them what is going on and why they are in court. Today's case is not one of those occasions: they're thrown into a room together with the scantest of information. Any minute now Lucy will be interrupted or called into court to present her client's position regarding the council's application to remove her child. The problem is, she doesn't know what that is.

'Hello, my name is Lucy, I am your lawyer,' she says. 'How are you feeling today?' She explains that she's been sent to represent her by her solicitor. 'Can you tell me what you know about today's hearing?' Lucy asks, to little response.

'Do you know why you are here?' Lucy asks.

'No,' Mia says.

Lucy explains that the social workers are arguing her drug use means her home is unsafe for her daughter and that they want to remove her into care on an emergency protection order. 'I'm your lawyer,' says Lucy again. 'I am here to listen to you, advise you on your options in this court case, and to follow your instructions. Now, can you tell me what's been happening?'

Mia is eyeing her suspiciously. Lucy is well aware that she comes across as posh and elite, though she feels far less so than some of the barristers that she argues against in court; she tries to use the most accessible language she can. Mia explains how she came to be here, that she left her toddler at home overnight and neighbours called the police because they found the child crying in the hallway outside their flat at four in the morning. She insists the child was fine and that she had to leave to work for a short period (she is a sex worker) and admits her addiction to heroin.

Lucy is soaking it all in. She remains entirely dispassionate, and doesn't wince at the details. She's trying to work out her tactics for court. How is Mia going to manage in court? Probably badly, she's sullen and withdrawn and loses her train of thought easily. She's jittery, maybe because of the stress of the situation; or perhaps because she needs a fix. Lucy considers two options in terms of the advice she might give at this stage: fight removal now, or wait until her client can show the improvements she's making in her life. She weighs up what she's seeing and in this case it doesn't take long for her to make a call. 'My advice to you is that given the neglect witnessed by the police it's unlikely that they are going to let you take your baby home. Let's work out a longer-term plan to put in place all the things that will convince them you can safely look after your child later,' she says.

Mia's demeanour changes gear in a second. It's like the world has shifted against her and her body braces into fight mode. From monosyllabic her voice becomes clear, and loud: 'You're not on my side,' she shouts as she stands and heads for the door.

She hesitates only to deliver a stream of accusations at Lucy: 'You're on the social workers' side. I saw you talking to them before. You've stitched this up and all you want to do is take my baby to meet their targets on adoptions.'

Lucy has lost her. She knows that the best thing for her client is to get her calmly into court, to work with the system, rather than fight it – to avoid a damaging contested hearing where the client will probably give more ammunition to the local authority. She is in a bad place to be arguing against removal, but she might have a window over the next few months to evaluate her life, to make some changes and to get her kid back.

Lucy takes a deep breath and looks her in the eye. 'Wait. Please can you sit down a minute before you go? Listen – in this room, my job is to listen to you and give you my best legal advice – even if it's not what you want to hear. My advice is that you might make things worse by fighting this today, and you have a better chance of getting her back if you play the long game. That's just my advice, and everything we talk about outside the courtroom is private. Whatever you decide to do, that is what I will run with in court. I work for you.'

Her client pauses with her fingers hovering above the door handle, and starts to take in what she's saying. They are called into court, and at the end of the hearing the order is given for the baby to be removed, another barrister takes on the case and Lucy never sees Mia again.

Lucy recalls cases like this because it changed the way she communicates with clients.[1] She has dealt with countless similar cases since – sometimes the clients take her advice, sometimes they don't. She works the case according to their instructions either way – sometimes situations are less clear-cut and she is able to persuade the local authority to back down, or to convince the judge that removal isn't justified.

No matter what the time pressures are now, when she first meets a client she sees it as a key part of her job to educate them about the whole process. In nearly every case her clients don't know why they are in court, they don't understand how lawyers operate, the documents or terminology, and they don't know what is expected of them. What's worse is that many will come in with preconceptions about the system and deeply held distrust of it. It might be that they had social workers who let them down in the past, or that removal has been threatened before and they have been on the Facebook groups and websites that give free – and very often inaccurate – advice to parents in this situation.

Lucy can represent any of the parties in the case. Chameleon-like, she might be the council's barrister in one case, the parents' in another, the children's in the next. She's part forensic investigator, part social worker, and part wrangler of the various elements of the legal process. Wrangling comes in when things go wrong. The courts are feats of logistical organisation and Lucy keeps the cogs of justice turning. They depend on the cast of characters and huge bundles of information in lever arch files being in the right place at the right time. After Covid-19 hit they also depend on video calls working and clients having enough data to join them by phone.

Lucy invites me to observe a case she is involved in. She canvasses all the parties in the case, which is being heard remotely during a lockdown, via video conferencing, in order for me to attend and observe. She secures their agreement. I dial in, and give verbal assurances that I understand the court reporting restrictions. I turn off my camera and watch two of the four days of evidence, dogged by delays and interruptions, concerning a court application to remove siblings from their mother's care.

Lucy is speaking on behalf of the children's guardian, an independent social worker who represents the children's best interests. She's precise in her language and never expresses an emotion in court. Lucy works diligently throughout the process of the days I observe to keep things on track, to give the judge the right information at the right time and to achieve a fair process. But she does it in a way that focuses everyone on the task in hand – every suggestion is helpful, humble and pragmatic, designed only to edge forward to a resolution.

I watch a witness struggling to convey her message. She can't locate the facts she needs, or build a credible argument. She's at risk of crumbling under cross-examination. Lucy coaches her back on track, teasing the information out of her that builds the case for Lucy's client. It's gentle, humane and very effective.

In the course of writing this book, what constitutes a courtroom became a more fluid concept. The coronavirus pandemic flung an institution based on precedent and traditions into the digital age. When I first observe family lawyers, in the courthouse in Leeds, it strikes me that they belong to a club. In the courtroom they are the pictures of professionalism. You couldn't read their opinion on the circumstances that they are peeling apart in front of the judge. It set a stage for impartiality, a backdrop that lends tragic circumstances the gravity they deserve. In the corridors of the courthouse they are colleagues, exchanging jokes, checking in on other cases they share in common and asking about the kids and holiday plans, like any other workplace.

After Covid, like so much else, the courtroom dramas were reduced to a chequerboard of characters on a video conferencing screen. Each character is like a chess piece, with different moves it can make and power it can exert or be subjected to. There is of course a judge, and usually (but not always) a clerk for the court that keeps proceedings running smoothly and clicks 'record' on the video call; then there is a barrister and a lawyer for each of the parties in the case, witnesses and the parents. The wider families might attend, plus social workers and the children's guardian. It's not unusual to end up with a dozen people in the hearing.

Lucy lists the skills you need to be a good barrister: you have to be able to absorb information very quickly; to read your client and build rapport; to win their trust by listening to them, so that they listen to you.

As a witness to the system, Lucy's deepest concern is 'the breakdown of trust between families and social workers. There's a legitimate reason why people feel that way sometimes. There's a lot of lawyers going off into a room or a huddle in the corner. Parents' antennae are up and they are primed not to trust lawyers. They are reading awful things on the internet about us, then they see us having a joke in the corner. There is always a certain level of banter and teasing – you need to lighten it to survive. I'm much, much more sensitive to how things appear – we joke somewhere private now.'

That sense of alienation is compounded by the power dynamics in the family courtroom. In the vast majority of cases, as we've examined in earlier chapters, the poshest person in the room is the judge, the poorest person is the family member. 'I'm significantly more privileged than a lot of my clients,' says Lucy. 'There are some hearings where you have really posh, plummy Mulberry handbag-carrying lawyers with manicures. That feels difficult for me, let alone a client. I try not to have airs and graces.' She pauses then adds: 'The truth is I don't have any anyway.'

The legal profession has a ringside seat to the rising numbers of children going into care in recent decades. Like Lucy, most barristers act interchangeably for the council, the children, their parents or the wider family; multiple perspectives which make their testimony invaluable.

Lucy has witnessed a growing eroding of faith in the system. It's not a system that families ever really loved, but it becomes harder each year to make it function under the weight of the suspicion of the people it serves.

She describes the internet-fuelled rumours of baby-snatching courts, shared on websites and Facebook forums that also advise parents to sack their 'professional loser' lawyers and cut off social workers. She names one man who runs one of the most prominent of these websites. He claims to pay for women to flee the country to avoid their children being removed. She has learnt to spot when her clients have found such sites – their language and disposition is different. They talk about social workers being motivated by targets to adopt babies, and foster carers and lawyers only being involved for the money.

The consequences are profound: it compounds families' problems. 'When they behave in ways that demonstrate a lack of trust, they are told they can't work with the local authority and that's another black mark. Unless they can get to grips with it and build a relationship the whole thing gets really toxic.'

Sometimes among the complaints of bias, lies and unfairness there is legitimate criticism of individual social workers – or more often the way in which a council has failed a family. Lucy has on occasion run with these complaints, successfully proving misconduct which has changed the course of cases – but the trick is judging which are provable poor practice, and which deflect from the real issues; whether raising them is likely to help the parent keep or recover their child.

Restrictions mean I can't report the details of the case I see Lucy work on – a care proceedings case where the council is seeking to remove children. But safe to say the window on the screen into the mother's life, the details we hear about her relationship with her children and the difficulties she faced, couldn't feel further away from the comfortable life Lucy lives in a town just outside Bristol. She works, in lockdown, from an office which she's plastered with pages of weekly law reports. Her husband, a stay-at-home dad, is in the garden with their kids experimenting with six different ways of growing tomatoes.

Lucy's children have names that suggest a far more bohemian hinterland to a woman who in court appears as straitlaced as, well, a judge. Her American husband used to run a youth hostel in California. They spent ten years in London, where they met, then moved near Bristol to start a family. Her oldest is named after a character in a cult film.

Lucy resisted the family courts originally, rebelling against the pigeonholing of women in the family court system, while men did the more prestigious and lucrative corporate law. But the more she experienced the more rewarding it became. 'I love getting to know the clients, working out what the issues are, helping them make good decisions, to at least feel like they've had a fair shot and someone has fought for them. A lot are disadvantaged and have had so much shit in their own lives.'

*

Lucy's testimony on the breakdown in the trust in the system feels to me like the heart of what's going wrong. A system designed to help and support is now seen as a bigger threat to the families it enacts its powers on. I read the wild conspiracy theories online and the conviction with which people feel the injustice.

I track down the man Lucy speaks of behind the 'forced adoption' website on the Côte d'Azur in the South of France. Ian Josephs is dressed in millionaire leisurewear – white tracksuit and trainers – and lives in a comfortable villa behind a high metal gate.[2] He's holding a ringing phone as he opens the gate. He doesn't stop to say hello as he answers and stalks back into his beautifully tended Mediterranean garden.

At the end of the line is a woman about to go to court to plead to be reunited with her children who were removed by social services more than a decade previously. Ian barks instructions: 'Don't have a lawyer whatever you do. You won't be able to speak.' He listens carefully. The swimming pool glitters in the dazzling spring sun, palm trees catch in a cool breeze and a cat strolls past. 'Why did you speak to a social worker? I told you, don't speak to them. You're the parent, not the adopters. You've not committed any crime.'

The call finishes. Somewhere in England the woman, should she take his advice, prepares to face a judge with high hopes and without legal representation. Back on the Riviera, Ian explains how he, an eighty-seven-year-old English tax exile operating his businesses out of Monaco, became a vigilante – not of the criminal justice system, but of the child protection system.

Ian pays pregnant mothers' travel expenses to flee the country to France or Ireland if they suspect social workers are planning to remove their babies once they are born. He does this for around five women a year. He estimates he's spent £40,000 over the years and advised hundreds more on the phone. He tells mothers to stonewall social workers and sack their lawyers. He advises that they shouldn't report domestic violence or abuse of their children, claiming they will simply lose their kids.

His main beef is with social services, which he refers to as 'the SS'. 'The way they behave is like Nazis, in various ways. Of course you distrust these horrible people ... They have one thought in their mind. Not to keep a family together, but to steal their children,' he says.

'It's better for the judge to just be suspicious than to work with social workers, which means giving up their children. Then they've got no chance at all.'

Back in England, Lucy deals with the consequences of his advice as clients try to fight against the system. They often lose. The situation reminds me of a prototype argument for the fake news rows that have surfaced on the internet and particularly around elections: rumours gaining speed in private message groups, then fuelling real-world outcomes.

Ian has a life story with the plot twists of *Forrest Gump*, and he tells it with the populist zeal of Nigel Farage. A middle-class boy at a top English public school, he fought his way to Oxford, despite low grades, to study law, sharing a room with Michael Heseltine, who later became a Conservative politician, before they went into the hotel business together. Ian expanded to bigger hotels, then language schools. Along the way he became a world-rated chess player, stood three times for parliament and was elected to Kent County Council. It was as a councillor in the 1960s that he first encountered the child protection system and started giving free advice to parents. In 2002 he moved to Monaco and launched his website. The website is a rambling diatribe of accusations, the punctuation randomly scattered and mostly replaced with bright red capitals where he wants to emphasise a point. Removed children might end up as sex toys, he claims, in between references to *Mein Kampf.*

He describes this morning's call as typical of the two or three he receives every day. 'Can you think of any reason, even if a woman is on drugs, to take a child away without giving her any chance to look after it?' asks Ian. 'I'm not pretending the women I've helped are saints – I'm not one myself. They've got flaws, as everyone has, but that doesn't take away their rights.'

Why would a well-off man, who lives surrounded by his family in the South of France, spend what should be his retirement meddling in a system hundreds of miles away? He says his motivation is to satisfy the lawyer he wanted to be. He claims he couldn't practise law in the UK because he was 'too flamboyant'. He doesn't like people telling other people what to do, and believes there is a huge injustice at play in which parents – mostly mothers – are being punished without a crime being proven.

Ian is, undoubtedly, fuelling the suspicion between state and family. But like so often in this story, there are elements of truth in his warnings – once in court, parents *are* often separated from their children. It's true that families do feel the system is stacked against them. He is an extremist in this story – and both a cause and a consequence of the breakdown in trust that is happening across the system and the desperation that families are feeling.

*

Periodically there are murmurs that maybe there could be a different way of running court processes, one that doesn't create the one-way 'conveyor belt' to care and feels less adversarial. There's also a question of the costs involved to councils and courts – this is a multi-billion-pound operation. One lawyer's daily fees for a final hearing are around £500 to £700, depending on whether they include a small uplift for extra big 'bundles' – the files of documentation that are produced with the cases. For the lawyer it is arduous work, with hours spent watching interviews describing traumatic details of abuse and neglect, and many more trawling through tens of thousands of pages of phone records, all for no fee. Meetings are done free of charge, simply because they need to be done.

But it all adds up on the public purse. Legal aid costs for families amount to £125m a year alone but with multiple lawyers in every courtroom in the country each day, plus the councils' legal staff, the guardians, social workers and judges' salaries as well as the bill for maintaining the court system, the true cost is mountainous.

Other countries have found different ways of doing things: in Scotland, cases are heard by a jury-like panel of volunteers. In Denmark, only the parent has legal representation and a panel of experts, politicians and a judge make the decision.

Parents argue that there must be a way to avoid disturbing cross-examination. Victims of domestic abuse are regularly re-traumatised in courts by having their experiences questioned. Cross-examination is critical to get to the truth – but it is also inhumane.

One of the most radical schemes has been trialled in

England. It's called the Family Drugs and Alcohol Court, where a parent struggling with addiction is given a chance to keep their children. For a set period, they regularly go to court to meet with the judge, but for problem-solving sessions in which they are coached and supported to parent better and tested to ensure they are drug-free. The problem solving, combined with the tough conditions, has been proved effective. The judge can insist on these sessions with the full force of the law. If this 'problem-solving court' fails to have an effect, the family is sent back to the regular courts.

An *Economist* journalist attended one such hearing and reported:

> A mother arrives for her first hearing, cradling one nine-month-old twin in her arm as she pushes the other in a pram. Everyone sits in a semicircle. The judge tells the mother to picture herself at the school gate in five years' time, on her children's first day at school. 'It's not an unrealistic dream, is it?' he asks. 'It is your right and we should be very careful before stopping a mother or father having that right. Work with us and make it happen.'[3]

Lucy believes the court process is necessary, that where there is no consensus over whether to remove a child you need to properly scrutinise the evidence. 'There is a reason we have trials,' she says. 'Where there are different versions of events, and when the court needs to know which version is true to make good decisions, someone is going to have to decide who is telling the truth. You need a human exercise in weighing everything up, and you need to hear what people have to say about things. That's a trial. There are cases which, on paper, look entirely plausible and possible but the minute they are in the witness box you realise it's a complete house of cards. Things can shift in the course of a trial.'

One significant change that Lucy has advocated for is more transparency in the system. In 2014 she set up the Transparency Project along with a group of like-minded lawyers who had been blogging about family law and the poor reporting of it in the mainstream media. It is a charity whose purpose is to open up the system to scrutiny, demystifying and challenging the status quo.

Currently, the family courts sit in private; members of the public are not allowed to attend hearings. Stretched news operations very rarely send reporters; there are just a handful of regulars who cannot identify the child or anything presented as evidence. The children's right to privacy, in these most intimate and sensitive of situations, is paramount.

It is only since 2009 that journalists have been able to attend family court proceedings at all, but they are not allowed to receive documents or report on what they see. Judges can be asked to consider whether journalists can see legal documents, including witness statements and expert reports, but to report on them requires additional steps to secure a judge's permission. Sometimes a judge chooses to publish a judgment on a judicial website[4] – this can be reported, but great care must be taken to avoid extra details that could lead to jigsaw identification. In no other part of the state would a journalist report judgments unquestioningly. As this book was going to press, important and progressive changes were being announced to open up the family courts to more scrutiny in recognition that the lack of transparency has not helped the system.

As a journalist, sitting in on a court hearing feels critical on a professional level to ensure the system is fair and justice is done. It can also feel intrusive; you are party to the most intimate details of family life and you watch as other people's parenting is methodically ripped apart in a room full of strangers. But what it most often feels like is bewildering and frustrating. The language is foreign and complex and nothing quite makes sense to laypeople. But you still witness extraordinary scenes about which you can't report.

At the Transparency Project, Lucy and her colleagues were noticing patterns when parents contacted them for advice. 'We were hearing that courts are not fair, the idea that social workers are trying to steal our babies to meet their targets. We were trying to bust myths and explain the law, so we started producing guides for families.'

Lucy now believes that the restricting laws should be reformed. Anonymity of children and families is still paramount, but otherwise the details of what happens in court should be more readily reportable. Lucy doesn't believe there is widespread malpractice going on – but that transparency will lead to a healthier system all around.

Louise Tickle is a journalist and member of the Transparency Project, and through careful, precise and obsessive reporting and understanding of the legal process in the family courts has helped open up the workings of the family court more than anyone.

When we talk about it, her voice is shaking with rage. She has been hauled before a judge whose case she is observing, after she was accused of breaking the confidentiality deal by tweeting about the process, though she was careful not to name any of the specifics. She knows the law and that she is well within her rights, and the judge understands this too, but she is furious that she was subject to what she believes was a blatant attempt to stifle her reporting.

Louise says: 'The family courts are one of the very few areas of unscrutinised and virtually untrammelled power exercised by the state over our lives. If you don't have effective scrutiny and open justice, if it becomes impossible for any party to publicly complain, then you have a state authority which can remove a child for ever with virtually no means of holding those decisions to account.'

She doesn't for a second argue against anonymity for children, but points out that rape victims and young people in criminal cases have anonymity and the media in the vast majority of cases currently abide by the law. The secrecy of the courts has another consequence: without scrutiny, bad habits can flourish and go unchecked. Louise says: 'I think there is an arrogance that starts to grow when anybody is unexamined. You become immune from effective criticism. It's that arrogance that I observe that the families find the most painful aspects. Their views are of so little value.'

Louise is well respected in the courts and among social workers. She is the go-to journalist for parents who believe they have been mistreated. She is fuelled by a sense of injustice. 'When I started reporting on the family courts I found all these blocks to reporting things that I thought were important,' she says. 'There's the bit of me that doesn't cope well with authority, that doesn't cope with being told I can't do something without a good reason. When you come up against that level of pushback to something in every other part of society that is seen as normal and useful, well I just get indignant and angry. I want to do something about it.'

Lucy and Louise, along with a number of lawyers and a couple of judges, have progressed the transparency agenda. New guidance has been produced and, as I research this book, the most senior family judge in England and Wales – the President of the Family Division – is publishing a review of procedures, heralding a new era of transparency.

The secrecy around the courts has created a breeding ground for unaccountable behaviour and, ultimately, poor decision-making. Those 80,000 children in care in England and separated from their parents are there by secret processes. The system making those decisions isn't itself judged. It needs a light to shine on it, so we can examine it and make it better.

But we need to do that carefully and respectfully. Lucy says there are moments that are private and should stay so. She describes what happens when a final decision to remove a child is made: sometimes there are dramatic, emotional scenes in court, but less often than you might think. It can be obvious before you reach that point what direction the case is going in, and parents don't often hang about for the final legal judgment.

'You just have to try to do your best to prepare a client. I always try to get out of the courtroom as soon as possible to talk to them outside,' says Lucy. 'Sometimes they are just gone. They run away.' In those moments the pain is too much to discuss with a lawyer.

Gabrielle's story

'We could have done it – with support'

Race, ableism and the postcode lottery

Gabrielle and her adult daughter, Aayla,[1] sit in the court waiting room alongside dozens of other people. Most are gathered in small groups, for support; a toddler wanders past but there are very few children around. I see furrowed brows. It's a quiet mix of boring and tense; people are concentrating on just getting through. Barristers lounge in the hallways, chin-wagging to pass the time. Their light banter jars against the numb backdrop of families at the tipping point.

Aayla is fidgeting. It's a long wait until their case is called into the courtroom and she's uncomfortable in the formal surroundings. Aged thirty-six, she appears much younger, dressed awkwardly in an oversized suit jacket and a short skirt that she tugs down to cover her thighs. She holds a blank expression that could seem hostile if you didn't know that she has learning difficulties, specifically autism. She struggles to make connections with people. I only meet Aayla once, in that court waiting room. She's at the heart of her daughter's story, by her absence.

Extended families are the hidden heroes of this story. More often than not that means grandmothers, aunties and sisters stepping in to pick up the pieces when parenting is deemed to be failing. They are the first people the state turns to when things go wrong. It makes for uneasy relationships all round.

Jada exists in a legal limbo. Aayla is her parent by birth, but hasn't lived with her for eleven years and is barred from caring for her. Aayla's fifty-seven-year-old mother Gabrielle, who Jada has lived with all that time, has never had full legal responsibility for her. Neither does the council, because, somehow, the case has slipped through the cracks. Loved and cared for by her grandmother, Jada is in a no man's land. Everyone knows where she belongs: at her grandmother's house. But not in the eyes of the law.

To understand how a little girl arrived in this legal limbo, and lived in that state for so long, is to enter the byzantine world of the court and social care process. I ask Gabrielle why she is in court today and it takes her three attempts to explain it. 'No idea,' is her first response. Then she begins to talk, finding her way through more than a decade of twists and turns in her family. Finally, she puts her finger on it. They are there to decide the legal responsibility for her granddaughter. She says that it's often hard to know what her court appearances have been for. She just turns up and hopes someone will take the time to explain things to her.

Jada moved in with her grandmother just shy of her second birthday. Her mother, Aayla, was struggling to look after her, hampered by her own learning difficulties, just as her daughter's autism was starting to emerge. Aayla was finding it hard to establish any kind of routine for Jada – feeding and sleeping schedules were all over the place and Gabrielle was worried. Aayla came to the attention of social services after Jada's nursery reported a bruise to her head, the result of what was accepted to be an ordinary accident for a two-year-old. But the concerns lingered because the toddler wasn't gaining weight and had started to show signs of anxiety, including pulling out her own hair and eating paper.

Things escalated after police witnessed Aayla shouting at her daughter for running into a road. They told her they were coming to her house to interview her, at which point she panicked and brought her daughter to Gabrielle, fearing they would remove her. 'That night, social workers and the police came to my house. Jada was in bed at that time and they asked to see her so we went upstairs and pulled the covers back and they examined her while she was sleeping, and they were happy and said Jada wasn't to leave my home,' Gabrielle recalls. 'So then I think the next day another, different social worker came and that's when they said Jada was going to be there under a "voluntary" agreement, and I wasn't to let Aayla take Jada. Jada has been with me ever since.'

Jada was placed with her grandmother under a legal provision of the Children Act 1989 known as Section 20. It allows a parent to volunteer that their child be cared for elsewhere, usually by a member of their family, without going to court – the parent delegates responsibility to the council. Around half of all children who enter the care system start off on a Section 20. A Section 20 is only legally valid if it is truly voluntary on the part of the parent. The problem is it's quite hard to know what voluntary looks like, when the alternative card on the table is an order for the children to go into foster care. 'The use of Section 20 must not be compulsion in disguise,' the high court has previously ruled.[2] In practice, there is an inherent contradiction here: as Gabrielle recalls, her family were 'told' that the agreement was voluntary.

Eleven years later Jada is still with her grandmother, on that Section 20. While Section 20s can be used for extended periods of time, it should be with good reason. In Jada's case it has just drifted. Eleven years on a Section 20 is practically unheard of anywhere in the system. Social workers I meet gasp in shock when I mention the case.

On a sprawling council estate on the edge of the northern city where the family live, Gabrielle has the heating turned up full and an air freshener puffs out a strong scent every few minutes. The walls are decorated with Caribbean art, celebrating her place of birth. Toys are stacked on every surface. It's just her and Jada in the two-up two-down house. Though they have apparently lived in legal limbo since that night, events have unfolded – and at times unravelled – around them. The family's version of the story reveals the complexity of the decisions the state has to make, and how the relationship between families and the state, when it goes wrong, can have dire consequences. It also shows how hidden layers of prejudice can play out in these decisions. At worst it hints at an authoritarian state that strips families of their rights.

After Jada went to live with Gabrielle, things stabilised for the family. She had regular contact with her mother. 'Since Jada was little they would laugh, they joke, they hold hands. They are affectionate to each other. They share a sense of humour and giggle at similar things. Jada can't understand why she can't see her mum more.'

After five years, Aayla got together with a new partner, and became pregnant again. Her new partner left; she went back to Jada's dad. When the baby arrived, a son, there were tensions in the house. Jada's dad, who also has learning difficulties, resented looking after another man's baby while his own daughter was living away from them. Gabrielle became worried when she noticed his carelessness with little Jason. 'They had come for Sunday dinner, he put baby on the floor, putting baby's coat on, put arm in the coat and let him bang his head. It was just a bit too rough handling. I said to my daughter, "You do for that baby", he doesn't know how to treat him right.'

A few weeks later things escalated further. The baby was crying and crying and they all knew something was wrong. Nothing would settle him. They visited a midwife, who sent them to the hospital where an X-ray revealed a fracture to the right arm. It was deemed a 'non-accidental injury', but there was no evidence as to how it had happened, or who had inflicted it. In these scenarios a list is drawn up of 'potential perpetrators'. Aayla was on it, her boyfriend, and Gabrielle, because she had also seen the baby. Jason was placed in foster care immediately. They never established who caused the injury so Aayla and her partner were both held responsible and permanently barred from working with children. Given the findings of the case, there was no chance of keeping him. Gabrielle and Sumaiya both wanted to help but were in difficult situations and a decision was made for him to be adopted.

The decision was made in court for the little boy to be adopted permanently. He was five by the time they had found a family for him.

'I don't think there was an actual moment when we realised we wouldn't see him again,' Gabrielle says. 'I think I always knew. Once they said in court that Aayla and her boyfriend weren't allowed to work with young children, I knew that they weren't going to get him back.'

Could she have cared for them both? Gabrielle pauses and says very quietly: 'Yes, with support.'

Her short answer betrays a heavy burden that is critical to this story. Had she had better housing, better educational support, more regular visitors, she believes the two children could have stayed with her and, more importantly, they could have stayed together. Her younger daughter could have fostered the boy if she had been given additional support to thrive instead of being tested. The 'support' Gabrielle refers to in that short statement might have kept the family whole.

It also gets to the heart of the politics of the debate: where does personal responsibility end and societal responsibility step in? In the traditional arguments of right and left, the right place the emphasis on the individual, the left on society. The debate has hamstrung the system and left us with a patchy picture across the country and no honest debate. Ultimately we have consented to a situation that we haven't thought through. Where should accountability sit? We haven't decided, yet it's resulting in those 26,000 children going into care instead of being supported to stay at home. That's too heavy a cost to bear behind closed doors.

Gabrielle nearly loses her composure when I ask about the last time they saw the little boy. He was four years old by then. 'It was at the contact centre. Aayla was there, her sister Sumaiya was there, I was there. It was quite sad. Quite harrowing. But by then we accepted we couldn't do anything about it. We played with him. I told him I was his grandma. I told him to remember us. I said I'd always live at that house so you can come and see us when you're big. He said he would. That was it then. They put him in the taxi and that was it then. Off he went. We never saw him again.'

Gabrielle seems resigned to the decisions that are made for her family. 'People say we were a very stoic family. No we're not. It hurt like hell. It hurt like hell but there was no way I was going to break down and be bawling and screaming and wrestling. They've got the say; there's nothing I can do. I don't need to show you my emotions. That's the one thing I've still got power over.'

What happened next is grimly predictable. Aayla got pregnant again. One in four women who has a child removed through the family courts is likely to return to have another taken away, and that number increases to one in three if they're a teenage mother. The cycle in child removal is even more intense if a parent has been in care themselves: four out of ten women who have multiple children removed grew up in care. More, a further 14% lived away from their parents in private or informal arrangements, while many more experienced disruptive, even chaotic childhoods. Inheritance has a tight grip.

Because of her history, social services were on alert from the first midwife appointment. Aayla initially hid her pregnancy from Gabrielle, wearing oversized clothes and complaining about getting fat. 'I told her she'd be silly to have another, they would remove it straight away. In court they had said she couldn't be in charge of the kids.'

Aayla insists to her mother that she was told during the pregnancy that there was a chance she'd be allowed to keep this baby. Gabrielle suspects this was so that she wouldn't do anything 'silly' – like try to have a late-stage termination. 'They went through this pretence of doing a viability assessment. There was no intention. The court had already said what they had said. That would stand,' she recalls. Aayla threatened to leave the country with her baby. Gabrielle stopped her. 'You should never have gone there,' she told her daughter. 'You've set yourself up for more hurt.'

After she had the baby, they let them stay together overnight in the hospital and the next day they came into the hospital and took the child away.

'I met the baby when it was born. They gave her to the same woman who fostered her brother. We went to the contact centre up until Angelina was two. She had entered her third year when they found a placement with the people who had adopted Jason. They said in court they would maintain contact between the siblings once a year. Social services were supposed to take Jada to go and meet them. That's never once happened.

'Jada's suffered two bereavements. She thinks about them but she doesn't know them now. She knows she's got a brother, she knows she's got a sister. She lives for the day when they are going to find her, she says. "They are going to find me, they are going to find me," she says.'

At the heart of Jada's legal process is the question of parental responsibility, and it reveals another Catch-22 in the system. Everybody agrees Jada should live with Gabrielle, but the situation has been allowed to drift without legal settlement for so long it's created a stand-off. Gabrielle would qualify as a special guardian, which would resolve the legal responsibility. But it would also remove her foster care allowance. She can't afford to live on the lower benefit given to special guardians. She would have to go back to work, as a nurse, so wouldn't be able to care for Jada. The alternative is that the council gets parental responsibility, and she continues to foster Jada. She is stuck between choosing between the finances that make their life work – £130 a week – and the legal right to decide for her granddaughter.

Gabrielle takes a pragmatic approach – and is also resigned to a feeling that the council always wins. Tensions came to a head when she disagreed with plans for Jada's education. Jada was in a special school with two-to-one care surrounded by children with very profound learning difficulties and Gabrielle fought for her to be moved to a lower intervention school – successfully, where Jada is now thriving.

'I feel very uncomfortable with social services having parental responsibility after they've shown how they've acted in Jada's best interest. I'm acting in Jada's best interest. But it's a big organisation and eventually they will get their will.'

What would she say to the social workers if she could?

Gabrielle pauses and draws breath: 'I think that everything that they did was all cloak and dagger and to save money. When the social worker came here and said it had been brought to their attention that Aayla was struggling, I said, "Can you not take my daughter to a mother and baby unit and work with her and give her the skills?" I talked to Aayla all the time and tried to instil what she should be doing but because she has learning difficulties she thought like a young teenager and that I was just trying to spoil her fun. Anything I said would end up in an argument. If there was a social worker who was working with her, who did want her to succeed, she'd be more likely to work with them because they are a stranger and there's not all that angst there.'

If Aayla had had access to services that taught mothers with learning disabilities key parenting skills at the beginning, it might have saved the cost of foster care and adoption for all three children – and the turmoil and grief Gabrielle's family went through.

Our long conversation starts in the waiting room outside the court and then continues in Gabrielle's living room, where the doorbell rings twice. Her brother stops by. Then a social worker bustles through the door to check in on them. The tea keeps flowing and Gabrielle welcomes everyone in with another pot. Jada is at school.

Gabrielle wants to talk about race in social work. She feels it was a major factor in her family's experience – that they were judged differently because they are black. 'It makes me feel like institutional racism is very much alive in the twenty-first century. And that the system is stacked against you and you are powerless,' she says.

As this book was going to press, the Sewell Report provoked outrage among antiracism campaigners for denying the existence of the institutional racism of the kind that Gabrielle speaks about. It seems clear that, similarly to the class prejudices that we examined previously, racial bias is also baked into the children's social care system in a way that makes families' experiences through that system even more alienating and difficult.

In Gabrielle's view, their racialised interpretation of Aayla as 'aggressive' was compounded by the fact that she has learning difficulties. 'They said Aayla couldn't bond with Jada, but that was because of autism. It affected them both and their relationship. The system should have accommodated that difference.'

'I know they will never ever remove Jada, it would cost them too much to place her with her needs. I know it would cost them a fortune if they had to do so properly. That's why they are happy for her to remain. It's the cheaper option. But the others, they are happy to take.'

Gabrielle returns to the theme of the conflict she had over the schooling. She has a way of describing the root of the problem. 'They were following a paper copy of Jada that was never really right,' she says. The council documents Jada's needs, abilities, and their family relationships, but never reflected the child Gabrielle knew. They underestimated her abilities, her problems were overblown. They ignored what she could do, and focused on what she couldn't. 'They didn't know who she is,' says Gabrielle.

A child's destiny can be unfolded in this paperwork. Each contact with a child and their family has to be meticulously documented to capture every warning sign and proof of parenting ability, so that if a case does end up in court, there is a record. Once papers are in court they are unreportable. But for many of the cases I have observed in the past year I have leafed through the court documents, bound in lever arch files. These artefacts of people's lives feel precious. They are deemed to be the truth of a child's story. The children don't see them at the time, but in future years, as they try to understand their personal histories, they can access them as the only account of what often turns out to be the defining moment of their lives.

Alice, the social worker from the second chapter, sweats over every word in those case files, knowing that in the future a child might want to read these records, and they replace the family photos that cement childhood memories for other people. She describes records that are strewn with spelling mistakes, where you can't always understand the point being made. In one case I hear of involving twins they are referred to interchangeably as 'one of the twins' rather than as individuals.

The poet Lemn Sissay, who spent his childhood in care, wrote his book *My Name is Why* about the experience of reading his files thirty-four years after he left the system. It took him that long to force the council to hand them over. It revealed how he was renamed Norman by a social worker called Norman, how his mother did actually fight to keep him (he was told he was abandoned). 'You stole my family, you changed my name, you gave me to foster parents that were inadequate, you imprisoned me and I suffered constant racism from the get-go,' he writes.

It's in the paperwork, the notes that are made, the short-hand that is used, that people's stories get distorted. Within the hard evidence of the cases social workers are making, what goes unrecorded is their starting point, the experiences and prejudices that shape their approach to what parenting should be.

Sissay's experience of being taken from his mother and suffering in the social care system was decades ago. What is the evidence around racism at play now?

Paul Bywaters' research exposes the link between poverty and children in care.[3] But he has also investigated the racial dynamic. He finds that you are much more likely to be in the care system if you are black or of mixed heritage than if you're white. There are strong patterns when it comes to ethnicity. Some 22 in every 10,000 Asian children are in care, compared with 64 in 10,000 white children and 87 in 10,000 black children.

But the intersectional discrimination in this system is very hard to disentangle. If you ask which ethnic groups are most likely to go into care, you get a story about race. But if you ask who is most likely to go into care, the answer, as mentioned earlier, is poor white families in the poorest areas of the country. 120 of every 10,000 white children in poor areas are in care – the highest rate of all.

A later study, in 2019, also by Bywaters, questioned why child protection investigations are different for children of different ethnicities.[4] Like so much in this story, there is no one driver but a mixture of social and economic factors, institutional biases and systematic differences. The key question is whether more children of black and minority ethnic backgrounds are in care because they need to be, or because they are treated differently. But there is no clear answer. 'None of the broad explanations (for example, artefactual, socio-economic, culture or institutional bias) are supported as single causes. As is entirely to be expected, it is clear that causation is multi-factorial, even in the absence of sufficient data relevant to all arguments,' Bywaters concludes.

Beverley Jones knows Bywaters' work well. She is one of those rare people with both academic and practical experience of the system. Having worked as a social worker for thirty years, mostly in the Midlands, she was awarded an MBE in recognition of her service. She now works at the Family Justice Observatory. Her job as Associate Director for Practice and Impact is to provide that link between research and the frontline. 'I am blessed with a lack of ambition,' she says. 'I never wanted to climb. I just wanted to make "good trouble", like the US civil rights activist John Lewis said.' She is also blessed with an ability to draw on those experiences on the frontline to shed light on the questions that the research asks.

Beverley is black – her parents were Jamaican and of the Windrush era. Where Bywaters' empirical research reaches the limits of understanding of how discrimination drives these processes, Beverley fills in the gaps with her academic insight and personal experiences. Listening to me recounting Gabrielle's story, she recognises the themes. 'Racial prejudices are working in two ways: social workers can think black families need less support because there is perceived to be a stronger kinship network. What you end up with is families who need high-level support not being recognised,' she says.

'On the other side there is a suspicion of black parents. You get a grandmother struggling with a thirteen-year-old getting involved with boys and wanting her to go to church.

Social workers see that grandmother as oppressive. They don't accept that we have the capacity to parent our children. There's always another dimension if you're black. I have seen examples of racist and biased practices. But it's often more subtle and about conservative Jamaican families versus liberal social workers. The trust falls apart.'

Racist prejudices about black aggression are relatively common too, she says – particularly for women. She's been accused of being aggressive in professional contexts just for expressing an opinion, in ways that her white colleagues certainly aren't. She cites a 'white lens' in social work, one that makes culturally disconnected judgements. Though social workers are taught to put aside their prejudices, they often struggle. 'We're all shaped by our own experiences. In social work you are actively trained to reflect on that, that there are different ways of seeing things. You have to learn to distinguish between what's harmful and what's just different to your experience. You have to work hard not to lose that perspective.'

But unconscious bias plays out in complex and surprising ways. 'People judge families through a white *and* middle-class lens. It's so hard not to see the extremes of poverty as neglect, but the truth is if the structural problems were fixed, there would be less damage to those families.' Then there are social workers, sometimes black, sometimes religious, sometimes neither, who struggle to build relationships with families where parents or children are questioning their sexuality, or are LGBTQI+, because it doesn't fit with their preconceptions of a family. There are so many dimensions to how discrimination might play out,' she says.

Beverley's combined experience of the frontline and

academia has left her pensive about the future and trying to find ways to shift the mindset of social work. 'As I've got older I'm less interested in the state intervening and more about creating spaces where people can regulate themselves. We need to be quite clear about what is harm, what is abuse. We need to tolerate more. Young people may be experiencing adversity, but that doesn't mean it's significant harm. How can we help?'

She describes her favoured approach to social work as 'radical tenderness'; challenge and support backed up with empathy and with a concept not often talked about in the context of social work: love. This is an idea that we will come back to and explore further in the concluding chapters of this book, exploring other models for the state to support families.

From the red-brick Victorian turrets of Royal Holloway University just outside London, Professor Anna Gupta forges another link between the academic and social work world, doing research and training social workers. She says the racial discrimination that undoubtedly exists within the system is very hard to quantify because the numbers are small and because cases play out so differently in different parts of the country. The overarching figures about patterns of children of different ethnicities going into care mask hundreds of local dynamics that all tell different stories.

There are countless variables: the ethnicity of the families, of the social workers and the attitudes and prejudices those bring. In urban areas religious social workers, who are often from black African backgrounds, might bring a set of values to a conversation with young mothers doing sex work that could alienate them; in rural areas with homogenous cultures, an ageing white workforce might hold prejudices against immigrants who arrive in the area. 'We all come with our own identities and beliefs about parenting practices,' Gupta says.

Relatively low rates of children in care among Asian populations, or middle-class ones, might not be a good sign, she also adds. Cultural prejudices go both ways and assumptions can be made that kids are OK, when in fact they are not. Assumptions about strong family support networks in Asian families can mask problems.

Once a child is in the care system, social work teams strive to find 'culturally agreeable' foster placements. The principle is to match children with culturally similar homes to limit the disruption in their lives. But there aren't enough foster carers from diverse backgrounds, despite huge efforts to recruit them. In England, 24% of children in care are children of colour, compared with 13% of foster carers.[5] In 2012 David Cameron's government intervened to relax regulations around cultural matching for good reasons: children of colour were being placed in long-term foster homes and found adoptive parents at a much slower rate than white children. The system wasn't working for them.

Cameron argued that it took twice as long to find an adoptive home for black children than white children, and that it was 'absurd' that cultural sensitivities were being prioritised over speed in adoptions, given the evidence on the impact of delays. 'This government is going to tear down the barriers that stop good, caring potential adoptive parents from giving a home to children who so desperately need one,' he said.

In her seminal book, *Why I'm No Longer Talking to White*

People about Race, the author Reni Eddo-Lodge describes this as the 'ultimate act of colour-blindness', the doctrine whereby predominantly white people believe that by ignoring race they can create a more cohesive multicultural society. She acknowledges that the move was not without goodwill – the process of adoptions for black children needed to be sped up.

> 'It was a cunning linguistic sleight of hand that the politicians insisted that considering a child's race was actually fuelling racism. Meanwhile, white parents who adopt children of colour take on a new responsibility to be race aware. They embark on a very new journey of self-discovery, and they have a duty to no longer commit to the limiting politics of colour-blindness. They have this duty because a black child cannot be burdened with the responsibility of weathering the world's prejudices on their own.'

Her point is that pretending to be colour-blind ignores all the structural racism that exists in the UK, and the history of white supremacy. Within adoption it ignores the differences children of colour will experience – and it risks further alienating a child who has already faced intense pressures. A lot of love and some good race awareness training might mean it works for some families; but for other black and minority ethnic children adopted into white families it creates a life-long feeling of otherness.

Poverty and race intersect to form patterns in child protection inquiries. But for many families there are further

aspects that compound their problems. People with learning difficulties, such as Aayla, are far more likely to be in
court proceedings with their children than other families,
and once in court they are more likely to have their children removed despite the fact that many can and do parent
successfully. One shocking study, conducted in Scotland,
suggested that between 40 and 60% of families where one or
more of the parents has a learning difficulty have had their
children removed from their care.[6] Another study surveyed
children going through the English court system, finding
that almost one in six had at least one parent with learning
difficulties.[7] That proportion rose to almost a quarter if parents with borderline learning difficulties are included.

Learning disabilities opens up a whole new frontier of
discrimination against parents because, by the very nature
of their conditions, people with learning difficulties stray
from the norm. But learning difficulties, learning disabilities
and specific conditions such as autism, have such a huge
spectrum of symptoms and traits, that it's almost impossible
to set any rules around what support should be available to
help them parent, or whether different standards of parenting might be expected of them.

If we return to the idea of the decision to remove a child
from their parents as a prism through which to assess the
health of our society and its systems, learning difficulties are
another fault line on its surface. We don't account for the differences of people in our interactions or in how we structure
our systems of support. One study interviewed magistrates
about their experiences of making decisions about parents
with learning difficulties finding they felt hopelessly ill
equipped to understand the implications of a parent's specific

condition, sometimes having to draw parallels with the limited number of people they knew with learning difficulties in assessing how they might cope.[8]

The 1976 Race Relations Act was the first to make distinctions between direct and indirect discrimination: direct being the obvious mistreatment of people because of their colour, indirect being the application of a rule or requirement which systematically prejudices certain people on the grounds of race. A second study documents how the process of child protection and the courts discriminates against people with learning difficulties, describing the 'tick-tock' nature of the twenty-six-week deadline to resolve child protection cases in the courts as particularly discriminatory against parents with learning difficulties.[9] The nature of learning difficulties means that they need longer to understand situations; the time pressures of the courts work against this. Other conditions such as autism affect the ability to build relationships, another aspect that is tested in the courts. The fact that adult and children's social care is so disjointed means that the professionals supporting the parents for the learning difficulties might be different to those working with their children, meaning the system doesn't look at the family in the round, as a unit, but as discrete problems. The fact that families that aren't neuro-typical might need more support to stay together means that the scarcity of the right resources to support them to do so discriminates against their condition.

Since 2007 parents with learning difficulties who are facing court proceedings should be given an advocate to help them navigate the legal system and understand what is happening. It's one of five elements of best practice in these cases, which also includes clear information, transparent processes, support for the parents as well as the children, and long-term support, if necessary.[10] But there have been concerns in more recent years about the withdrawal of these services as budgets in councils are squeezed, further disadvantaging these families.[11]

So ableism is another scandalous feature of the child protection system: people with learning difficulties are directly discriminated against, but also indirectly discriminated against as a side effect of the systems and lack of funding across the system.

These are the layers of societal discrimination that intersect in the courts: poverty, racism and ableism, built into an assumption of what a 'good enough' family is, and removed from people who weren't lucky enough to inherit it. There's one more to add: geographical inequity in the support system for families.

This is one of the most worrying trends in this story: the fact that family separation is a postcode lottery. There is huge regional variation in the rates of children going into care. In Richmond upon Thames, south-west London, 23 out of every 10,000 children were in care last year. In Blackpool, in the north-west of England, that figure was 185 for every 10,000.[12] The north–south divide is clear, with a band of authorities across the north of England standing out. Gabrielle lives in a council that is judged to be failing its children, next door to one that is held up as a model of good practice around the world.

There are statistical tricks you can play to attribute the difference between local authorities to known factors, such as poverty and funding cuts. But there remains about a third of the difference that it's impossible to account for. These are the cultural differences that exist locally: the norms and behaviours, the tolerance, or intolerance, for poor parenting that informs how decisions are made.

Children are being removed from their families in one area of the country who might have been supported to stay together in another. At the margins, your human rights depend on where you happen to live, rather than what you do. It's simply down to luck.

Many of the cultural reasons for this variation are soft – the expectations of managers, the relationship between social workers and the communities they serve, the attitudes they hold. But elsewhere it's hardwired into the rules. Andy Bilson, professor of social work at the University of Central Lancashire, has investigated the postcode lottery in children's services.[13] 'This variation is an injustice,' he says. Each area has a local safeguarding board that publishes thresholds for social workers' interventions, which are made publicly available. Bilson has picked through these documents. He found some alarming discrepancies.

For instance, he examined the thresholds for investigating bruising in babies, which lean heavily on National Institute for Clinical Excellence guidelines issued to the NHS. They suggest that bruising is uncommon in pre-mobile babies. He challenged these guidelines with research that suggests that bruising at that age is actually relatively common – one in fifteen babies experience an accidental bruise every day, even though they cannot walk or crawl.

Yet in the threshold documents, Bilson found five local authorities where social workers are instructed to formally investigate such bruising, even if they believe a straightforward explanation that it was an accident. These are the so-called 'Section 47' inspections that remain on a parent's record and could prevent them from, for example, being security cleared to work with children. Bilson says: 'I don't think that's fair at all. It's not only unfair, it's actually dangerous because where there is massive over-intervention there's a real danger that parents will be unwilling to take children with bruises to medics, and there's a risk that children will die because it turns out they've got septicaemia, that can actually kill you.

'There were huge differences across the country in terms of how this guidance was given. In some local authorities, they went as far as to say that any child with a bruise should immediately be subject to a full child protection investigation which quite often led to children being removed just on the basis of a single bruise. At the other end of a spectrum, there were local authorities that didn't have a specific policy.'

The prism of child protection has many facets and each one of them reflects the inequity of our society: one for classism, one for racism, one for the prejudices that people with learning difficulties face, and another for the postcode lottery and geographical injustice.

Gabrielle says that the 'white lens' she experienced left her feeling disenfranchised and, alongside the symptoms of her daughter's autism, compounded a view that Aalya was 'aggressive'. She's jealous of families in other local authorities, which she thinks do a better job. The system didn't listen to her or understand her problems were about poverty, housing and the learning difficulties her offspring faced. It's the intersections of prejudice that are more subtle, harder to pin down, that really bore down on their experience.

But for Gabrielle, observing what her family went through, she saw a chasm between her daughter's experiences and those of the baby's father, who was white. 'They automatically saw a black family, the baby had been hurt, it could never have been the white parent,' she says. 'The dad was seen as gentle. Aayla was black, a brute; the idea is that it's within our DNA to be aggressive because of slavery and that kind of thing.'

There was an attempt to be culturally sensitive towards Gabrielle's family, but it was handled in the most ham-fisted way. The only time the family ever met black social workers was on the separate occasions they came to remove the two younger children. 'They took two children, and they were the only two black social workers we met. It's been white middle-class posh social workers all along,' she says.

A year after I first meet the family, Gabrielle and I speak again, this time on the phone during lockdown. Jada is now classed as a 'looked-after child', fostered by her own grandmother. This work-around means that Gabrielle can continue to receive the foster carer's allowance and to care full time for her granddaughter. But it also means the uneasy relationship with the social workers continues. The council is now ultimately, and unnecessarily, the corporate parent of Jada. Gabrielle knows that, periodically, she has to navigate around them to do what she believes is in her granddaughter's best interest. It's a compromise they have reached to make Jada's life work. Parental rights exchanged for parental resources. No one planned that, it's just a side effect of a system limited by inadequate resources.

Aayla still sees Jada, increasingly without the supervision of a social worker or her mother. They go to McDonald's together, a neutral ground that they both enjoy, which gives them a chance to nurture their own relationship in their own space and time. Meanwhile, the new school that Gabrielle fought for Jada to attend is far better. She is challenged to develop her skills, surrounded by children of different abilities. Her reading is developing, her social skills slowly evolving. She's learning to live.

For now, things appear to be settled. I can hear Jada bossing around in the background as we speak on the phone. She wants to go out to the park. Gabrielle worries about her being on her own, but as Jada is thirteen she knows she needs to start taking baby steps to independence. That's why she's encouraging Aayla to spend more time alone with her daughter. She knows there will come a time when she's not around. 'It will come full circle,' she says. 'It will just be the two of them in the end.'

Or maybe three. There's something more pressing on the horizon that could upend things for the family again. Aayla is pregnant. The cycle continues.

Angela's story

'We are blaming mums who don't have anything'

The 'toxic trio' and loneliness

Four hours after Angela gives birth to her second son, her partner arrives and strong-arms her out of the maternity ward and down to the post office to pick up the benefits he needs to buy drugs. Six weeks later she collapses with sepsis and a haemorrhage, the result of some of the placenta being left inside her. An ambulance takes her to hospital where, just hours later, her partner calls to say he will put the two boys – including their six-week-old baby – in care if she doesn't come home.

She discharges herself, against the doctors' advice. She makes it into the hallway of her house and collapses. Hours later she crawls into bed, from where he drags her, in her poisoned delirium, and throws her back down the stairs. In the beating that follows, including with a plank of wood, she suffers multiple injuries, bruises and broken ribs. She later recalls just a few snapshots of the sustained attack: the moment when her thumb broke is particularly vivid, as is another when he spat in her face. The ambulance driver who later comes to take her back to hospital is the same one who had taken her to hospital the previous day with sepsis.

A chaotic few weeks follow, which Angela spends mostly in a hospital bed recovering. A restraining order is put in place and a prosecution is underway against her partner. She lets herself hope that she and her children might be safe at last. But he continues to turn up at the house and torment her. She lives in fear that he will be sitting in her living room every time she walks in. She is physically incapable of looking after a baby, with one hand strapped to her chest and broken ribs. But social workers send a lady to help her with making bottles and bathing him. She is so grateful, not least for the company, until she realises a record is being kept of her every move. When she asks for help with bathing, it is recorded as her failing to wash her baby.

Ten weeks after the baby was born she walks into the social workers' offices and appeals for help. 'I can't keep him away and I can't keep my babies safe,' she says. 'Please help me.' Her older boy is five and has been in care before. They respond by removing the children from their nursery with police assistance, giving her no chance to say goodbye. When she next sees the boys in contact under the eyes of a social worker she can see the impact on her older boy in particular. 'I had promised him I wouldn't let him go again. It destroyed him. He's never forgiven me for that. You could see it in his face. He was shut down. The life was knocked out of him. The spark was gone. That was the beginning of the end.'

In the end she agreed to their adoption because she was

told she'd have more chances for contact with them as a result. By then she felt she was too broken to give them the childhood they deserved. She spent the final weeks buying gifts and putting together photographs for them. The last hour was an attempt to fit a lifetime into sixty minutes. 'I was told: don't cry, make it easy for them. I cried. I thought it was better for my eldest son to see that I was sad that he was going rather than looking cheerful. That seemed crueller. I carried them into the car and waved until I couldn't see them, and then I collapsed on the floor of the car park.'

Angela Frazer-Wicks, her new married name, had never really known a life without abuse. Now, at forty-five, she is a striking woman, with short punky hair, tattoos and a north-east tinge to her accent. For much of her life she was, in her own words, 'a mess'. Angela grew up in County Durham in a mining village. On the face of it she came from a nice family. Her mother was at the heart of the Church community; her father had secured a job as a telephone engineer so they owned their own home and car in an area where his generation had been blighted by the closure of the coal mines. It all appeared very respectable. But behind closed doors, she was suffering harm from both her parents: her father beat her, while her mother psychologically abused her, using her to protect herself from the father's violence.

'Once a year we'd go on holiday. A self-catering place somewhere. For a week we would all pretend we were a happy family,' she says. 'We'd have fun and not shout. Then we would go home and the shouting would start again.'

By eleven Angela was self-harming, by thirteen she was drinking heavily. By sixteen she was taking her first drugs, wandering the streets at night and falling in with the wrong people. She was twice attacked and three times thrown out of school. She was mentally very, very unwell, but her mother, the school and Church made her feel like she was evil, rather than ill. She was labelled a freak by a teacher, a label that stuck with her throughout school.

She first saw a psychologist for an evaluation after she started to display violent behaviour. Angela stared at her, willing her to see what was really happening. Locked in her own head, she silently begged for help. The doctor agreed with her parents: it was just teenage hormones.

As she grew older the beatings stopped but her parents would ground her, locking her in a room for weeks or even months. There was a bucket in the corner. Those imprisonments were when the agoraphobia kicked in.

Day after day she wished for someone to come and save her and take her into care. There were so many missed chances. One morning she boarded the school bus with an obviously broken arm, the result of her most severe act of self-harm. The bus driver sent her to hospital but didn't tell the school. The receptionist in the hospital knew her by name, so regular were her visits for self-harm injuries. Back then this brought more judgement and stigma; she was made to wait while more 'deserving' patients were treated first.

She left school and home at sixteen determined to get away, getting herself on to a government-backed training scheme to do administration in a legal office, dreaming of becoming a paralegal. Before she had her first child at twenty-three she had married, divorced and fallen into a pattern of losing employment. She was really good at the office work, but what by then had become full-blown alco-holism meant she couldn't hold down a job. There was one serious near-fatal suicide attempt, after which her mother severed all contact with her. Suicide, in her mother's view, is a mortal sin.

When Angela found out she was pregnant, the result of a fling with a drug dealer, it focused her mind. She went to social services and asked for help to set up a proper home for her and the baby when it arrived. At that point this area of the north-east had a relative wealth of services: she was given counselling and housing support. She was creating a base. But then things turned even more dramatic. At six and a half months pregnant a new partner beat her up. Reaching for a knife to protect herself and her unborn baby, she stabbed him. His accomplice lied and said she instigated the fight. She was awarded bail but told she had to leave the area and everything she was building in anticipation for the new baby to arrive. She set up home near a friend who was also a single mum and tried again to settle down.

When the baby came she remembers only delight and relief. 'I was really ecstatic and laughing hysterically at his pointy head. He was perfect. He was perfectly healthy and such a good baby. You know when you're just really lucky. He was content and happy and he slept and he ate.'

When she was discharged from the hospital she asked again for help from the social workers. They sent a family support worker, Christine, who Angela describes as a 'guardian angel'. She helped organise benefits, food, furniture, hospital appointments. When she went back for sentencing, Christine found a babysitter. Angela got probation. She saw a single parent adviser at the job centre, got on to a college course and went one day a week. 'Everything was quite calm and stable. I was making friends through college. I started to think, Maybe I'm going to be all right.' She spotted a job for a paralegal in the paper, got it and went back to work full time when her son was one year old. She began to think about buying her own home.

On the surface, everything was stabilising for Angela. But inside she was grappling with the aftermath of her upbringing. She still lived fairly locally so would bump into her mum or the unsavoury characters of her wild days. Worse still, she grew addicted to the painkillers that were prescribed to her after her Caesarean wound failed to heal. Then she met the man who would go on to ruin her life.

She struggles now to even remember what she first loved about him. She describes how he dismantled her friendships, undermined her confidence and played out his paranoia on her. Physical abuse was becoming a normal part of their lives. Then it transpired that while she had been at work, he had been stealing the rent money and had spent the deposit she was saving for a house. They were evicted. He was on a waiting list for a council house and when she and the baby's name were added to his, they were immediately prioritised. But it meant that instead of her owning her own home, she was reliant on him for the council house because it was in his name. 'My life went from nearly being great to this horrendous situation,' she says, sounding like she still doesn't quite believe it happened. That's when she became pregnant again; he beat her more than ever before and eventually both sons were removed.

After their adoption she fought for 'letterbox' contact – annual letters to keep in touch. That kept her going as she rebuilt her life – with each exchange she wanted to have good news to share with them. She received the last one four and a half years ago. 'My eldest hit his teens and struggled with his identity and what he wanted. I told him, "If you need to let go, let go." I've had to let go of so many people. Sometimes you have to. I get it. They live abroad now and have wonderful lives. Then my ex died. It was finally all over. The boys are OK. He's gone. It's OK.'

To understand the rise in children going into care you can listen to the experiences of the people involved and understand what led to the decisive events in their lives. But you also have to look the monster in the face. A broken family looks like Angela's mother, using her daughter to shield herself from her husband's blows. It looks like Angela repeating those patterns and choosing a new partner who also beats her – then covering for him because that was the only love she knew. It looks like parents passed out on drugs while their children raise themselves, the addiction that takes away the pain of abuse and medicates undiagnosed mental difficulties and trauma. It's ugly.

In the statistics it is sanitised. Officially, every removal is given a label. In 2019, 59% of care orders were for 'abuse or neglect', 2% because of the child's disability, 3% because of a parent's illness or disability, 8% for 'acute family stress', 3% for socially unacceptable behaviour, 13% for 'family dysfunction' and a further 13% for 'absent parenting'. In the official figures a further category is provided: 'low income'. None were recorded under that label.[1]

The classifications confuse me. What's the difference between family dysfunction, absent parenting and neglect?

When would you use one of those descriptors over another? Why are abuse and neglect lumped in together where they suggest such different things: abuse, the proactive harm of a child; neglect, an absence of care or the ability to provide that care? Care doesn't mean an absence of love. Both abuse and neglect can harm and even kill, but the spectrum feels too broad for one category. I ask the social workers I meet, but their answers are instinctive and inconsistent. And while we know that poverty is the most common underlying factor, it is not ever noted as a reason for removing children.

In social work circles, if you ask what is going wrong in the families that need their help the most, people will instead talk about the 'toxic trio'. These three key drivers of family breakdown are: substance misuse, domestic violence and mental health problems – all three of which Angela experienced. It's a hated term, because it labels people, parents and their families as toxic. Some talk about the 'trigger trio' instead. MP Nadhim Zahawi, who is the children's minister responsible for the system when I interview him, uses it as a shorthand for why the state intervenes in family life. 'Clearly, the children's social care system is under pressure,' he says. 'Now, the pressures are varied, but essentially you've got the toxic trio: so you've got mental health, domestic abuse, and alcohol and drug addiction.'

You'll also find the term scattered through published court judgments. The following is just one, an extract from a judgment published by Judge Cameron.[2] The council was seeking to remove the children because of the issues highlighted in this extract. It's a partial portrait of the toxic trio in a family's life.

'The oft quoted "toxic trio" has been operating here in these particular children's lives for far too long and for many years in the case of S [the child]. There is that proven excessive and chronic use of alcohol by both these parents. That has made particularly the mother at times simply not available to her children. I am satisfied of that.

Leading from that there have been the alcohol-fuelled heated arguments, the pushing and shoving and the physical violence too which father finally accepted in his oral evidence to the Court yesterday that he has indulged in, that each of them have indulged in, and accepting that it was not 50/50. A man is always going to be physically stronger than a woman. It seems to me from the reports that I have read that the mother came off the worse for wear rather than the father.

Most or all of that, until it was taken out into the street on the 20th October of last year, was witnessed and/or overheard by the children. Then of course they had the horrendous experience of seeing the aftermath of that in their mother's damaged face and her no doubt being emotional and distraught and the atmosphere being very, very tense and frightening at times.

They have seen and witnessed at first hand that poor quality of their parents' relationship at times. That does not take away from the fact that, at times, these have been very good parents. Certainly the mother is well able to provide a good quality of basic care. The children are well presented. There is food in the property. It is an attractive home and so on and so forth. However, that has simply not been consistent enough. The mother now accepts that, as does the father, given their helpful concessions in relation to Threshold.

There has been a disastrous and worrying cyclical history here and a real revolving door of Social Work input, improvements demonstrated, case closed and then the whole ghastliness starting up all over again. That cannot go on any longer, particularly for S, and for the younger children too. They are all highly vulnerable and particularly in the case of S because she is very, very close to her mother and has this issue about paternity too which she has had to come to terms with.

However, very belatedly indeed, the mother has taken some significant steps and made significant changes which the father too has recognised and acknowledged. There are therefore positives for which credit is due to this mother. There is therefore a scintilla of hope that she can sustain those changes consistently and honestly and hopefully consign the toxicity to history for the good of her children.'

The judge decided to give the family 'one last chance'. The anonymity of the judgment, which protects the identities of the clearly very vulnerable children, also makes it impossible to know whether he made the right call and the family stayed together in the longer term.

Domestic violence is a 'hidden crime', the national crime survey says, and can manifest as psychological, physical, sexual, financial or emotional abuse. 'Over recent years there has been little change in the prevalence of domestic abuse ... while the number of cases recorded by the police has increased. However, the majority of cases do not come to the attention of the police, and many of those that do, do not result in a conviction,' official figures show.[3] In the year ending March 2018, an estimated two million adults in the UK aged sixteen to fifty-nine years experienced domestic abuse in the last year (1.3 million women, 695,000 men). When the pandemic hit, the domestic violence charity Refuge saw a 60% rise in calls to its helplines from people seeking help with their abusive partners.[4]

Where police are called to investigate allegations of domestic violence and children are present, they automatically have to consider the welfare of those children and if deemed necessary inform social services. In 2018, 201,656 referrals were made to social services by police in these circumstances.

One mum I interviewed, from the north-east of England, said: 'There's more domestic abuse where I live. Relationships are old-fashioned. You see it in the school yard. The women are together, the dads are out at work. Women are still having kids earlier, staying at home to look after them, we just haven't experienced the same kind of progress – particularly in rural areas. Domestic violence is rife.' In Durham there are fifty incidents of domestic violence reported for every 100,000 people in the population; in Surrey that rate is twelve per 100,000.[5]

Opioid addiction is rife in the north-east, too. A report by the journalist Paul Caruana Galizia for Tortoise Media details how misuse is higher than anywhere else in the country.[6]

'While the North-East is not significantly more deprived than other areas, it is significantly different in one respect: it suffers from a much higher rate of social trauma, resulting from domestic violence, abuse and adverse childhood experiences. And pain consultants find that this history of trauma is the single factor most likely to lead to problematic use of opioids.

Looked at through this lens, the North-East suddenly seems like a place apart. There are 65 per cent more domestic abuse incidents per capita here than in any other area of the UK, 30 per cent more child protection cases, and 62 per cent more child sexual abuse cases.'

The mother from the north-east laughs bitterly at this report. 'I got addicted to opioids after an accident,' she recalls. 'They helped numb everything.' Angela's experience was similar. This chain of events describes how difficulties like family separation and domestic violence link back to substance misuse, creating an unacknowledged phenomenon of 'social trauma'.

Our definition of domestic violence, meanwhile, has changed. In 2015, a new offence of 'coercive control' was introduced, which describes a form of abuse characterised by being intentionally isolated from friends and families, deprived of basic needs, monitored, having your clothing, sleep patterns and finances controlled, and persistent humiliation. By 2018 there were just short of 1,000 charges under this offence; prosecutions are even more rare and the punishment is five years in prison, a fine or both. The low number of charges means the authorities are not holding people to account for this crime.

Instead, it has changed the nature of child protection. Social workers now have a broader understanding of what constitutes emotional harm to children, and when they identify it, it tends to be the mother who is punished through child removal, while the father walks away.

Cathy Ashley, Chief Executive of the Family Rights Group, says that an earlier change to the law, which meant that children witnessing domestic abuse could be classed as having experienced significant harm, has also affected this. 'Witnessing domestic violence is now largely labelled emotional abuse and the big rise has been in relation to that,' she says. 'Women may indeed move on to a safe and loving relationship in the future, but social workers are fearful of predicting that. You hear of children removed for future risk of emotional harm – that their mothers may get into another damaging relationship. How can you prove that?'

Progress has therefore created a fraught moral dilemma. The mother is the victim of abuse, but she effectively becomes the perpetrator of abuse against her children if she fails to protect them from seeing it. There might be sympathy for her, and no blame overtly attached, but if her children are removed she is effectively punished for the abuse she has suffered.

The journalist Louise Tickle has reported on even more Kafkaesque scenarios whereby social workers tell a mother she must leave her abusive partner or risk her kids being removed.[7] The mother does as she's told, only to end up back in the family court that would have removed her children, forced to allow her partner contact with the children. It's a trap of breathtaking cruelty.

It exposes the misogyny that runs through the whole system. Women are punished for their partners' violence against them; men are ignored and again the pattern emerges of responsibility heaped back on women for their perceived inaction (partly down to the lack of resources given to support families). So more often than not it's the poorest and most marginalised women who are victimised.

Current political narratives invoke a zero-tolerance approach to domestic violence, fuelled by decades of well-intentioned and important women's rights campaigns to simply get the subject on the agenda. But some academics and campaigners are now calling for a more nuanced understanding of what domestic abuse can be – to acknowledge the difference between, on the one hand, the sustained terrorisation of someone (most often a woman) within her own home, in which she has no control over her life, such as Angela experienced, and on the other, the fights that can erupt between couples under pressure.

It's a profoundly controversial debate, which suggests that in some cases couples can be coached to stay safely together with their children, rather than issuing a blanket statement to any woman that they should leave an abusive partner. Critics are concerned that offering support to couples struggling with domestic abuse legitimises or downgrades violence against women.

Perpetrator programmes focus on men's behaviour and support them to change, but they are extremely challenging and rates of success are variable. Charities, such as Respect, have championed this work, sending the message that we need to stop asking: why didn't she leave? Instead we should ask: why didn't he stop?

When the evidence suggests that people often don't leave violent partners, and that children still need relationships, even with their violent fathers, making women and children responsible for the failings of men is doubly punishing them. Instead of writing men off, we need to hold them to account and make them responsible for fixing their own behaviour and healing their families.

The toxic trio – mental health problems, domestic violence and addiction – is widely recognised in social work. They could all be the result of social trauma – but they are also the cause. Doctors in England privately use the term SLS – 'Shit Life Syndrome' – as a catch-all label for someone suffering the multiple effects of poverty. Sarah O'Connor, who first reported the phrase in the *Financial Times*,[8] wrote: 'People with SLS really do have mental or physical health problems, doctors say. But they believe the causes are a tangled mix of economic, social and emotional problems that they – with 10- to 15-minute slots per patient – feel powerless to fix.' The toxic trio is a similar shorthand, when the problems are too big and pervasive, too stitched into the social fabric to even start to address.

The truth is that drug addicts can parent well. People with mental health problems can parent well. Victims of domestic violence can parent well. People with none of these issues can parent badly. The presence of these problems is not in itself a trigger for social services to act. In most cases one factor alone wouldn't lead to a child being removed. But a combination of two or more can tip over into harming and damaging children's lives.

At the most catastrophic end, in a review of serious cases conducted after a child has been seriously injured, or has died, you confront the correlations between toxic trio characteristics.[9] The review found evidence that about two-thirds of cases featured domestic violence; mental ill-health of one or both parents was identified in nearly 60% of the families;

parental substance misuse was reported for 42% of families. In the toxic trio Venn diagram of 139 cases, 20% showed signs of all three parts of the trio, 35% displayed two factors and only 14% excluded any part of the toxic trio. 'While, singly, parental substance misuse, domestic violence and parental mental ill-health may pose risks of harm to the child, this analysis reinforces findings [...] that it is the combination of these factors which is particularly "toxic".'

I hear of this happening time and again. A mother suffers from anxiety and depression, but it's not clear whether being unable to leave her abusive relationship is a cause or an effect. She drinks to help her cope. She loves her children; they love her. Everyone agrees on this. But the spiral means she can't put them first, or help but draw them into the depressive cul-de-sac in which she is caught. She says all the right things about wanting to change, but is considered to be in a 'pre-contemplative' state, meaning she cannot truly envision the change she needs to make, or even why it's needed. There is support that could help her develop these skills, known as Mentalisation-based Therapy. MBT teaches someone how to think about their own mental processes, to understand their thought patterns and reflect on their instincts and reactions.

All too often it is not available soon enough for the court to give her the chance to save her family.

Her children go into care.

Beyond the toxic trio, I believe there is a fourth risk factor. Social isolation.

At a conference I asked a group of fifty practising social workers what the difference was between a family suffering from the 'toxic trio' who get separated and those who stay together. There are two: first, the councils' resources to support the family. Second, how isolated a mother is. Whether a parent has family and friends willing to lend a hand might decide whether they can keep their children.

Social isolation is the rotten root beneath many of the stories I have reported on for this book. It's not considered part of the 'toxic trio', but it's just as omnipresent. Caitlin, from the first chapter, had no safety net because she had moved to escape her abusive partner. This is common for people who are fleeing abuse; they are told they must separate to protect the children, then they go through the upheaval and disruption of setting up in a new area, far from family or friends. Caitlin recently met with a mum in an abusive relationship with all the hallmarks of her own situation, and the reason that woman's kids are still with her is because she has parents to support her, lend financial assistance and she's got cousins and aunties and friends to check up on her. 'If you're isolated and have no one to turn to, you can't cope. I know a lot of people who don't have anyone. They just have a couple of friends. Not everyone has family, not all of us have a good family. How is that my fault? So every single person who doesn't have a support network shouldn't have children? Surely that's when the state should help?'

With council resources cut to the bone, the safety net of the welfare state, designed to catch families that are struggling, has worn so thin that intervention often comes down to the parent's immediate support network.

I hear of a child adopted after his aunt was refused a special guardianship for him rather than being given the support that could have made it work. One parent told me the pressure of adopting her two children estranged her from her wider family. A foster carer describes the web of relationships she had to draw to prove to the adoption panel that she had back-up. The opposite can prove the case: Francesca, from the fourth chapter, kept her children after her headteacher, vicar and the local community sprang to her defence. Each case shows that one determining factor for the outcome of their cases was the isolation they as parents were – or weren't – facing.

Social isolation is studied by psychologists as a factor that can drive brain degeneration in the elderly. But in recent years, work by the British Red Cross has exposed the fact that loneliness is not the preserve of the older generations.[10] Younger people, newly moved to a new city, and new parents in particular, are suffering social isolation in a way that we have not previously recognised. The lockdowns of 2020 heightened our awareness and empathy for loneliness. The effects are mental and physical, but they also play out in the network of your life and your ability to do things such as parent.

Social isolation is seen as a growing problem across Western countries. The debate was kicked off in 1995 by the Harvard professor Robert Putnam in his paper 'Bowling Alone', which documented how the spectacular decline in bowling leagues and other social groups in the US is eroding political participation and connectedness.[11] Social capital – the shared understanding, norms, values, trust, reciprocity and engagement – has also crumbled alongside social participation. Political theory mapped the correlation with the rise of populism, extreme views and, more recently, the notion of 'culture wars' – confected battles over totemic issues, often played out in the digital sphere, that further drive polarisation.

The economist Noreena Hertz examines the phenomenon in her book *The Lonely Century*. She describes social isolation as the defining condition of the twenty-first century, driven by longer working hours, social media, the rise of automation and the polarisation of societies. In Britain, she writes, one in eight people don't have a single close friend they can rely on – up from one in ten five years previously. But while economists have examined isolation as an economic theory, and political thinkers have looked at the demographic consequences, it's less understood within the fabric of the family. Yet it's stark in the patterns of child removals: in the eyes of the system, you are less likely to be able to look after your child without a support network.

What could the state do about this? Caitlin visited her local children's centre, hanging around after sessions to chat to the other parents and workers, in a bid to avoid her abusive partner. Social worker Alice worked in a children's centre with abundant services to offer families before trouble even started. Universal schemes that catch families earlier are designed to build connectedness between people and between the state and communities. Previous efforts around Sure Starts and children's centres have been shut down in the era of austerity; some studies suggested they were hijacked by middle-class parents who didn't urgently need them.[12] But the point of universal services is that it's very hard to track their true impact in the long run; it's hard to prove causation.

There's another fundamental schism in the state that fails to mitigate social isolation in general and mental health problems in particular. It's in the flawed structures of the state. Social services are divided into children's and adult social care. Child social workers are concerned with the children, rather than their parents, but the ability to support and improve their lives lies in the parents' hands. This is demonstrated by the fact that parents struggle to get pre-emptive mental health care before their children are born, because there is no child at that point that qualifies them for it; there is very little aftercare for parents whose children are removed, because no children are at risk, despite the fact that many parents go on to have more children before they are deemed ready, creating a cycle of removal.

We need to see children as part of complicated webs of people, and families, who might hold some of the solutions. Instead, we see them as sinking ships in a sea of problems that need a lifeboat.

Angela describes the time when she was hemmed in by the toxic trio: using drugs to numb her emotions, seeking out awful relationships, repeating the abusive patterns of her childhood. The drugs, drink, domestic violence and her mental health problems were all interlinked. But in the eyes of the state they were like different parts of a car that she needed to fix. 'There was a lack of transparency between agencies. All these things were seen as separate issues. But they were three symptoms of the same problem. There was a link between everything and that link was me. I was the problem but everyone was looking at the symptoms instead of me.'

She also describes the crippling loneliness she experienced. 'I would say it was more than being isolated. I felt like I didn't exist,' she recalls. 'The only people I saw at some points were social workers. But what they were doing was surveillance, not support. It sends you crazy.'

Today Angela lives in a very different place. Her home is on a farm in Norfolk. Her daughter Elizabeth watches the combine harvester and tractors at the back window; the front window looks over her beautifully tended garden to fields of peas stretching to the horizon. Her garden is her sanctuary. There's a corner for Elizabeth's trampoline and a veg patch that feeds her neighbours. A proud pink rose dominates the front beds, planted for her boys. 'It's a nice feeling. To have the life you never thought you'd have. To go from all of that to complaining that you have too many courgettes.'

After the boys were removed she met a woman called Norma, from a charity called After Adoption, who helped her grieve for their loss, to get clean and then to find a new purpose in supporting other birth families and sharing her story to train social workers. She moved to Norfolk during a short-lived and ill-fated relationship, but once she got there met a man called Paul, the son of her landlord. He was kind, and he listened to her. They have been together for twelve years, married for six, and their daughter Elizabeth is now eight years old.

Angela still has to manage her mental health problems every day – she has PTSD and Borderline Personality Disorder as well as anxiety and depression – but she's learning how. Her only addiction now is to the tattoos that cover her self-harm scars. Across her shoulder is Cinderella's carriage, only halfway through transition from a pumpkin – a nod to her past and future. The boys' names are tattooed across her lower back, done in the aftermath of their removal when she still thought she had to hide away the shame of her parenting.

Angela lives with a painful paradox. She knows that

ultimately the state did the right thing by her boys, but it went about it entirely the wrong way. A different approach might have had a different outcome. 'I don't think there was any other option but adoption by that point. I needed so much help that I had to lose them in order to fix myself. I was so ill.'

We talk about blame versus responsibility, and about how as a birth parent you are subject to so much judgement that it's hard to move on. 'I was responsible because I was the adult. I made the wrong choices. I can see when I could have done better. They were children and they needed me to protect them better. I should have done better. But I also understand that I was ill. I was controlled by my ex, the local authority and my mental health.

'Social workers come into a family's life when everything is crumbling. The walls of their life are falling. As a practitioner they can be the mortar for rebuilding – or the wrecking ball that levels everything. You have a choice about how you work with a family, how you see a family and how you treat that family. You are the one that has the power and control. Acknowledge that, understand that, help a family past that. The best social workers are the ones who say, "I can't imagine what it's like for you."'

What Angela wants people to understand is that there is a problem of blame within the system. 'Everyone is so defensive they are blaming someone else,' she says. 'The fact that they are calling it the toxic trio sounds like they are blaming. None of those things are people's fault. Mental health is an illness; I was a victim of domestic violence. Yes, perhaps you could blame me for the drug abuse but really it was just about self-medicating and coping.

'We are blaming mums who don't have anything – not even a support network. It's like it's their fault. I didn't have a mum or a sister. I didn't have anything. I needed help.'

Each factor of the toxic trio bears a weight of personal responsibility for the parents – usually mothers – who experience them. They are concrete problems that can be assessed by a social worker and presented to a court. Women are blamed for them. But they are things that are largely beyond an individual woman's control that I've examined in this book: poverty and how the state safety net is failing; social isolation and the gradual erosion of our social capital; and the misogyny and intersectional prejudices against women, poor people, those with learning disabilities or neurodivergence and, in different ways in different places, people of different ethnicities. It is cruel and unjust.

These are the things that are the fault of wider society and that the state should fix to help families stay together, but they are also the things that aren't being addressed or funded. They are too big to be tackled by social services alone. They require safe housing and children's centres and social networks that join communities together. These are the responsibilities that our society and the state have shirked. Instead, the system focuses on the factors it can measure, and the ones for which we can blame women.

As this book went to press Angela's story took a different turn, again. Sixteen years, five months and fifteen days after they said goodbye, she was reunited with her older son whose adoptive mother had helped him track her down online. Out of the blue she received an email that started 'Hi mum'. They are now slowly, but with commitment, getting to know each other again. Elizabeth has met her big brother.

PART THREE

Consequences

My story

'What is good enough parenting?'

The judging of families

When my daughter was two years old she skipped across the living room and into a freshly boiled cup of herbal tea. Her socks were drenched in the scalding liquid, burning the skin away from her feet as she made a terrifying, unrecognisable noise. We instantly knew she needed to go to A&E and bundled her into the car, forcing her screaming into the car seat and strapping her in for safety.

My daughter was always an extraordinarily composed child. I remember sitting her on the countertop next to the knives aged eighteen months, as I cooked and she babbled, knowing that she would never come to harm. She wouldn't walk or crawl until she was fifteen months, not until she had studied how other people did it, and then one day she got up and strode purposefully across the room. Thanks to all her natural caution, she didn't know pain, and now I didn't know how to console her because I'd never really had to before.

My husband concentrated on driving as I tried to soothe her and stop her kicking the pain away. With every bit of friction the injured skin was coming away from her feet and I could see the dirt from our grotty family car contaminating her wounds.

We got to the door of A&E with her still screaming. I couldn't hold her. We lay on the floor in front of the receptionist's desk. I was utterly focused on her; everything else was a blur as I waited for a doctor to come and do something, anything, to make it better. Instead, the receptionist told me to fill in a form. My husband was parking the car. I begged the receptionist to get a doctor and when she pointed at the form again I lost my composure and burst into tears.

I don't remember what I said but I remember her cold, hard stare next to a sign saying that rudeness would not be tolerated against NHS staff. I couldn't stop crying and felt a deep shame that I hadn't kept it together for our daughter.

Moments later, a doctor materialised, whipped out a syringe full of morphine and shot it up Ivy's nose. She passed out and in the peace that descended I finally stopped crying too. I turned to my husband at just the moment that he burst into tears.

It was stressful and frightening, and a rite of passage for first-time parents, one that is experienced daily in A&E departments across the country. I learnt a few important lessons: herbal tea without milk is incredibly hot; if you have a burn at home wrap it in clingfilm to prevent infection; and that baby skin heals miraculously quickly.

A few weeks later I was spending my day off from work

at home with my daughter. The cleaner had just left. Our house was in that pristine state that lasts for the first hour or so after the weekly clean. It was a particularly intense time at work and I was determined to do all my good parenting that day, knowing how precious those hours were. It was one of about only three times in my daughter's childhood that we painted pictures together. We were both wearing aprons. The doorbell rang.

The two women at the front door introduced themselves as a social worker and a health visitor, and asked if they could come in. I felt instantly on the defensive, wondering on whose authority they were asking to see my home. They explained that the A&E trip had surfaced in the records and they just wanted to check that everything was OK. There was mention of a missed vaccination as well. I assumed that two flags had been raised, triggering the visit. I managed my instinctive reaction, reasoning that it was good that the council was checking in on kids. It showed they were looking out for people.

As the women walked in, I saw them clocking the situation: the tidy house, the child-led activity, the calm, happy demeanour of my daughter. The social worker laughed and joked with my normally serious little girl, putting us at ease. Her manner defused the initial tension I felt about their arrival. The health visitor gave a little lecture about vaccinations, which rankled a bit with my time-strapped-mum defence mode. They went on their way, and that was that. It became an anecdote I told friends when the subject came up; how I got lucky when the social workers came at the moment that I looked my best as a parent.

When I started to report on families in the care system,

this relatively inconsequential episode kept playing on my mind. I wondered what factors would have to be different to trigger more scrutiny. How much chaos in my home would have meant further visits? Six hours earlier, before the cleaner came, the house had been pretty grubby, but I don't think it would have triggered alarm bells. A year later, when I was in the depths of depression after a string of miscarriages, there were days when I would have answered the door in my pyjamas and with a bleakness in my composure that would have worried anyone. What if they had come the morning after our Christmas party when I was still half drunk, the floors were sticky with spilt beer and our daughter was deposited in front of a screen for most of the day?

Through my investigations into this subject I ran these scenarios past dozens of social workers. None thought any would have led to serious consequences for me. But most agreed on a different picture that might have. What if my house had been very small, there had been more siblings vying for attention and fewer resources to help? What if it was a mess and the fridge was empty? What if my cat had just crapped on the floor and I hadn't noticed? What if my daughter hadn't had her breakfast yet and was hungry? What if I had been in care myself as a child? How would it have looked to them then?

We all have lapses in standards sometimes; but being comfortable enough to have those lapses is a privilege in itself. I'm confident that I'm at times a poor parent. I look at my phone too much, I worry that I went back to work too early when they were babies and I have zero patience. I leap on the research that says you only had to be good enough half the time and that kids can tolerate pretty lazy parenting. I believe that I'm a good enough parent. But what is 'good enough parenting' in the eyes of the state?

When a social worker knocks on a door with concerns about a child they will be looking for signs of neglect as well as abuse. The government, in guidance to the social workforce, defines neglect as the 'persistent' failure to meet a child's basic physical and/or psychological needs resulting in an impairment of their health or development. It says:

> Neglect may occur during pregnancy as a result of maternal substance abuse. Once a child is born, neglect may involve a parent or carer failing to: provide adequate food, clothing and shelter (including exclusion from home or abandonment); protect a child from physical and emotional harm or danger; ensure adequate supervision (including the use of inadequate care givers); or ensure access to appropriate medical care or treatment. It may also include neglect of, or unresponsiveness to, a child's basic emotional needs.[1]

Most local authorities use an assessment framework in the shape of a pyramid. The child is in the middle and three aspects are considered: their developmental needs – their health, education and social relationships; the parenting capacity in the family – how they deal with basic care, safety, stimulation, boundaries and warmth; then there's the environmental resources – their family's housing, employment, income and community networks for support. This simple 'child, carer, context' model is really the basis of social work.

Health　　　　　　　Basic Care

CHILD'S DEVELOPMENTAL NEEDS

PARENTING CAPACITY

Education　　　　　　Ensuring Safety

Identity

Emotional & Behavioural
Development　　　　　　Emotional Warmth

CHILD
Safeguarding
and promoting
welfare

Stimulation

Family & Social
Relationships　　　　Guidance & Boundaries

Social Presentation　　　　Stability

Self-care Skills

FAMILY & ENVIRONMENTAL FACTORS

*Department of
Health 2000*

Community Resources　Family's Social Integration　Income　Employment　Housing　Wider Family　Family History & Functioning

But interpreting that is more complex. A source sends me a toolkit used to assess new referrals in one area of London. This 'child neglect toolkit' runs to fifty-five A4 pages and documents things you might find in a child's home, asking the professional to, quite literally, tick boxes against what they are seeing. Social workers give a score of 1 (good) to 4 (bad) against the markers for neglect. A 1 for food, for example, would be nutritious meals, served with order and regularity with the family sometimes eating together. A 4 would be when the child is regularly going hungry, has no set meal times and the food they receive is poor, processed and sugary. For housing, a 1 is a home in good repair. For 4 it suggests a home that is dirty and squalid, with the smell of damp and even visible faeces.

The same tick-box exercise is used to assess love and care in the home. A 1 for warmth and affection; a 4 when a 'carer speaks coldly and harshly about [the] child and does not provide any reward or praise and is ridiculing of the child when others praise'. On substance misuse, a 1 would be someone who, if they do use drugs and alcohol, ensures they are stored carefully at home and are not impacting on the family's finances. A 4 would be a carer who blames their use on their child or involves them in their substance abuse.

It's a grim roll-call of the spectrum of parenting, simplified into a handy checklist for social workers to deploy as they visit families at home. It's in these dispassionate lists that the state determines what it takes to be a responsible parent. In reality, of course, these standards are subject to human judgement, enacted by social workers who all come to the job with their own set of unconscious biases and prejudices. One senior social worker who has worked across the country tells me it's the warmth factor that sways it most with her. You can forgive a lot of mess and chaos if there is obviously love between a parent and a child, with proper care and attention.

In an effort to standardise the system, councils have locally set thresholds that guide social workers on the steps they can take. These thresholds are set locally to let them account for regional differences in culture and population. The thresholds also influence the resources available for children and their families, and the level of need that automatically qualifies them for support or services. The thresholds present a conflict: between dispassionate assessment of a family's needs and the inevitable weighing up of what can be afforded by a council. The muddying between the two is obvious to families, and plays back later in court as the justice system seeks to balance the threat of harm of staying with a family within the context of the support available, with the threat of harm from removing that child.

Imposing definitions of good enough parenting has unintended consequences. The official standards are internalised. As one mother, who has had several children removed, says: 'There are two ways women can go: you blame everything on the council and social workers and refuse to work with them; or you face up to your own shortcomings and do everything you can to get your kids back. You become a "professionalised"' parent. Suddenly you're talking about "age-appropriate" toys, because that's the language they use. It changes you as a parent.'

Thresholds demarcate the court system too – there are particular benchmarks that must be met at all stages before a case can progress, and then during a case, other thresholds determine the action a judge is able to mete out.

Three critical hinges determine the next stage: how likely are the parents to change and improve their situations? How well are they working with the authorities to improve their family's circumstances? And how much support is there in the community for the parents?

The demands might be to stop substance misuse or to leave an abusive partner. I have come across dozens of cases where women have convinced social workers that they have severed ties with an abusive partner, only to continue the relationship secretly. This is getting harder to conceal in the courts now that digital records – emails, text messages and social media – can be harvested for evidence. The question comes back to timescales – will a child spend five years bouncing in and out of the care system while a parent quits drugs, and will the damage already be done by the time the parent is clean?

For the majority of children removed, one significant factor was the inability of their parents to collaborate with social workers. But as Isabelle Trowler, the Chief Social Worker for England, has pointed out, the onus can't just be on the parents to work with the authorities, but on social workers to nurture the right relationships. As Lucy, from the seventh chapter, experiences in courts every day, the trust has often been destroyed long before a social worker meets a family and it's an uphill battle to win it back.

Carol Atkinson, the Designated Family Judge for East London, describes how parents are increasingly oppositional to the courts. Some seem to be cutting off their nose to spite their face, willing to risk losing their children to resist working with the authorities. 'We're seeing more and more people who see the haves and have-nots. People who feel that the judicial system and family justice system is part of the establishment and they are not part of the establishment. We have to work very, very hard to make sure they understand we are just people as well. It's an ever-increasingly important part of my job.'

She pauses and embarks on what appears to be a tangent but actually might be the heart of the problem. 'I think it's like Grenfell. That's a perfect example,' she says. 'The mistrust of the whole inquiry process. Twenty years ago you got a high court judgment and people accepted it. But now there is mistrust of the system. Mistrust of institutions. It's the whole "Enemies of the people" thing in the press. We have to be aware of this.'

After the Grenfell disaster, I was working at the British

Red Cross, running their media operation as they launched a fund for victims and deployed volunteers. As we tried to make people aware of the help available, I felt the suspicion from a local community marginalised and let down by the authorities. Even the Red Cross, in their eyes, was part of an establishment that hadn't bothered with them before.

Plummeting trust ratings in governments, charities, the media and business over the past twenty years are reflected by the rise of populist politics and anti-establishment rhetoric. The social services story is perhaps the most acute case of this: where the state meets family, the power balance is out of kilter and those at the sharp end, some of the most disaffected people in our society, feel they have to fight against the system or become its victims.

The flip side to that distrust, seen through the academic work of Robert Putnam and his 'Bowling Alone' theory, is the scourge of loneliness, the hidden factor fuelling the rise in family separations. These huge structural changes are putting new and in some cases intolerable pressure on family life, yet it still tends to be the families who are held accountable for them.

Parents feel punished when their children are removed according to rules that they don't understand.

'Society's ideas about what is considered to be acceptable parenting shift sometimes imperceptibly,' Isabelle Trowler tells me. 'At other times, these changes are accelerated by a heady mix of political discourse, media interest, community scandal and personal tragedy.' That shift is invisible day to day, but viewed over the past twenty years it is huge. The rules of the game have changed.

The mechanics of deciding whether to separate a child

from their family are made up of uniform structures and boxes to tick. An algorithm could be created that standardised the system across the whole country – indeed, algorithms are being used by some councils to trawl families' records and look for patterns of neglect or abuse. But that disregards the need for judgement, instincts and humanity.

The question is: what is the underlying purpose of child protection and family separation? Are we trying to keep children safe or improve their life chances? Are we rescuing children from poverty and disadvantage or from abuse and neglect? Are we removing children from homes with extreme political views that will make them outcasts for life or are we only saving them from physical and emotional harm?

There's a judgment that courts return to again and again when trying to define good enough parenting. Judge Hedley, a family court judge, ruled in 2007:

Society must be willing to tolerate very diverse standards of parenting, including the eccentric, the barely adequate, and the inconsistent. It follows too that children will inevitably have both very different experiences of parenting and very unequal consequences flowing from it. It means that some children will experience disadvantage and harm, while others flourish in atmospheres of loving security and emotional stability. These are the consequences of our fallible humanity and it is not the provenance of the state to spare children all the consequences of defective parenting. In any event, it simply could not be done.

It would be unwise to a degree to attempt an all-embracing definition of significant harm. One never ceases to be surprised at the extent of complication and difficulty that human beings manage to introduce into family life.[2]

Baroness Hale later built on this, in a judgment in which she ruled:

We are all frail human beings, with our fair share of unattractive character traits, which sometimes manifest themselves in bad behaviours which may be copied by our children. But the state does not and cannot take away the children of all the people who commit crimes, who abuse alcohol or drugs, who suffer from physical and mental illnesses or who espouse antisocial political or religious beliefs.[3]

Yet this is what I witness in the stories I've heard and the cases I've watched. A shifting in the standards of parenting by invisible forces that rewrite the rules of family life. It results in the mass removal of children from the poorest, most disadvantaged homes, placed into wealthier families. Rather than solving social problems, we are breaking families up to socially engineer the problems away. Paul Bywaters, the professor of social work at Huddersfield University, has the research that evidences this. On average, foster carers and adopters are richer than the children's birth families. To qualify, they have to have a spare room, immediately putting them into a higher socio-economic bracket. Foster carers receive more benefits from the state than birth parents or kinship carers do.

'Children have been removed from families in extreme poverty. Placed in homes with more assets to start with or given large fostering allowances,' says Bywaters. 'Then comparisons have been made between affluent families and the birth families who were living in poverty. It could be seen as social engineering.'

Judge Carol Atkinson is very aware of the limits of the decisions she makes. 'We're looking for good enough. Not to socially engineer,' she says. 'People harm their children day in day out. It's got to be proportionate to the risks. We're not in the business of improving parenting beyond getting them to an acceptable level.'

But one Central London social worker is in no doubt. 'There's certainly an element of social engineering. It depends on the social worker. Some have ingrained ideas about what good enough care is and what families should be.'

She gives very practical examples where social workers may have different suspicions. 'For some social workers it's so frightening if an adult is sharing a bed with a child or having a bath with a child. There are terrible assumptions being made. Sharing a bed or bath doesn't always ring alarm bells for me. If I have a mum and a kid in a one-bedroom flat, yes that's a problem. That's not her fault. That's not abuse; that's a housing issue.'

I've heard this prejudice all the way through my research: when Lucy Reed, the family lawyer we met, described the families who use 'sexy' as a term of endearment and how that panics social workers because of the difference in semantics; when Daniel's social worker was so surprised that he cooked fresh food; when Caitlin talked about the policing of 'people like me'.

The problem is that social engineering the problems away doesn't work. It might feel like it makes sense, to remove children from dysfunctional homes. But it creates different social pain in the families left behind and the children taken away.

The fact is we're all somewhere on the spectrum of good to bad parenting. There is a lot of poor parenting that happens without disastrous consequences, and that's as it should be. 'They fuck you up, your mum and dad,' Philip Larkin wrote. 'They may not mean to, but they do.' The system is trying to draw an impossible line between the inevitability that we fuck our kids up, and the moment it's the state's responsibility to step in.

Throughout the research of this book I've reflected at length on my own parenting. I meet a mother whose children were removed by the police after she left her teenager in charge of the smaller ones. I do the same. There are no firm legal limits to define what abandonment is, how old kids have to be to be responsible for their siblings or for how long you can leave them. When does the 'time out' method for setting boundaries, used by Francesca, become an act of cruelty? The rules aren't written down. It's bewildering and it makes parenting a lonely place for us all. We're supposed to know, but the truth is we're all making it up.

My own brief brush with social services, however innocuous, kept bothering me. What was the process they went through to come to my house, what flags had been raised, and what about the visit made them disappear and never come back? Was there something about my character and actions in the hospital, in my heated exchange with the receptionist, that made people think I was a questionable parent? I can't remember what I said to that woman, but I know I wasn't in control and I might have spoken harshly to her. Had I made a mistake in that moment and been reported?

I contacted the council and asked to see the records pertaining to my daughter. There were none. They suggested I contact the hospital, who also said there was no record. A social worker had put it on their lists to visit my home, and yet the paper trail was invisible. My search came to a dead end. It looks as though I'll never find out why they really came to our house, or what they thought of what they saw there.

Nancy's story

'As normal as it can be'

Foster care and love

Sandra walks into a room buzzing with enthusiastic adults with fixed grins, over-compensating for nervous, weary teenagers. It's her first fostering day – which is like a speed-dating event for new foster carers and children living in care – and a chance to find a match. The first child she sees is Nancy, who she knows from the local youth centre she runs. They move together like magnets, full of relief that they've found someone they know. 'Can I come and live with you?' Nancy asks. 'Of course,' Sandra replies. It really was as easy as that.[1]

There are many horror stories about the care system – children left in dire conditions, or removed from loving parents before they've been given a chance. There are also numerous cases where children's lives have been improved, and sometimes saved, by the state intervening. Somewhere in the middle of those two extremes lies the quietly heroic work of simply trying to make things a bit more normal and a bit less bad than they have been.

Nancy is twelve when we meet at her foster carer Sandra's Midlands home. She dances in and out of the room when I visit, checking me out, then retreating again as I chat to Sandra. She's wary of strangers; there have been many in her life. But she is also interested in my work and keen to tell me her story – once she's got the measure of me.

She circles the open-plan kitchen-diner, observing us as we talk. Sandra cooks a spaghetti bolognese. Nancy hangs back, listening to our conversation, then jumps in with questions about my children. She wants to know what my teenage daughter is like, what she enjoys doing, and asks to see a video of her playing the guitar. She's not easily impressed.

Nancy has a wicked sense of humour and a knowing way of talking about her situation. She describes herself as a 'vulnerable' child, placing a comedic emphasis on the word and cocking me a look. She knows the system and she knows the lingo.

She guides me through the world of being in care with patience and authority. 'A LAC is a looked-after child. In a LAC meeting, you talk about education, home, contact with your birth parents. In a PEP you just talk about your education. You talk about your levels and everything you do with education. I can't remember what PEP stands for. You get a pupil premium to buy help with your education. I get a laptop; but you can also get tutoring. I get Stagecoach – that's acting, singing and dance lessons. Sometimes you have a reviewing officer and the reviewing officer is there as, like, a back-up social worker. When you're sixteen or seventeen you get a PA. A personal assistant. They help with transition to independent living.' She never questions the logic of it, it's just how it is, but it needs explaining and she wants people to understand.

She can recite every significant date in her shifting family status: leaving her birth family; arriving in foster families; and then when she saw Sandra at the fostering day run by the charity Coram, the awkward 'speed-dating' event for foster children and their would-be carers. There's a stigma to being a foster kid. 'I'm not going to lie, it's quite secretive, isn't it?' she says. 'People have just heard about it, they make assumptions of what it is, but they don't really know what it is.'

Nancy's foster home is spacious, looking out over rolling fields. The cupboards are stocked with chocolate treats and her favourite drinks. Her bedroom is pristine and peaceful, fairy lights hang above her bed and the walls are covered with pictures of her birth family. She says it's different to the house she was born into, but doesn't really want to talk about her birth family or what went before. This isn't her first foster home.

Nancy's fourteen-year-old foster brother comes in for a snack. He won't meet my eye and isn't up for talking. It's his first time in care. Sandra's parents drop off a bed for him. Archie, Sandra's birth child, who is seventeen, also comes in and raids the fridge. He describes the forms he has to fill in about his feelings on fostering. 'I don't really have an opinion,' he says. Sandra looks on at the comings and goings, enjoying the bustle and the noise.

There are an estimated 44,500 families fostering at any one time in England – 55,000 across the UK. The scene in

Sandra's house might feel secretive to the individual children in it, but it's a huge operation to create this army of back-up families for kids who need them. Sandra is a bubbly ball of energy, gently teasing and playfully chatting with the kids as they drift in and out. Everyone is 'babes' or 'darling'. She calls them out and indulges them, neutralising the things that might trigger bad memories, making them feel safe and cared for.

The paperwork that comes with being a foster carer stretches to pages and pages of forms to fill in, reports to file and a handbook that explains what she can and can't do, down to the stipulation that the kids all have to have dressing gowns for walking around the house at bedtime or in the mornings. She knows the limit of her parenting, which decisions she has to consult the social workers about, and what boundaries she can decide for herself. 'It's a very long process and some people can find it really uncomfortable because they need to know everything,' she says. In Sandra's house, the dressing-gown rule is not enforced.

In some ways Sandra is trying to create the happy childhood she missed out on. In her thirties she had lots of therapy, specifically CBT (cognitive behavioural therapy), to help her manage the aftermath of a childhood scarred by domestic violence. She was working in medical sales when she started volunteering at the youth centre. She had always wanted a full house and to foster, but her husband didn't feel the same way – he worried he wouldn't be able to let go of the foster children if they needed to leave. When they separated she saw her chance to do it as a single mum.

Sandra's natural ease with the kids masks a deeply strategic approach she takes to the home she has made for the kids. They have team meetings to discuss what's happening. Everything is talked through, their privacy is respected and the difference between their foster home and birth homes kept clear. 'We're a unit all together,' says Sandra. 'We live our lives and deal with problems and have a laugh. But we've got the brilliance of their family still being there. Nancy has the best of both worlds.'

Foster families are just normal families in Sandra's view. It's not a job, but a vocation with subtle differences to parenting. Children love their birth parents unconditionally, and they not only don't automatically love their foster parents, but they can arrive full of resentment at even being there. It's a different dynamic, a relationship that takes work.

She sees certain problems in the system. Each time the social workers come Nancy is questioned about the things that were on her mind at the last visit, which might have been a month ago. 'Everybody has bad days. Sometimes the system doesn't allow for that – everything is trauma-based. But it might be that you've not had enough sleep.'

Nancy is listening in. 'It can be difficult. Everybody is just talking about my life,' she says. 'It's my life.'

Each morning Sandra takes Nancy and her foster siblings breakfast in bed. It sounds like the height of indulgence, five-star fostering, but actually it's a carefully thought-out tactic to set up their day in a quiet and calm way. When you've lived in stressful homes, mornings can be flashpoints. Chaos can be a trigger, making them hypervigilant. Neutralise that and there's less potential for conflict; they wake up feeling nurtured. 'My house is a picture of calm in the morning. That helps them all day.'

There are not many families that start their day like that.

Her household is built on rules and relationships and a lot of laughter. 'I can't reiterate it enough. It's just normal family life. I know, I keep saying it. Is it coming across?'

Nancy looks at Sandra fondly. 'Yes,' she agrees, then gently corrects her: 'It's as normal as it can be.'

For all the good reasons you might remove a child from their birth family, to mitigate a risk, reduce a harm or give a child a future, it can only be judged a good decision if the child is given a better alternative. Once in the care system, it's incumbent on the state to provide a better alternative to one they faced at home. That is implicit in the social contract, when the authorities have assumed responsibility as 'corporate parent'.

The care system has a bad reputation. Revolving doors through foster placements, multiple changes in social workers who don't provide the stability they promised, a fast track to a life of institutionalisation.

By every academic measure of success, care leavers underachieve: in school, college and at university. Over 30% of those who are homeless have been in care at some point in their lives, according to the children's charity Coram.[2] Some 22% of female care leavers become teenage parents – three times the national average.[3] Care leavers are estimated to represent between 24% and 27% of the adult prison population.[4] This is despite less than 1% of under-eighteens entering local authority care each year. From this vantage point, the care system is a conveyor belt to prison, especially for boys.

Once out of the care system, one in six young people return to their family homes anyway; half of them as soon as they can, the NAO found.[5]

At the time of writing, nearly 80,000 children are in the care system in England. In 2019, 72% of those children were in foster placements, 12% were in council facilities such as children's homes and secure units, 7% were placed with another parent, 4% were living independently (post sixteen) and 3% were placed for adoption.[6]

The lives and experiences behind those statistics are hugely varied. Of fostered children, many are placed with extended family, and these are usually the most successful. Some foster carers are employed directly by the local authorities, but many come via agencies that vet and approve foster carers, but also charge a substantial fee. There is a market in foster care. When councils struggle to recruit they turn to agencies, the majority of which are profit-making and increasingly backed by international hedge funds who see this as a sound investment. Agencies compete to provide placements for the kids. It's become such a murky market, that's not always providing the best care for children, that the Competitions and Markets Authority, at the time of writing, had launched an inquiry into the system. As if it needed saying, the Chief Executive of the CMA, Andrea Coscelli, pointed out: 'Children's care is not a market like any other – our clear and overriding priority will be about identifying ways children can get better care.'

For example, foster carers aren't always where they need to be for children who need them, so some 16% of foster placements are more than twenty miles away from their birth homes, requiring children to change schools as well.[7]

The NAO (2014) also found considerable variation in local authority spending on foster care. It calculated that the annual bill for a child in care for a council ranged from

£15,000 to £57,000 for their own foster care provision, and £18,000 to £73,000 for private providers' foster care.

This market also creates folklore about carers' motives and what they are paid. A government review in 2016 revealed how the financial rewards were significant in carers' decisions whether to start and remain fostering.[8]

But Sandra has no truck with these suspicions. 'A lot of people feel it's a vocation. There are a group of foster carers locally and we all get together. We do it for the right reasons: to give young people an opportunity and help them grow. I imagine there are some who just do it for the money, unfortunately. But really not many – it's too big of an ask.

'The money is just enough to provide everyone with a nice lifestyle but I also work. I think it's good for the kids to see you work to get the money. That gets us the nice holidays, the trips to the cinema. I probably am rare in that I'm a single person, working, with two foster children.'

Coram Voice is a charity that advocates for children's experiences within the care system. They conduct the biggest annual survey of children in the care system.[9] In many respects this finds children in care living emotionally at the extremes: feeling happy and positive about the future; or unhappy, worthless and negative. The system, as it stands, is working very well for some children and making it worse for others. This data also reflects children's prior experience: if you remove children from their parents who had been very neglectful and abusive, their life improves. Children in care, for example, report feeling significantly safer than other children where they live.

At the same time significant numbers (one in five of the total) couldn't name their social worker and say they haven't really been told why they are in care; 27% of children inter-viewed had had three or more social workers in the past year. A parliamentary report in 2016 found that in significant swathes of the country, children in care aren't getting the mental health support they need and in some cases aren't even being assessed. 'We believe that looked after children should be viewed as a priority for access to mental health assessments and never refused care based on their placement or severity of their condition,' the MPs concluded.[10]

By educational measures, by prison populations, by the homelessness and teenage pregnancy stats, it seems that people who go through the care system are failed. But it's not a fair comparison. Comparing children in care with chil-dren who have never been in care just proves that they've had more disadvantages that have disrupted their lives and limited their success. It also reinforces the fallacy that removing – or 'saving' – a child from a harmful home will have a fairy-tale ending. They still carry with them the harm that went before and the emotional fallout.

One study attempted to shed light on the benefits of the care system. Led by Oxford University in 2016, it compared the educational outcomes of children who had been in care with those who hadn't and those who were on a 'Child In Need' plan (where social workers have identified problems in a family that don't warrant removal, but do necessitate additional support).[11] Children who have never been in care do best, followed by those who have been in a long-term stable foster home, followed by children in need, with the lowest-performing category children who have bounced around the care system on short-term placements. This offers a different perspective: that where fostering works, it really works. But where it doesn't, creating more instability and upheaval in a child's life, it does serious damage.

The emotional costs of separation, the severing of a sense of belonging and the loss of unconditional – even if traumatic – love take their toll on children in the care system too. Cathy Ashley, the Chief Executive of the Family Rights Group, says: 'Their educational outcomes might be better than if they stay at home. But longer term, their well-being in terms of their network, identity, their chances of having employment is much more questionable.

'People need to feel wanted and like there are people out there for them. The care system, however amazing some foster carers are, is not so good at that.'

Trying to understand whether child removal is right or wrong is a complex exercise in weighing up damage against benefits. You can measure these by education, by rates of looked-after children who end up in prison or at university. But what's harder to quantify is the effect of love, or the lack of it. Sir Martin Narey, who advised the then education secretary Michael Gove on child protection matters, told me he'd never met a mother who didn't love their children, but that sometimes that wasn't enough. Alice, the social worker, described the child she was working with and the desperate, primal love she shared with her mother, who despite all the love in the world couldn't parent well enough. Caitlin and Angela know that they loved their children, but they also know they struggled to protect them. If love isn't enough in parenting, what place is there for it in the care system?

When a child is removed from their parents, the local authority that starts the proceedings becomes what is known as the 'corporate parent'. Lemn Sissay, who grew up in the care system and has campaigned for its reform, believes it is exactly the responsibility the state should take, but the child never needs to know it in those terms.

'I had very little conception of the state. I meet young people now who try to articulate emotionally what a corporate parent is. Mainly it irritates them emotionally,' he says.[12] 'Put those words together: corporate and parent. A child thinks a parent is a parent; you're then asking them to think of a parent as a corporation with different facets that can serve a child. It's an impossible ask. It's not going to work emotionally. For the institution the idea of the corporate parent is the best idea. It means that every part of local government is thinking about how we're serving a child in care. For the kids it's not working, it doesn't sit right.'

That system, in his view, can erode a child's concept of their own childhood and build their experience around the way the council works, rather than the way they live their lives. 'What I needed in care was one person to travel with me through the whole journey. The one thing that was consistent is that everyone disappeared within a year. And I was supposed to be sound of mind at eighteen?

'It's all about love. How do we account for the greatness of love? Our care services are told to not be emotionally involved in our cases. Social workers said to me, "I can't be emotionally involved." That's an emotional statement in itself. It's a violent one.'

Traditionally, social workers have put up rigid boundaries to protect themselves and their clients. Some are starting to challenge this, opening themselves up to the families they are working with. James built his relationship with Daniel on shared experiences of parenting young boys. Otherwise, as Sissay puts it, the state is replacing the love of a parent with the practicalities of parenting, but awkwardly avoiding the more difficult question about how we make up for the love that is inevitably lost. For all the hundreds of people I spoke with for this book, the word love was all but invisible, limited in court to fleeting references: 'Mother loves her child but ...' – then outlining her deficiencies rather than examining the capacity for that love to translate into better parenting.

How do children experience love and abuse, side by side, and how can the care system replace the loss of the love of a parent, even if it did come hand in hand with abuse or neglect? Steve Bambrough is Associate Clinical Director for Children and Family Services at the Tavistock and Portland NHS Mental Health Trust, which has deep expertise spanning social services, the courts and the roles of child and family psychology within them.

Bambrough agrees that it's extremely rare to meet a parent who doesn't love their child. Rarer is a child who actually wants to sever ties with their parents. In twenty-five years of social work he can recall only three children who didn't want to go home. 'They don't want to be separated, they just want their parents to change,' he says. What he does see is confused definitions of love, born of generations of getting it wrong. 'Abuse can distort people's concept of love. It can be specific to their own history. That's the platform or model for their expression of love to their children. When you point this out to them the response is often, "It happened to me, it didn't do me harm." Actually it did. You don't see it as harm because it's an internal world.'

The Tavistock tries to teach care leavers the practice of warmth and relationships that have been missing in their lives. Really, they are trying to train them, for the sake of their future relationships, to correct the corrupted view of love they've grown up with. In that, they are also trying to disrupt the endless cycle of children going into care through generations.

The list of ten Adverse Childhood Experiences on page 18 doesn't explicitly include family separation or a childhood spent in care, despite the evidence of harm. Bambrough believes that is partly a symptom of a system that struggles to acknowledge the damage it does. His approach is to see the trauma in people's experiences – most parents who come through the courts have experienced a trauma; going to court is a trauma; being separated from your child is a trauma. 'The system doesn't like to think about what it does as being traumatic. That's a real flaw,' he says. 'They put the trauma at the door of the parent. It doesn't acknowledge its responsibility.'

The state doesn't try to replace the love that's lost from a child's life when they are separated from a parent. It tries to create the conditions of parenting and enforce the practice of parenting, but love is undoubtedly lost. I suspect that sometimes that might be a relief: I meet one teenage daughter who chose not to testify in her mother's defence. You can see the guilt and shame she carries for abandoning the mother she loves but knows cannot care for her. Bambrough says this shame and guilt is carried by 99% of the children he's ever worked with – for life. In Angela's story we heard about the shame that is poured on mothers, but this too is passed down through generations to the children the system is supposed to protect. It's the paradox of a love that is treasured above all, but also the source of the problem.

At the beginning of this book I quote the Joy Division lyrics:

Do you cry out in your sleep?
All my failings exposed
Gets a taste in my mouth
As desperation takes hold
And it's something so good
Just can't function no more?
Love, love will tear us apart again

They might seem inappropriate: a song about romantic love applied to a story about parental love. But those words encapsulate something for me about the coexistence of the dark and light sides of love.

The author Jon Savage, dissecting Joy Division's lyrics, writes: 'At the core of the song is the paradox that love and intimacy – "something so good" – can destroy as well as uplift. And, as the lyric insists, it will continue to do that as long as two people keep on coming back for more, as long as they fail to find resolution.'[13] This is the paradox that runs through the story of family dysfunction and separation. It's the story of violent, broken relationships that the women I meet can't let go of. It's the story of the love between a child and their parent, despite the parent repeatedly letting them down and neglecting them. Love isn't enough.

In these lyrics I see the pattern of destruction that plays out through the system: when social workers give too many chances; when they intervene too quickly. But there is also fearfulness in the state's response of how they can replace the love. Social workers are told not to emotionally engage, but as Lemn Sissay points out, this withholding of love is abusive in itself.

What is the nature of parental love? Sheena Webb is a clinical psychologist and lead at the Family Drugs and Alcohol Court (FDAC) in London. Her job is to assess the psychological state of parents and make recommendations to the court about their suitability, weighing up the psychological impact of the poor parenting, their capacity to change, and the potential damage of the removal. 'The parents we work with love their kids. It's how they show their love that matters, and how their experiences get in the way of them showing it,' she says.

'Love doesn't work unless it's felt by the recipient. You can be loved without feeling it. A lot of individuals really love their children, but intimacy and closeness is triggering for them so they can't express it in a way children can feel.'

She describes how love can mean different things to different people. Some think their kids are amazing; for others it's a biological link; others feel like love is equivalent to ownership, possession. What matters is how it's manifested. It needs to be unconditional, consistent and attuned to the children's needs. Hardest to measure is a sense of 'warmth' that evades definition. 'You can't describe it but you know when it's missing,' Sheena says.

On the term 'corporate parent' she is definitive. It's a 'revolting' way to describe a system that is so inconsistent and fundamentally loveless in its care. 'The state is hugely conditional: you can only phone between these hours; you can only have money for some things. It does absolutely none of the things a parent should do.'

I think about Daniel's Congolese saying about learning to listen to the beat of a child's drum. Nancy's words echo in my ears: life in foster care is 'as normal as it can be'. For children removed from their parents, the love they lost is 'something so good' that can't function any more. The next best thing is stability. There are no fairy-tale endings.

Emma and Sarah's story

'There are no fairy-tale endings'

Adoptions and afterwards

Sometimes moments are just indelibly scratched into the memory. It was a morning in April 2012 when Emma put her six-year-old son Seth into the back of someone else's car and buckled him in.[1]

She then turned to her three-year-old, James, and strapped him in on the other side. But by the time James was secure, older brother Seth had let himself out and was clinging to his mother. She put him back, only to find that James had wriggled free and jumped out the other side.

Like a terrible nightmare, where you've lost all control, every time Emma secured one of her sons in the vehicle, the other would slip away and clutch at her legs again. She tried to be as honest as she could, telling them she would see them again, one day, when they were grown up. 'I'll always be waiting for you,' she said. It lasted just a few minutes before the car could pull away, but it felt like the most torturous episode of her life. Both boys defied her expectations; the one she thought would go to pieces kept it together more than the son who usually put on a brave face. You can't predict how people will behave in moments of trauma that will reverberate through their lives for ever.

Watching the scene was a social worker, holding a camera and filming these precious, desperate last moments of Emma's motherhood. Emma doesn't know whether this was to show they were doing it properly, or to show the children in the future. It's a thought that keeps her up at night still. Somewhere there exists a video of the worst moment of her life, and she doesn't know why.

The story of how they got there is, as is always the case in child protection, complex and messy. Emma noticed some bruising to one of her boys and took him to the doctor. Blood tests suggested he had lymphocytosis of the blood, which is a trait of both leukaemia and thyroid disorders. She went back to A&E shortly afterwards when she noticed further bruising. They kept them in over the weekend, observing her and her son. Then she and her partner were questioned by police and a social worker. The boys were sent to live with her sister and she was placed under a curfew that prevented her spending the evenings with them. At the time she didn't believe her partner was responsible for the injuries. Now she does. She believes that the fact she had had dysfunctions in her own childhood – she experienced sexual abuse and spent a short amount of time in care – were further factors that the social workers noted.

The boys spent the next few years in foster care, but maintained regular contact with Emma. Later they were adopted, without Emma's consent. That's when Emma found herself

struggling to get them into the car. They were being separated for good, but as Emma remembers: 'I refused to say
goodbye. I didn't want them to know it was the last time.
But all they saw was a broken-hearted woman.'

Nearly one hundred miles away from where Emma was
struggling with her children at the car, Sarah, the boys'
chosen adoptive parent, was getting ready to welcome Seth
and James to their new home. She was a single mother;
it was her daughter who had first seen the boys in *Be My
Parent* magazine. They had similar heritage to Sarah's birth
children. It felt right. She was told the kids had been in a
stable foster home and were ready for a new start. Sarah was
also a professional, a social worker, so she believed she was
equipped to cope with any issues the young brothers would
bring with them.

Sarah wasn't a complete stranger by the time the boys
came to live with her. They had been meeting on and off for
a while to get to know each other. She picked them up from
the social workers and stopped at a restaurant on the way
home for a treat. There James kicked a waiter. Sarah saw it as
a test for which she wasn't quite ready. 'I'd been their parent
for two hours, I didn't know what to do,' she remembers.

On the surface, the boys began to feel at home with
Sarah. At heart, there was something not quite right. The
first sign was bed-wetting. Their behaviour and moods
fluctuated. The boys eventually told Sarah about the pun-
ishments they had received while in foster care. 'It wasn't a
one-off. They were very clear on what they said and very
upset,' Sarah says.

'Seth was very angry. He did not want me to be his mum.
He had a mum, thank you very much. He really struggled,'

says Sarah. 'They would imagine Emma lived next door and they had a tunnel into her house. They could just go and see her. They wanted to know she was OK.' What the boys needed more than anything were answers. Why had they been removed from their family to keep them safe, then not properly looked after in care?

It seemed a reasonable question for the boys to ask, and Sarah pushed the council to explain. They refused to investigate the children's complaints, a decision that was subsequently criticised and overruled after Sarah went to the local ombudsman. The whole process dragged on. The result for the boys was a short, official letter from the council and a small compensation payment. It did not satisfy their sense of injustice.

In the children's absence, Emma, now with a new partner, had given birth again. She spent the pregnancy in a state of fear about what would happen. What does happen when a parent has had children removed previously, and is pregnant again, varies widely from authority to authority. The law states that legal action about a child's parental status can't be taken until the child is born. Through the pregnancy councils can do an assessment of the parents' capacity to care for their child. But how this is done varies widely from area to area. There is no national guidance, and there are risks – if a mother believes the child will be taken away, they might seek a late-stage abortion, or attempt to miscarry. Or they might try to flee the jurisdiction and hide out elsewhere. Parents are known to have left the country, moving to Ireland, France or Spain, in particular, to remain with their babies.

Emma was in touch with social services through the

pregnancy and her experience of it was of deep uncertainty. Just like Caitlin in the opening chapter, there was 'parallel planning' going on. In the midst of labour, she resisted pushing. 'I thought if I pushed I'd lose him,' she says, and shivers. When her little boy arrived they wanted her to leave him in the hospital. That week, she went to court to contest his removal. 'I couldn't even say goodbye. I broke my heart coming out the hospital thinking I wouldn't see him again. I got to the court. My boobs felt like they were going to explode. My bits felt like they were hanging out.'

The family thought there was no precedent in law for parents who have had children permanently removed being allowed to keep a subsequent child. They combed statutes and legal records and found a relevant judgment by Lady Hale, the Supreme Court judge. 'The judge ruled our research was correct and there was no reason, given I had improved my lifestyle and mental health, that I couldn't keep my baby. Family agreed to visit every day. And we would all support and call social workers if there were any doubts. I'd done it.'

By the time her next baby, a little girl, arrived, she didn't even have a social worker because they were confident that she could cope.

Meanwhile, Sarah was struggling to manage on her own with two young traumatised children pushing against her. Her family relationships became increasingly strained and her mental health started to suffer. 'I was far from the parent I thought I would be,' she says. Her situation was even harder to accept because of her own professional knowledge as a social worker. She thought she understood the issues she'd be facing. 'So many adoptive parents struggle. I was like, "Yeah, but not me,"' she laughs. 'It might have been different if I wasn't so stressed about my own issues. I felt guilty that things had been so difficult. That I hadn't been managing.'

By this time, the boys were getting older and asking more and more why they couldn't see Emma, their birth mother. Seth and James had a few details of Emma's life through the 'letterbox' scheme, which allows birth parents to write to their adopted children via social workers. They knew she had become a mother again and was allowed to keep custody of her new children. The injustice was hard to swallow, it left them angry and confused, and that was playing out in their day-to-day behaviours and frustrations.

For Sarah, their adoptive parent, the constant battle to reassure her boys and deal with their questions led to a realisation that they were simply not going to settle, not until they had seen their 'Mummy Emma'.

It also occurred to Sarah that soon the inevitable would happen, and one of the boys would look Emma up and make contact online. So she called the social workers and set about persuading them to organise an extraordinary reunion.

Some parents can struggle to remember their kids' birth dates, but Emma remembers the date of every significant stage in her family's separation – and their eventual reunion. 'I was on holiday with my partner, feeding my son. I got this phone call and I was told that not only does Sarah want to meet me, but the boys want to see me.

'I can't speak. My partner grabbed me and I told them. We're both crying. I phoned my whole family. I needed to tell everyone. They are coming home. Not coming home for ever, but they are back.'

Emma and Sarah meet first. They sit in a coffee shop in a train station, where their drinks go cold as they swap stories about the boys. Emma looks through every photo on Sarah's phone as Sarah tells stories of the days she has missed. There is a bizarre intimacy between two strangers who come from different parts of the country; they know nothing of one another, but everything about their sons, because they are both mum to the same two boys. They also know, immediately, that for the sake of those boys they need to be in one another's lives.

They plan to meet again, this time with the boys, and two weeks later Emma sits in a grotty council 'contact centre', a building where families can spend supervised time together. She sits there as the clock ticks towards 1 p.m. and the boys' planned arrival time. It passes 1 p.m. and her heart is almost stopping with nerves. The clock ticks on and the boys don't turn up. Emma worries that Sarah has got cold feet. Or worse, the boys have changed their mind. At 2.30 p.m., ready to give up, she goes for a walk in the local park. Her phone rings and the contact centre says the family are waiting for her – their car had broken down.

Emma walks through the park to the contact centre, trying to steady her breathing. Her hands shake and her heart races, she's close to a panic attack. She enters the room and the boys fly at her like birds, nearly taking her off her feet. Sarah is there too, and the four huddle together. The boys are looking at her with starving eyes; it feels like they could consume one another, to make up for all the time and space between them.

When we meet, in 2019, Sarah ('Mummy') and Emma ('Mummy Emma') tentatively describe themselves as 'co-parenting'. The boys still live with Sarah, who has legal responsibility and is the primary parent, a two-hour drive away from Emma. They all meet regularly and the boys recently spent six straight days with Emma. When they have a problem, they put the phone on speaker and all four of them, mothers and children, sort it out together.

The two mums could hardly be more different. Emma talks at a hundred miles an hour and her house bursts at the seams with family and pets. She defines herself by the fact that she never gives up. People rarely see her without a full face of make-up. Sarah is quieter, more pensive. She speaks deliberately but doesn't sugar-coat anything. She has brought Emma back into the brothers' lives, even though it could threaten her own status as their parent, because that's what the boys need.

On a walk through a local park, Seth, the eldest, sticks close to one or other of his mothers, always maintaining physical contact, draping an arm or holding a hand. James, the younger brother, runs circles around everyone, dashing up and down hills, taking anything but the most direct route. They are easy in their mums' company and confident of their own stories, and the family speak openly about the unusual nature of their situation and the difficulties they've faced. What they want other people to know is that these situations are messy and not straightforward. There are no fairy-tale endings. It's still not easy.

Sarah says the judgements that social workers have to

make are all but impossible. 'Children are being removed at the risk of emotional abuse, so they might not have actually experienced it. But then there's the emotional impact of being separated – that's just as hard to assess – and how do you weigh up between them?

'I've lived through the fallout of separation. It's a big hole. Some people who have that bit missing can ignore it and focus on the rest of their lives. For others, that missing bit is the sole focus that's ruining everything else.

'If children lose a parent through death there is lots of support, but if they lose through adoption, it's assumed it's a magic wand, a clean slate. It's not always like that. People say adoption will give children a normal life, a fairy-tale ending. There's nothing normal about living that life.'

In England and Wales children can be adopted without their birth parents' consent. Non-consensual adoption – labelled 'forced adoption' by its critics and on the Facebook groups where those who have experienced it gather – is relatively rare elsewhere. Sir James Munby, previously the President of the Family Division of the High Court, noted in one judgment: 'England is unusual in Europe in even permitting adoption without parental consent, indeed in the teeth of parental opposition – what I shall refer to as "non-consensual adoption" – and even more unusual in the degree to which it has recourse to non-consensual adoption.'[2]

One paper for the European Parliament suggested that other countries do allow for non-consensual adoption – but do it in very rare circumstances.[3] In the year of that study, 2013, 5,050 children were adopted in England and Wales, the vast majority against their parents' wishes, compared with the next biggest cohort of 3,293 in Germany, where parents do have to consent.

Adoptions are often portrayed as a storybook ending: a child rescued from adversity and given kind new parents who are desperate for a child. The imagined adoption holds a promise: a new life for the children, a fulfilled dream for the parents. But the reality can be very different. Every decision that judges such as Judge Wildblood make is a choice between the risks of harm as they are understood now and an unknowable future harm of the separation from their birth family.

2013 was the year we hit a peak in adoptions. It was on the back of a government drive to encourage more adoptions, faster permanence for children, in light of all the emerging evidence of the impact, both social and personal, of unstable childhoods.

Three politicians in particular shaped this political appetite. Tony Blair laid the groundwork as Prime Minister when he called for a 40% increase in adoptions, recalling the profound positive effect adoption had for his father. Andrew Adonis, his schools secretary, campaigned for children in foster care to be sent to private boarding schools – something that had happened to him. Arguing for improvements to social work, he described his upbringing:

I say this from personal experience. I was in care until the age of sixteen and in a Camden council children's home until the age of eleven. I was lucky to have a remarkable ex-Barnardo's lady in charge of the home, who became a surrogate mother (we called her 'auntie'), and a brilliant social worker who took on Camden's social services bureaucracy to enable me to go to a boarding school at eleven, part paid by the council, as the best way of providing a stable education while returning to my family.[4]

After the 2010 change in government, Michael Gove took up the cause, tackling delays in adoptions and introducing targets to stop children bouncing around the care system for too long. 'That adoptions are at their lowest point for a decade means a cruel rationing of human love for those most in need,' he said in a foreword to an action plan he published in 2012.[5] A new rule demanded that all care proceedings are concluded within twenty-six weeks. At the time the average length between children entering the care system and being adopted was one year and nine months.

Gove was born Graeme to a single mother in Edinburgh. He spent his first four months in care and then was adopted by a childless couple of whom he says: 'That couple, whom to this day I call Mum and Dad, gave me the stable and loving family life that allowed me to enjoy amazing opportunities – to go to university, work in Fleet Street and Parliament and become a father.'[6]

With Gove's interventions, in 2012 the pendulum swung sharply towards faster intervention and quicker adoptions.

But in 2015 there was a rapid reversal after the then President of the Family Courts, Sir James Munby, restated the primacy of the right to family life in courts. In a judgment, called Re-BS, Munby argued that Gove's targets meant that too many cases were coming to court ill-prepared, seeking adoption orders without the evidence that merited such a serious decision:

We have real concerns, shared by other judges, about the
recurrent inadequacy of the analysis and reasoning put
forward in support of the case for adoption, both in the
materials put before the court by local authorities and
guardians and also in too many judgments. This is nothing new. But it is time to call a halt,' he said, urging courts
to ignore the twenty-six-week limit if they didn't feel like
they could make a fair decision within that timeframe.

Where the proposal before the court is for non-
consensual adoption, the issues are too grave, the stakes
for all are too high, for the outcome to be determined by
rigorous adherence to an inflexible timetable and justice
thereby potentially denied.[7]

The number of adoptions fell back to pre-reforms levels,
while the number of kids going into care continued to
increase. The fashion for intervention in families moves
in cycles.

Personal experience and passion coming from Whitehall
had been backed up by evidence-based arguments for the
twenty-six-week rule. Brain development in early years is
increasingly proven to be dependent on positive attachments
with a carer or parent. Without these, there can be permanent damage.

But the focus on Adverse Childhood Experiences, which
we examined in the first chapter, did not take into account
that separation in itself can be a damaging experience.

The longest-term study of outcomes for adopted children looked at babies adopted between 1958 and 1970 and
found that they did as well – if not better – in life in terms
of economic and social well-being as their peers. But that

study also acknowledged the patterns in adoption at the time, babies adopted at birth by relatively wealthy families.[8] Today there are relatively few babies, with more adoptions happening for toddlers and older children, who have been in care and who may have already sustained some damage from their experiences. Today's adopted children are very different from the generation our politicians were born into.

A separate attempt to review all the evidence about the well-being of children adopted from the care system made a sad conclusion: 'Adoption was associated with lower academic attainment and elevated levels of behavioural problems across childhood, adolescence and emerging adult-hood compared with non-adopted comparison groups.'[9]

A further study, conducted in Wales in 2019, looked spe-cifically at the rates of Adverse Childhood Experiences in adopted children.[10] Most had been adopted from care and the older they were, as is to be expected, the more adverse events they had experienced – triple that of the general population. But it also found that the mental health of the children they surveyed was worse than the UK general pop-ulation on all points, which, they said, stressed the need for more support for adoptive families to cope. The warmer, more nurturing and 'child centred' the family was, the better a child's outcomes would be.

Being an adoptive parent is challenging, as Sarah found. According to Adoption UK, two-thirds of adoptive parents face aggressive and violent behaviour.[11] Figures on the breakdown of adoption are not recorded and the last study to ask the question, in 2014, found that only around 3% of adoptions fail, although the implications for those children of a fresh round of rejection at a later age are profound.[12]

The idea that adoption is a fresh start for a child is baked into the system. Very basic things suggest this: when a child is adopted, the numbers that identify them are changed once the order is completed. In the eyes of the state they don't just move family, their identity is erased and they become a different person. However, attitudes to adoption are changing and becoming more flexible.

Open adoptions, with ongoing contact between children and their birth parents, are more common. As with Caitlin, who sees her children twice a year, more birth families are maintaining some contact with their adopted children. There might be annual meetings at a council contact facility. Other families have 'letterbox contact' – letters passed on via social workers – as Emma did. Very few adoptions are now entirely 'closed', as they've been historically labelled. But the contact is regulated and social workers are nervous of unrestricted access such as Sarah and Emma instigated.

Part of this shift is down to the internet. The anonymity of the pre-internet age meant that families couldn't easily trace their children and vice versa. But given our digital profiles, it's now quite difficult for people to disappear, especially if a child is older and knows their parents' names. They are too easy to find on social media.

But part of it is an acknowledgement of the damage that is done if we try to erase people's pasts. Sheena Webb, the psychologist we met earlier, also works with families going through care proceedings for fostering and adoption orders. 'People think there is no cost to putting a child into foster care. Some professionals do it because it's a safe option rather than understanding that you lose something. It's not just about love, but the unconditional belonging that comes with a biological link. Some foster carers and adopters will do a good job of making it feel it's unconditional. But what if that foster carer never adopts you? What does it mean?' she says.

She describes her clinical experiences of children who are adopted and go on to form very strong attachments with their parents, but there is also consistently something missing: a yearning to know where they come from and where they belong. 'They just need to know what happened and that everything was done to help them. Did everybody try their best?' she says.

'If they question why their parents didn't want them that gives rise to a sense of unlovability which can really damage self-esteem. A lot of these children will be OK for a bit – but then it hits in adolescence and adulthood. They carry a latent impact and vulnerability that's not addressed or responded to.'

Emma and Sarah talked about the 'hole in their children's heart' that they hoped to fill through their unusual situation. Having existed on both sides of the divide between social workers and parents, what has the whole experience taught Sarah about the system she works in? 'That it's shit. I don't know where to start. Just the underestimation of the impact that social workers have on people's lives. The huge impact of not being heard. The lack of sympathy and understanding. Things could be done so much better if people had the time and space to invest in people.'

Sarah now helps children to write their life stories, a technique developed to process trauma and unravel their own backgrounds. She says: 'It's about getting their understanding of the story and filling in the blanks. It can be very basic information, or very harsh information. They've often had no help to process it. Quite often people don't want to tell a child something horrendous that's happened. Quite often that child knows.

'We need to start listening to the impact we have on children in care. There are plenty who will say, "My mum was shit, it was right for me to be removed", but there is always an element of love that can never be replaced by ever-changing social workers.'

Her experience also gives her an overview of some of the bigger forces driving the system: 'There's very much an "othering" going on – they are not like us. Parents subject to child protection are put in a different category. These people are human, we're all human, we're all vulnerable to mental health problems. If someone had come in here when I was struggling they might have put us on child protection. I needed help to get back up. You can judge what you see on the surface. There are some families that need their children taking away because things aren't right. But we also need to get underneath people and build them up. Having social workers involved just makes things harder.' Her point is that the judgements of parents need to come with an understanding of the challenges they face, and a commitment to help them overcome those challenges.

Emma adds: 'Adopters are sold a dream that they want to believe for these children. Life is so much more complicated.'

Part four

Is there another way?

'To love is to act'

Relational activism and radical tenderness

Inside a disused café on a high street in north London, a few dozen residents are gathering to debate what they can do about the knife crime that has touched each of their lives in different ways. A hand-made banner declares 'To love is to act'. Parents lead the workshop. Toddlers play on the beanbags. One man introduces himself as a social worker. A woman boos. There's a split second of tense silence, then everyone laughs.

That social worker is Tim Fisher. He's a smiley man with floppy hair and a laid-back, slightly hippy demeanour that masks a fierce intellectual focus on transforming the social work system, one family at a time. He's relaxed about being the butt of this group's jokes.

The workshop splits into smaller sub-groups to debate what could prevent knife crime, and help people when it happens. One group asks for anti-gang education in primary schools. Another says that more bereavement services need to be made available. 'When my daughter was murdered, I rang up the bereavement counselling and they told me six months,' one mother says. 'What use is that?' They exchange information about local counselling services.

This is my local high street in north London, but despite the familiar friendly tone, it's a foreign conversation to me. The threats that haunt the lives of the people meeting here, knife crime and violence and sexual exploitation, hasn't touched my family's life just two streets away. Nor does the real reason they are here: the undercurrent to the conversation is that most of the families have had social workers in their lives, or have had children in care; two are themselves care leavers. One of the women facilitating the session is Caitlin, from the first chapter, who had her two children adopted against her will. While the conversation, on the face of it, is about knife crime, there is another trauma they are trying to address: family separation by social services, or the threat of it.

This is a restorative justice process, called a Full Circle. It's designed to build bridges between the residents, social services and other council workers. By identifying problems, and coming up with solutions led by the community, they hope to forge a better way of working together.

Tim is the Camden Council social worker behind the Full Circle project. He plays an interesting choreographic role, encouraging families to get together, then standing back and letting them get on with it. He's been quietly working away in Camden, trying to change the way social workers build relationships with families.

'Social work has too often been something that we've done to families, so the power dynamic is all wrong. We've set ultimatums and measured their lives through thresholds. That has sometimes done more harm than good,' he says. 'We want to change that. We call it relationship activism.'

A small group of local authorities, including Camden, is now insisting that families can and should be a part of their own solutions. Family Group Conferences, where the wider family is brought together to solve a problem that is causing suffering to a child, are gaining momentum across the country. The Full Circle is a bigger and newer community version of this, bringing everyone together to try to solve problems.

This nascent movement is responding to the problem we've identified in this book: the sour standing of social work within communities, hoping to turn it instead into a resource families might turn to for help.

Parent campaigners describe how even kinship carers – people who step up to look after children when relatives can't – feel tested, rather than supported, by the system. They say that sometimes it was as if social workers had had to detach from the individuals involved to cope with the stress of the job. Meanwhile, families can often only influence the system through the complaint processes, which are by their nature inherently adversarial.

Sarah, the social worker and adoptive parent we met in the last chapter, is an advocate of this new way of working: 'We're missing the relationships. We need to see past the pattern of what you think you know about the person and understand what they need to make their lives and families work. People become numbers in a massive caseload. Decisions are made without seeing the people at the heart of it.'

*

For relational activism to work, it needs careful calibration between buy-in from the very top and ownership at the grassroots. Martin Pratt, the Director for Supporting People in Camden, appears to be a quintessential local authority executive. He works in Camden Council's swanky new offices, which look more like a tech start-up. He is older and greyer (save for his Paul Hollywood blue eyes) than the team of social workers, lawyers and police who sit outside his office.

I first see him in action at a conference the council hosts on the outcome of a family-led inquiry into child protection called Camden Conversations, designed to find out how parents really felt about the system. Caitlin was facilitating that session too and told her story of losing her children. She's determined to describe every detail to the social workers in the room, so they really understand how it felt. Some of them are crying. As Caitlin finishes and the room claps for her, I watch Martin look her in the eyes and mouth two words: *I'm sorry.*

Such an exchange is all but unheard of in this world. 'It's just being human, isn't it?' says Pratt, when I ask him about it later. He looks uncomfortable that I witnessed it, so against the grain it is. But the system in Camden is trying to build on this notion of humanity.

'You need to do social work with humility and respect. If you get the relationship right it becomes purposeful and less adversarial,' says Pratt. 'If you are a parent whose parenting is called into question, there is a huge power imbalance there. You have to acknowledge that.'

Fixing the system by improving relationships can come across as 'fluffy' and hard to measure. He's keen to be clear that it's not about taking more risks: 'If the child is not safe, we will remove that child and make them safe. The end goal is not a nice relationship; it is the thriving of the child.'

From Tim Fisher's 'relational activism', to Beverley Jones's 'radical tenderness', to the work that Angela Frazer Wicks now champions in putting parents' voices at the heart of the policy-making process, people are trying to put parents at the centre of a new way of working. Indeed, Pratt is all too aware that to succeed, the ideas need to take root organically in communities. If it looks like it was imposed by the council from the top down, relational activism will struggle.

If these terms can seem a little woolly, there's one place in the UK where they have demonstrated hard results. In Leeds the council has reduced spending on children's social care as well as the number of children going into care by making families the solution, instead of the problem.

The Leeds Family Valued project is focused on the Family Group Conferencing (FGC) model, but at a scale seen nowhere else in the UK. FGCs began in New Zealand as an effort to improve child protection within Maori communities, which had historically been oppressed and brutalised. The relationships between community and the authorities there seemed beyond repair. FGCs have an element of restorative justice, with social workers having to reflect on their own decision-making as well.

Nigel Richardson led children's services in Leeds from 2010 to 2016, during the time the previously failing service was turned around. 'The fundamental proposition is about family: family is the way we do business,' he says. 'But what family means is different to different people. You need to think creatively about it. If the state intervening in the life of a family is a last resort, as the legislation around the Children Act makes absolutely clear, it's fundamentally about children being best served by being brought up in their family networks. Family is the most important, but the most forgotten utility of the twenty-first century.'

Richardson now has influence at a national level. He led the Care Crisis Review, convened by the Family Rights Group and funded by the Nuffield Foundation, which laid out in detail the problems in the system.[1] But he also has an acute sense for how it plays out on the ground.

'When you talk to families about what it's like to be on the receiving end of these services, time and again they will say, "You are not listening." And I mean listening to hear, rather than listening to respond,' he says, echoing the words of Daniel, the dad we met in the fifth chapter.

'The language starts to escalate quite quickly if they don't do what the social worker wants them to do. "You need to stop drinking to keep your children." That's "doing to". Instead, "doing with" is high support and high challenge. You don't minimise the context or concern, you're inviting the families to engage in their rights and responsibilities. It's not fluffy. It's hard-nosed.'

It's about choices of where to put your efforts. 'Absolutely there are children who would benefit from the adoption process, but we don't put the same resources into family networks. We talk about fostering and adoption and it has a warm feeling about it. But actually it's stranger care. If anything happened to my kids as they were growing up, what would I want to happen? I would want an exhaustive look at our family network in all its guises. People that the kids knew. I would not want strangers. Yet that's what we do.'

He describes a scenario where a child is at risk of going into care and how they look for a family member to step in and take the children instead of going to a stranger – even if that family member is in another country, or is not family by blood. Not just asking a question and writing off the family but really kicking the tyres on how to build a child's existing network to keep them safe.

The official evaluation of the Leeds scheme, Family Valued, found a reduction of children in the care system from 80 per 10,000 to 76 per 10,000 over the fifteen-month evaluation.[2] It's slow but steady work, having an impact where all else has failed.

It took initial investment: £4.3m came from a government innovation fund to set up Family Group Conferencing and the support services that are needed to help families, but the money is earnt back through the reduced costs of children going into care. The government is now funding a scheme to extend the way of working across the north-east, where some of these problems are most acute.

Other activists advocate taking the Family Group Conferencing model to tackle the wider contextual problems that young people are facing. A growing movement is also urging social work to look at the harms coming from outside the family, such as community and gang violence and Anti-Social Behaviour, which not only result in abusive and damaging experiences for children, but can disrupt previously thriving families. It's called contextual safeguarding. Instead of responding to community problems by criminalising the children, or moving children away from a supportive family to escape local problems, families and the wider community could come together to find solutions.

In a 2021 paper[3] making the case for Family Group Conferences to tackle community-wide problems affecting a child, the Family Rights Group, along with Kent County Council and the Contextual Safeguarding Network, said the processes could 'help change the narrative from expecting young people to "keep themselves" safe from harm to a focus on community responses to create safety'.

The Full Circle experiment, back on my local high street in Camden, has taken that idea one step further – not just Family Group Conferences to bring a child's family together to tackle the dangers they face, but a whole community coming together to tackle the broader problems they share. It's about empowering people to find the solutions to their own problems and build the network to solve them.

It's also about social workers stepping back and becoming trusted convenors, rather than statutory intruders in peoples' lives. It's a dramatically different role.

The social workers I've spoken to are under no illusion that the system needs a reset so that they can do their jobs better. Parents and children remember the ones that truly helped them for ever. Fisher sums it up: 'I want social work to be better so that when I say my job title people don't boo.'

This growing movement of reformists in England is taking inspiration from elsewhere in the world. New York City was closer to where England is now in the early 1990s, with 50,000 children in the care system. Today it has 8,300, the result of a concerted effort to reduce numbers.

I visit New York to hear more about how they did it. There is a spectrum in the debate for the city's foster care system that mirrors the conversation in England. At one end there are those who say that the city's poorest citizens just don't parent well and their children would be better off adopted into wealthier families to break the cycle of care. But at the other end is a more radical argument from abolitionists who say the whole system is built on prejudice against some families, and it needs to be scrapped so communities can be given space to heal themselves.

Miriam Mack, thirty-one, is a lawyer working out of the Bronx Family Court, which sits in the shadow of the Yankees baseball stadium, and is surrounded by an industry of justice that includes the giant civil and criminal courts, bail bond brokers and shop-front lawyers.[4] The family court shows little sign of concession to the children in its waiting rooms who fill the cold, fluorescent hallways with the sounds of their play. Juvenile criminals, who are also tried there, shuffle through the corridors with legcuffs around their ankles. The administrators who run the courts are in full uniform. They carry guns and wear bulletproof vests. One claims this is the busiest family court in the country.

A toddler sits on her grandfather's lap and plays with crayons at the back of one courtroom. A baby is in a car seat at the side of another, like precious luggage to accompany proceedings. By the court's entrance is a day care centre where parents are encouraged to leave their kids while they are in court. But it is like no other childcare facility. If the decision is made in court to separate the family, the parents aren't allowed to return to say their goodbyes. The courts encourage it this way to avoid the public horror of children being removed from their parents in the hallways of the courtroom.

'It is incredibly difficult to bear witness to the level of

disregard that our clients endure,' says Mack. 'Child removal is emotional violence. This is a system that targets and victimises black and brown families in particular.'

Mack works for the Bronx Defenders, which provides legal counsel to parents – paid for by the city but fiercely independent of it. Parents are supported by their lawyers but also by social workers and parent advocates – people who have been in their position and understand what they are going through. Mack currently has seventy different clients on her books. The majority, like her, are black.

She is clear about the difference she can make: 'As a public defender we can make structural change over time by resisting the day-to-day poor decisions. And if I can just lighten the load my clients bear under the child welfare system, that's enough for me.

'But I know I am trained to be part of a system that I think is inherently oppressive. I am trained to be part of a system that privileges people with resources, with race privilege, with class privilege.'

In court, Mack is cool and direct. In between hearings she works the halls of the courthouse. Just like Lucy Reed in the Bristol courts, she wrangles with the bureaucracy of the system. She gives 'heads-up' to opposing lawyers of her intentions, ensuring they have the right paperwork, making sure they are abiding by their court-mandated promises.

The texts from clients showing pictures of their kids playing by the pool, or enrolling in school, make it all worthwhile, she adds. At the end of the day Mack goes home and winds down by binge watching *The Bachelorette* reality show.

Mack's boss, Emma Ketteringham, who leads the family defence practice at the Bronx Defenders, says that expectations are made of poor black and brown families that just wouldn't be the case elsewhere. 'You read articles celebrating the "pot mammas" of Park Slope in Brooklyn, where white, wealthy people live. Then you come in here and have to stop children being removed just because their parents smoke marijuana.

'This system is the fantasy of someone who designed it without their own children in mind,' she says.

The Bronx Defenders are part of the parent rights movement in New York City that many credit with helping drive down the rates of children in care from their peak at the height of the Aids and crack epidemics of the early 1990s. Every parent the city takes to court has the right to legal representation from specialist lawyers. And from their first meeting with the authorities, parents are provided with a 'parent advocate', someone who has been through the system themselves, to help and support them. The city pays for advocates, but activists, including the Bronx Defenders, also provide independent parent advocates.

Martin Guggenheim is a lawyer and professor of clinical law at New York University. 'The parent advocacy community in New York has really changed the conversation,' he says. 'Twenty years ago if you argued against a child being removed from their parents, you were condemned for not caring about children. Now judges question the harm that is done by removing children. That's minor progress. But it is progress.'

But others say that the reduction in family separation has given way to a surveillance culture that causes a different kind of damage to families.

Erin Miles Cloud is co-director and founder of the

Movement for Family Power, a national group campaigning for the abolition of the child welfare system in its current form. There is now a movement that questions the very existence of the current child protection system, following in the footsteps of campaigns in America to abolish the prison system on race grounds. She says: 'I think it is positive that fewer children are being removed, but the intense scrutiny and experience of surveillance cannot be told as a success. It creates a second-class citizen of parenting.'

The state has a system of mandated 'reporters' who because of the roles they hold – as teachers, day care workers, doctors, therapists – are legally required to report any suspicions of abuse to a state hotline. The city then, by law, has to investigate those complaints.

Cloud claims this surveillance culture weakens communities and divides families. In addition to mandated reporters there's a huge expansion of support services that are being supplied to families to tackle mental health, drug addiction and domestic violence. 'They might call it services, but they also frequently and interchangeably call it supervision,' she says. 'They often say they want "another set of eyes" on those homes. I don't think everyone is evil and wants to do harm. But the reality is not about support in the home. It's about surveillance. It doesn't come from bad people but from bad systems.'

The system, led by the Administration of Children's Services (ACS), which runs child welfare services, has also become weaponised within and between families. One young mother from the Bronx describes, with some shame, calling the ACS in revenge on her aunt after her aunt was given custody of two of her children. Cloud says this is common and can cause rifts between generations, siblings and communities that never heal.

'When your family is threatened, you clench to defensiveness and frustration and people point fingers,' Cloud says. 'Instead of de-escalating that, ACS uses the finger-pointing to get information out of family members.'

The Administration for Children's Services has its headquarters in downtown Manhattan, occupying a block between the 9/11 memorial and Wall Street, far from the Bronx and Brooklyn communities that take up the bulk of its time. Its grand art deco entrance gives way to grey cubicles. Kailey Burger is the Assistant Commissioner with the $330m annual budget responsible for the recent huge expansion of prevention services in New York. Her strategy is rigorously evidence-based, trying to situate services, via the agencies that deliver them, as close as possible to the communities they serve, despite her Manhattan base.

'If you're asking what we prevent, it's increased incidence of child abuse and neglect, it's worse harm to children and it's removal of children,' she says. Four out of five families complete the programmes they start. Of those, only one in thirty-eight families have another child welfare investigation within six months. For those who enrol but do not complete preventive services, one out of seven have a repeat, substantiated investigation within six months.

But Burger recognises the reputational problems the ACS has in the communities it serves. 'We are one house, with one side taking children away. The other side is trying to help, to be a friendly warm face. There's some dissonance there. That works against us,' she says. 'The other thing that works against us is this history of oppression. ACS was not always so progressive.'

I relay the stories of the 'surveillance culture' I've heard from Cloud and other parents I met in the Bronx. Burger, who is white, doesn't dodge the question and addresses the racism that Mack and others mention head-on. 'These things are real and we need to hold that every day when we're making decisions, because we're in a position of power and authority and that can very easily become oppression.

'The reality is that every government institution is racist; it's a system of oppression and things are designed intentionally to create poverty. That's the way government institutions work. And so if you want to shift that, it takes a lot of time and it takes a strong focus on justice and it takes a strong focus on listening to people and it takes a focus on building things that people have more ownership over.'

The communications officer from ACS, sitting in on the interview, gets nervous and intervenes. But Burger continues: 'If you have a president who is saying things about immigration and we're saying we're a sanctuary city and everyone is welcome here, people are hearing mixed messages.[5] It's about how do we as a government work towards this vision of the long arc of history bending towards justice? How do families have access to what they deserve and an equal opportunity? I just think to ignore the history of our country and the president of our country and things that are going on at our border is wrong.'

She seems beaten by the sheer scale of the systemic problems they are trying to fix. 'The whole country has a racist history,' she says. 'It's about making sure that everything we do is about moving forward to equality and fairness and equity.'

The movement in the UK towards a 'relational' approach to social work and supporting families, championed through official channels in Leeds and through grassroots activism elsewhere, shows there is a growing consensus that we need to find another way. New York offers both inspiration of how this can have an impact, reducing the numbers who are in care and better supporting parents, but it also flags a warning of its unintended consequences. For the starkly racially divided society in the US, this has resulted in black communities feeling policed and monitored. Already, families in the UK who have social services involvement feel supervised in ways others aren't, held to standards that they don't understand.

All these lessons tell us one central truth: that social workers alone can't fix the issues plaguing our most troubled families. These entrenched, complex problems can only be tackled with a cross-system, cross-society effort. New York's problems are made worse by a racist, breathtakingly divided society in which social services are just one visceral manifestation; in Leeds a critical part of fixing the issue was engaging the entire authority, putting a child-centred approach at the heart of everything they do.

The social work system is a plaster on the self-inflicted wounds caused by poverty, inequality, prejudice and isolation. Social workers are sent out to try to undo layers of dysfunction so far outside of their control, and without the tools they need. The prism of family separation and how the state goes about it reveals a decay that goes well beyond a narrow part of the state designed to support families and extends to every part of society. In England it needs a radical intervention but there's a lack of will because of how invisible this process is, cloaked by secrecy but also masked by marginalisation.

The system has been allowed to drift under a blame culture that corrupts its own processes, and free from scrutiny because the victims at the heart of this story are not only poor, marginalised and voiceless but are also the perpetrators of the biggest crime in society's eyes: poor parenting. This is behind closed doors because we don't want to see it; it's too painful an indictment on our society.

This system, that 'others' and marginalises the families within it, does us all a disservice. We're all on the 'good enough' parenting spectrum. This isn't happening to other people; it's happening to us. This isn't the fault of social services, or the courts or other authorities; it's our collective responsibility. Because looking after the most vulnerable children is what a society does. We are the sum of our society. We are each other's safety net.

A thought experiment

There were some things I heard through the research for this book that stuck with me and became guiding principles.

'When I really needed social services they failed me again by sweeping everything under the carpet and saying, "You've done this, you must suffer the consequences,"' a mother told me.

'This system is the fantasy of someone who designed it without their own children in mind,' a New York lawyer told me.

'You have to decide what's really going on. Everyone has a whole range of incentives to say and believe certain things,' a Whitehall mandarin told me.

'We could have stayed together, with support,' a grandmother in the North of England said.

'It's as normal as it can be,' a twelve-year-old girl in a stable foster care placement in central England said.

Each is understated in its own way but together they propelled me through the long conversations I had with the people I met for this book.

The first encapsulates the cycle of mistrust in the system that is passed down through generations. The second describes oppression, alienation and the dehumanising of families. The third tells us that the whole debate is riven with belief systems about the role of state and family that stop us seeing the wood for the trees; the fourth that we, as a society, are simply failing people who need our help. The last betrays the fact that, at the heart of it, is a dream we tell to make ourselves feel better. We tell ourselves that there are solutions to these problems. But there are no happy endings, every story I heard was about loss that stemmed from a broken family.

Pretending they can be 'fixed', that children can be rescued from their own parents, denies the complexities of the human relationships and the profound need for love and belonging that they are built on.

This is the paradox: that love and abuse are intertwined in the lives of everyone in these stories, and so often in their parents' lives and in their parents' parents' lives, too. Of course there are children removed for good cause from emotionally, physically or sexually abusive or neglectful parents, and there are stories of children's lives made a little better, or a little less worse, giving them a chance. But simplistic 'rescue' narratives seldom tell the whole story: separating children from their families always has some fallout. It doesn't mean we don't have to do it sometimes, but we should always be questioning how and why we're doing it and whether we've got into a habit of doing it before we've exhausted every option to help people stay together.

As a reporter I'm used to getting stuck into the most fraught subjects. I've dug deep into education policy, health inequalities and worked at the heart of the political hothouse of parliament; I'm used to examining policies, comparing them to the reality and navigating the intense political battles that accompany them. The surprise in this story is not about the division or intensity of those battles, but the consensus that I found. People have different views on how to intervene to protect children, and in particular how many chances parents should be given before we remove their children and how much we can really expect people to change; but nobody is defending the status quo.

From Whitehall to the Royal Courts of Justice, from town halls to schools and living rooms across the country, those who work in and experience this system know something is going wrong: that the current rate of children going into care is neither desirable nor sustainable and that we are an international outlier. The postcode lottery of who goes into care is an all too common injustice. No one is really confident that we are consistently making the right choice between an abusive or neglectful home, and the current care and adoption system.

Each decision to remove a child might be justifiable in that moment, but up to a third could have been avoided had more been done to support the family earlier – remember, that's 27,000 children each year. We've cut the early interventions and universal services that can help families thrive, and we haven't worked hard enough to establish ones that are proven to work. So we are getting to children too late, leaving them in terrible circumstances, then 'fixing' the problem by separating them from parents who, despite everything, they still love.

Something always breaks when you remove a child from their family. The child loses something, the parents lose everything, and the state creates a generational cycle of family failure and a life-long obligation to make up for that separation. The state rarely fulfils this obligation. The consequences are not just felt by the child who is removed, but by any subsequent siblings and generations to follow; all of them internalise the heartbreak and with it a distrust of the state.

I would never argue that we don't have to remove some children. Of course we do. We need to, in Nancy's words, make life 'as normal as it can be'. Separation should only come when all else has failed, and it's in that moment that the state proves itself as the safety net we consent to.

The truth that flows through every conversation I've had is that of the creeping drift towards removal before the state has done everything in its power to help the family. Separation should be a last resort. It's not. We are not giving families a chance to stay together before the state intervenes. I write 'we' because this is not the responsibility of social workers alone, or the courts in their decision-making, but it's about the kind of society we want to be. These actions and decisions are a function of a society that has lost sight of its purpose.

Through this book I've explored the layers of policy decisions, changing social norms and events to try to explain why family separation has proliferated in the UK over recent years. Those layers are complex and the whole thing is encased in a political conversation that makes it hard to see the truth. The prism of the decision to remove a child reflects back at us the many changes that have happened in society that are almost imperceptible in the moment, but hugely significant over time.

Fundamentally, our understanding of abuse has shifted

over the last few decades. We understand that emotional abuse can be as damaging as physical abuse. We understand that neglect and a lack of love can in its own way be as brutal and harmful as a beating. We understand how destroyed people can be for life if they go unseen for a whole childhood.

The toxic trio – of substance abuse, mental health problems and domestic violence – feed into that. But currently the system focuses more on the things that are seen as within the individual's control rather than where society is failing. We ignore the undercurrent drivers of poverty and structural inequality that consign some families to a lifetime of struggle, and which have hampered social mobility and our ability to improve the circumstances we were born into.

We ignore the compounding effect of social isolation, the symptom of a weakening society and declining social capital. It's our mutual responsibility to be part of communities, willing to help our neighbours.

We ignore the discrimination that plays out in our judgement of other people's parenting in myriad ways: privileged people judge poor people's parenting; liberal social workers judge conservative, religious parents; white workforces judge non-white communities; and a largely female workforce marginalises men and heaps responsibility on women. The best people in the system work hard to understand their own prejudices, born of their own position and experiences. Not enough of them succeed.

The system varies from council to council, social worker to social worker. In pockets of the country you can reverse nearly all of the national trends we've witnessed, producing a confusing, often contradictory pattern in the postcode lottery of decisions that means where you live dictates whether your family stays together.

At the extreme, the effect is that we are punishing lonely, poor, marginalised mothers for the failure of our society to do its job and provide a safety net. Then we are blaming them too for self-medicating with drugs, or succumbing to mental illness, or repeating the patterns of their childhood experiences by 'allowing' themselves to be abused. These cases are built into community folklore that then infects trust in the whole system, perpetuating the cycle.

The ability of the state to form that safety net has in the past decade been severely hampered by austerity. Drug rehabilitation services, domestic violence resolution courses and mental health provision have been whittled away and social workers are left looking on, powerless, at families who are in distress and struggling. They have fewer tools to help.

The courts are now pushing back, demanding that more is done to help families before they are taken to court. As soon as that 'conveyor belt to care' that the Chief Social Worker Isabelle Trowler denounced has been switched on, relationships break down. Once in the courts, the adversarial nature of the system makes it harder for families to work their way out.

Add to that the ongoing fallout from the high-profile cases of Peter Connelly and others, and you create a profession that is risk averse, removing children rather than taking the time and effort to respect human rights laws and keep a family together. If the only action a social worker feels they can confidently take is to push families into the court process, and by doing so shift responsibility to a judge, that's what will happen. Put all that together, and it's no surprise that we are removing more and more children.

What's also true, and takes some mental acrobatics to understand, is that we are missing more children. Thinner resources, applied via a narrower definition of need, means that social workers are picking up on things too late, when they have already hit a crisis point. Early intervention is increasingly a myth. Kim's experiences trying to support the families who don't qualify for social services interventions in Tipton speak to this. This is a system that manages to both remove too many children and at the same time leave too many in substandard homes, suffering without a sense that anyone cares.

Politics is a factor. The 'saviour' narrative, born of the Blair era and enthusiastically and personally championed by Michael Gove under the coalition government, prized adoption and fostering as a solution. Remove children from struggling homes, place them in homes that want them, and the problem ends. The fact that adopted children don't just change parents, but their entire official identities, says a lot. We think adoption or removal is an endpoint, but the ramifications play out for years to come. You see this narrative in the thinking that flourished after Victoria Climbié and Peter Connelly: prioritise the child's needs over the parents' at all times. We are saving innocent children from bad parents. Blaming mothers, mostly, in the process and labelling them as almost untouchable. But in this something was lost: the understanding that a child and their parents are part of a whole; separating them has consequences.

Children love their flawed, broken and sometimes useless parents. You punish the children when you remove them, pushing them into a shameful and, as Nancy described it, 'secretive' world of foster care.

Blame and judgement percolate through the whole system. Courts blame the social workers for being ill-prepared for hearings. The child protection social workers blame the referral team for slow responses. National politicians blame local politicians for poor practice on the ground. We all blame the parents. Mothers shoulder disproportionate amounts of responsibility; dads are allowed – and even encouraged – to disappear.

The guilt and blame also extends to the very people the system is designed to protect. Children feel it. They see the impact of a separation on their parents, they understand themselves to be the cause of it. It is a crushing, painful outcome.

The prism shows us not broken families, but a broken society. Is there another way?

In Whitehall, the people who think about these things are under no illusions about the problems in the system. 'Clearly, the children's social care system is under pressure,' one minister told me. Isabelle Trowler has exposed some of the problems I've been reporting on. There are efforts underway to tackle them. The Leeds model is being expanded to other councils. The Family Justice Observatory, funded by the Nuffield Foundation, is trying to fill the evidence vacuum in the system. The government-commissioned What Works for Children's Social Care systematically reviews the sector and shares best practice between social services. The President of the Family Division of the High Court, Sir Andrew McFarlane, is evaluating the public and private law systems. In November 2021 he announced fundamental reforms to improve transparency in the family courts. Local safeguarding boards have recently been formed, bringing services together to take joint responsibility for caring for children in local areas. Josh MacAlister will this year deliver an independent review of the system, which has already, in interim reports, begun to out some of the problems in this book. 'Our children's social care system is a 30-year-old tower of Jenga held together with Sellotape: simultaneously rigid and yet shaky,' he reported.

Left to its own devices there are signs that the system is holding itself to account, trying to become more evidence based, tackling inequities and attempting to become a fairer system.

Then two things happened. First, the coronavirus pandemic struck. The system was frozen overnight, couldn't do its job, right at the point that new pressures were piling on to already troubled families: joblessness, isolation and widening inequality. Domestic violence reports went up. Reports of the most serious incidences of child abuse involving death and serious injury increased in the first lockdown. At the time of writing we don't know what the true impact of that will be – indeed, it might not all be bad. Perhaps families have proved more resilient than many assumed, and advances in the digitisation of the courts and contact between birth families and children might force the system to modernise. What's certain is that it has set in train a cash crisis in public spending that will cast a long shadow. Second, as this book was going to press, the story broke about the horrific murder of six-year-old Arthur Labinjo-Hughes, focussing public attention on the system, including a new government review that will spotlight rarer cases of deadly child abuse. There is a risk that the full spectrum of problems in the system will be neglected.

Covid-19 and Arthur's murder have forced urgent questions where our systems, already under pressure, have to be reimagined and rebuilt. Everything is changing. Can we change it for the better? So, here is a thought experiment – not a fully worked policy proposal but a provocation for action and reform. What might be done if we let ourselves think the unthinkable? What could happen if we dismantled the current social work system and started again?

Throughout the writing of this book the idea that emerged was of vulnerable families punished for their perceived failings, whereas in fact many of those are the structural things they can't control; poverty, geography, isolation, race, ableism and gender inequality all play a part.

Rather than fixing a housing issue, we remove a child. Rather than removing violent partners from the equation, we remove a child and punish their mother. The people the state employs to support families need the tools to do it. Those tools are practical – access to better housing, support with childcare, safety from a violent partner or support that stops the violence. Sometimes it's as simple as some money to buy food.

This support needs to be more universally available – embedded in the fabric of our society through the structures of the state that have no shame attached: through education, health and communities.

These tools are pragmatic, but they also need to be provided within a dynamic that is humane and based on the emotional relationships social workers can build with families. The radical tenderness and relational activism we heard about – instituted through Family Group Conferencing to properly engage families, or through the Family Drugs and Alcohol Courts to properly support parents – are about attitudinal shifts away from blame and towards what actually works. What Leeds has learnt about prioritising family, being creative about what constitutes family and paying much more than lip service to strengthening the families they work with, the rest of the country should benefit from.

Many of the problems we heard about from the people I interviewed demand this different approach: for police to prevent domestic abusers from being near families, rather than for the families to be responsible for keeping themselves safe; for more men to work with the invisible fathers in these stories; and for a way that we can look at families without prejudice and work out where their strengths lie, as well as their vulnerabilities.

Arming social workers with the practical and emotional tools to do their jobs makes sense. It also creates a reset moment for the structures within local authorities. The disconnect between children's and adults' services is a disservice to communities. They are organised around the council structures, not people's real lives. In reality, the support services for a parent made vulnerable by learning difficulties, poverty or addiction could be the most important thing the state could do for their child. But the family is treated as separate unrelated entities, rather than as deeply enmeshed parts of a whole. The state needs to reflect the way families live.

What Leeds has got right, what Camden is striving for

and what New York has attempted is putting families at the heart of things, and seeing them as a potential solution, rather than as an inevitable problem. They see the whole family. It's about opening minds to people's strengths as well as their weaknesses and looking for those capacities, rather than the risks and threats in isolation. It's about building relationships that are robust enough to challenge parents to change their behaviour.

And it's about holding people to account, which you can only do in an impactful way when you've earnt their trust. That takes time – and inevitably resources. But it also takes skills that are sophisticated and can't be replaced with protocols and tick boxes. The 'doom cycle' that Josh MacAlister described, where social workers' standing is eroded by process, needs to be replaced with status and better pay in recognition of the crucial work they do. It couldn't be a more important job.

They need to have the intellectual imagination to engage with men, rather than write them off as the problem. They need to have the time and space to support a lonely, isolated parent to build a network to support themselves. And they need to have the muscle to demand that other services are provided – housing, mental health provision, employment advice – so the family can fix itself. They need the tools to tackle poverty and disadvantage, instead of the power to remove a child.

The political barriers to these ideas rest on the left-right dichotomy over the duty of the state to support versus personal responsibility to change. I saw the effects in some of the people's stories I reported on: the dependent relationship between social workers, services and families rather than a mature relationship-based model where support workers can challenge families to improve. I don't think there is a golden age we should return to – even when the system had enough money, it was not evidence driven.

Money, as always, is the elephant in the room: this sector needs more money. We can't just keep trying to do the same thing with less money; we have to try something different. There needs to be accountability on public spending, but we also need to spend on areas that are backed by evidence. Many of the services available in the early 2000s were not rigorously tested. There were pots of money that were badly spent – Jemima's mother's counterproductive trip abroad, paid for by social services, which ended up with her son in care, speaks to that. It would take smart investment – but remember, in Leeds an initial investment in earlier support and intervention now pays dividends in the form of reduced child protection costs.

We are not as a state and a society doing everything we possibly can to keep families together. We know that even when it's been impossible and after everything has been tried, if a child and parent can't stay together, it matters hugely to that child as they grow up that separation was a last resort. A glaring gap I saw was in mental health support services, which are chronically underfunded across the board in the UK, consisting largely of emergency services that step in to section people and keep them safe, followed up by low-level, often online CBT services. There are no real resources to help people struggling in the middle group of profound-but-coping mental illness and personality disorders. Indeed, these are often only diagnosed during court assessments, when there is no hope to treat them 'within the children's timescales'.

It is a scandal that we would separate a family just for the want of adequate mental health treatment. It saves nothing and creates a new generation that feels betrayed by the state. We need to prioritise families on waiting lists for mental health services. This is controversial and won't feel fair to those who don't have children, but it will save so much more in the long term.

We also need far better mental health services for conditions such as personality disorders, which are a common diagnosis among parents facing the removal of a child and for whom parenting courses are all but irrelevant. Personality disorders can stem from trauma. It's rare you will find a parent in these cases who hasn't themselves been traumatised, but it's ignored. One psychologist said to me: 'If you are female and you self-harm and sleep with too many people and you're a bit shouty, you'll likely end up with a diagnosis of borderline personality disorder. What they don't see is the trauma behind your experience. That needs the attention.'

The Boston-based psychologist Bessel van der Kolk, author of the best-seller *The Body Keeps The Score* makes an impassioned plea for the impact of trauma to be recognised, arguing that many diagnoses of mental health illnesses are actually masking the very real impact of trauma on people. Drawing on Bowlby's attachment theory, he argues that the scars of trauma are passed down, generation to generation. Indeed, one major flag for social services is whether a parent was themselves in care. Trauma runs through every story I hear. We need to break this cycle with new therapies that allow people who have experienced trauma to break free of the fight or flight mode their body is trapped in.

Social workers need the tools of time and space to build

relationships and work more closely to support families to find their own solutions. They need the training and capacity to sit with risks, mitigate them and know when to say enough is enough. They need power and resources to tackle the underlying problems of family dysfunction, trauma and mental illness, to get better access to housing, health services and to tackle poverty.

But the question that I have found impossible to ignore is this: even with the resources and this different approach, is the current system now so corrupted by thirty years of distrust that it is beyond repair? Is there just too much generational baggage in the relationship between troubled families and the state for us to fix the current system of social work?

In the US, the Black Lives Matter protests put a campaign to defund the police on the agenda. Advocates of defunding the police say that they are so discredited in the communities they serve that they now do more harm than good. Defunding, rather than abolishing, means redistributing funding to community groups to pay for housing, education and support services to families instead of policing and controlling them; building people up, instead of imprisoning them in their own neighbourhoods. Proponents argue that if you invest in these communities, if you strengthen social and economic circumstances, then the need for policing will naturally be reduced. Incarceration rates will decline. You create a virtuous cycle.

In the US case, proponents of defunding the police also call for social workers to be given a role in supporting families. But I met people in New York who argue social work should be defunded for similar reasons. They say that the social work system has simply become an extension of the crime and punishment system, monitoring families, and causing more problems than they fix. In her forthcoming book Professor Dorothy E. Roberts, the American scholar on race and rights, argues for abolition of social work. *Torn Apart: How The Child Welfare System Destroys Black Families – and How Abolition Can Build a Safer World* will ignite the row over ending the child welfare system in the States. The only way to stop the destruction caused by family policing, *Torn Apart* argues, is to abolish the child welfare system and liberate black communities.

From my conversations with hundreds of people across England, I have come to believe that social work as a concept is now so distrusted, so toxic, that the model is irrevocably broken. The disruption of a pandemic might be the opportunity to reinvent it.

That 'enemy' reputation of social work loads the dice from the start. While nationally social workers are scrutinised for their perceived failure to protect children, in communities up and down the country a folklore has built up about interfering 'baby snatchers'. It's an unfair picture of an almost impossible job, but there is just enough truth there to reinforce the belief, which is deeply felt. The latest generation of a family that has experienced decades of soured relationships with social workers arrive in the conversation already feeling oppressed by the imbalance of power.

Brilliant social workers, such as Alice and James, can just about find a way through that. But it takes skills that many social workers don't possess. They are set up for a fight, not a genuine relationship in which they will, together, help families find a better way to parent. Crucially, that relationship can't be built on what resources a social worker can bring, or how popular they can be with a family, but on how they support a family to support themselves – and that means being able to challenge as well as charm.

To build a better way of doing social work, maybe we have to start again.

What if we scrapped the role of social worker? Decommissioning social workers would not mean decommissioning social work. What it could look like is splitting the role into two workforces: a smaller team of child protection officers, who investigate abuse and neglect; then a larger fleet of community workers, who provide earlier support to families who are facing difficulties. Behind the scenes in councils this is how it actually works – you have family support, then child protection and more social workers who are responsible for looked-after children and placing children for adoption.

But in the eyes of the communities that have lost faith, they are all just social workers – one tribe who go back to the same office and share information about families behind the scenes. If you separate out these two jobs into new roles, there is a potential to both refresh the profession in the eyes of the public and recalibrate the dynamic between supporting and – as a last resort, sometimes swiftly decided upon – separating families.

It would make the system more accountable for the support it provides to families and help shift that balance in spending to focus on earlier intervention. It would prioritise the universal services to prevent families falling apart, rather than tools to dismantle them. Right now the same social workers support families when the problems are at a lower level, then build the case to take the same family to court if things get worse instead of better. It makes it harder, as Angela experienced, to go to a social worker for assistance, because a cry for help might later become evidence in court that you're not coping. Caitlin even covered up for her abusive partner because she felt his stalking of her would result in her being further punished. In child protection we have criminalised the abuse, rather than the abuser.

Parents should seek out support when they are struggling, like they do already when their children have a Special Educational Need. But they hide problems from social workers for fear of the repercussions. We heard about this in the cases of domestic abuse, where mothers are held responsible for emotional abuse because they haven't controlled the domestic abuse they are experiencing – the cruel irony being that the very effect of experiencing domestic abuse is that you have no control over your life. Community support workers, employed and trained locally, valued and paid more, could be part of the answer.

Scrapping social work and starting again with two different brands of community support workers and child protection officers gives the system a chance to reset, but they need the resources and services to do the job better than they have done before. The challenge is always how to pay for it and where to divert money from. But in this circumstance, there is potential for the system to be cost neutral. As Leeds showed, an initial investment in reform to reset a system will pay for itself longer term. It is more expensive to remove a child than to keep them with their families. If we put some of that spending into supporting the family, through earlier interventions, then you save the costs through fewer child removals.

I hear whispered ideas for radically reforming social work mooted in Twitter threads shared between social workers, by parents I meet, and by social workers who want to go back to what they came into the job for: to help families. I raise the idea in senior settings with policymakers: they don't blanch as much as I thought they would.

This reform would not be a punishment for social workers – though I acknowledge it would inevitably be seen in the press as a failure of the profession. It should be about liberating them to focus on tasks and valuing what they are good at. There need to be higher standards as well – and an end to the revolving door that sees poor performers evading accountability by rotating through different councils. The new roles need to be highly trained professions; more so, they need to be the smartest people. This doesn't mean Oxbridge graduates, but people who know how to reflect on their own experiences, prejudices and assumptions and to keep an open mind. The New York experience of supporting families with advocates who have been through the system themselves, if adopted, could also build a pipeline of community workers into the profession – empathic and experienced, who can truly relate to parents.

Social workers are state actors. They become the visible personification of the state and authority in many families' lives. Reinventing social work and funding it in a smarter, more strategic way can't happen in isolation. It needs to be part of a bigger change in society to create stronger networks. This needs joint responsibility and universal services. Community workers could work in devolved, empowered teams, learning from the Buurtzorg model that the Frontline organisation is advocating for: that means in schools, GPs and reinvigorated children's centres. They already work in these places in pockets, but that's where their homes should be, stitched into the fabric of our communities.

New Labour explored some of these ideas in the 2000s with the introduction of Sure Start children's services, which were criticised for being hijacked by families who aren't struggling with the problems that really need the support. The scaling back of this programme, rather than learning and iterating, was a missed opportunity to localise and institutionalise family support.

We need a new era of 'relational activism' and the 'radical tenderness' that humans require in order to change. If we gave community support officers the time and support to take this approach, they could be the glue that helps rebuild relationships, that safely reconciles partners, that finds the friends, relatives and neighbours to take some of the load. A reinvented profession of community support workers would build the relationships in which to hold parents to account with kindness, candour and rigour.

But they won't do it in isolation.

Even a radical intervention, such as scrapping social workers and replacing them with community support officers and child protection officers, can't be expected to fix or make up for the underlying problems in society. Poverty, isolation and discrimination wear away at parents' capacity to parent, and the state's capacity to help them. These underlying causes are so big that they have become invisible. To fix this, we need to nurture a stronger society.

A stronger society means less poverty, less isolation and stronger social networks. It means more understanding, and realising that simply cancelling men, for example, doesn't fix anything. It would understand that the saviour narrative of rescuing children from broken homes doesn't account for the love lost. It just stores up future traumas. These are huge and seemingly insurmountable problems. But if we don't even question them we are perpetuating an injustice where the most vulnerable people are being blamed for something that is built on all of our shoulders and should fall on all of our consciousnesses.

Nancy told me that her life through the child protection system, and now in care, is a secretive one. She shouldn't have to keep that secret. A society's work to help families and protect children shouldn't be something that we are ashamed of, something that remains hidden behind closed doors. It should be our greatest achievement: a strong society able to build up families, instead of tearing them apart.

Author's note

I came to this story by chance. A brilliant editor, James Harding, who edited *The Times* and was director of news at the BBC, gave me months to go out into the country and try to answer the fundamental question: are we removing too many children from their families? I wrote a series of reports for his slow news start-up, Tortoise, which he founded with Katie Vanneck-Smith, formerly the president of the *Dow Jones* and publisher of the *Wall Street Journal*. They believed in the story and the need to give it the time and space to tell it properly.

Tortoise does journalism differently, holding events called ThinkIns to build communities around the stories that help shape and research the stories. ThinkIns are an exercise in organised listening, they put listening at the heart of the reporting process. A lot of the stories I heard came from those events, bringing together people from social work, the justice system and families to debate how the system works – and how it should work.

But despite the generosity of reporting resources the editors at Tortoise gave me, I struggled to encapsulate the full story that I was seeing. Reporting calls for clean narratives.

This story twists and turns and is full of contradictions that have taken me the process of writing this book to understand. How can it be that more children are getting swept up in a legal process that senior government officials damn as a 'conveyor belt to care', but at the same time teachers across the country are desperate for more intervention? How can it be that we are intervening more than ever – and still missing the suffering of so many kids? How can social workers be responsible for enacting this, yet be so horribly uncomfortable with its results? How can parents be abusive and neglectful, and at the same time be victims themselves?

For me, the stories in this book, and the 'slow-news' Tortoise way of reporting that preceded it, challenged the need to clean up those difficult and contradictory narratives for easier consumption. It's in those contradictions that the real story lies.

Throughout my career as a journalist I have worked to demand accountability where systems go wrong. In order to get that accountability, we need to work out who is to blame. I grew up as a reporter with a 'heads must roll' mantra, but through my career and with the rise in social media, I have seen that morph into a cancel culture that constricts how we debate nuance and delicate subjects where there might not be a right or wrong.

I still believe accountability to be vitally important and a principal motivation for my career as a journalist. But throughout this story I've seen the limits to this approach. What if there are no real 'baddies' in a story, but a systemic breakdown with multiple root causes, each interacting to produce devastating results? Before we try to fix the fissures in our society, we have truly to understand them.

I've found that there are very few villains in this hidden world. There are parents who believe they would do anything for their children, but can't. There are social workers busting a gut to help people, but failing. There are judges striving for a fairness that they just can't deliver. It's in these grey areas and apparent contradictions that we can really understand what's going wrong.

Our narratives often demand perfect victims – entirely blameless people who are sympathetic casualties of circumstances. That's a limitation on the truth because the truth is always messier and more complex. Just like there are no real 'baddies', there are no pure 'goodies'. Our rush to judgement and to put people in boxes eats away at what makes this story so fascinating – the interplay between people and society and where our responsibilities begin and end.

People who experience the system, who lead it, who work in it and the academics that challenge it through their research know what's going on. But too often this story is told in one-dimensional ways that just add to the breakdown of trust.

These are complex stories to report in many ways. Anything heard in a family court is subject to strict and important reporting restrictions designed to protect the identity of the children. To be able to report these stories, in some parts I've had to heavily anonymise the people I've interviewed. In others I've only been able to report one person's side of the story, and as you've seen these are all complex, highly emotive cases. Each account is told from detailed interviews with the people who experienced them. People recall traumatic events poorly, and where they have been judged as failing they create their own narrative of what's happened, justifying or only partially acknowledging the full horror of what they have done. None of the parents I interviewed claimed to be perfect. Many knew they had done horrible things. Because of the necessary secrecy of the processes, I couldn't always fact check their version of events. That's the reality of the darkest episodes of people's lives in a system that, for good reasons, operated in the dark.

My research has been a combination of reading all the research that is being done in this area, interviewing the most powerful and influential people in this field, and comparing that evidence with the experiences of people on the ground. I have organised the interviews to give an overview of individual experiences within the system, rather than definitive accounts. This book is the result of listening to people who aren't usually heard, and for that reason I quote my interviewees at some length. Their words matter. I wanted you as a reader, through these people's stories, to understand the multiple truths of this system.

In this book you've read the word 'we' a lot. That 'we' is important. It raises the fundamental question of why we as a society are removing so many children from their families. Social workers and the courts might be the final actors, but behind them is a vast, creaking infrastructure in which we all play a part. We have a collective social responsibility to step in where families are failing. And we fail as a society when we leave children in desperate circumstances or brutalise them further by severing their family ties.

Child protection is shrouded in secrecy, hiding the horror some children live through when their parents are cruel and neglectful. But it also masks the brutal nature of splitting up families. Both the neglect that children experience and the

88ff>8

decisions to remove them happen behind closed doors. We have sanitised, rationalised and dehumanised these stories. You can see this in the language used. 'I know when a child has a social worker because they say "sibling" instead of brother and sister,' one welfare manager in a school told me.

At the same time, on internet forums and WhatsApp groups around the country, a populist narrative is building about child-snatching social workers, one that is making their job of supporting families even harder. The responsibility I took in writing this book was to reveal the full horror of how we are treating families, without fuelling that populist narrative. I hope I've done the story – and all the people in it – justice.

Acknowledgements

This is a book about people. First and foremost, I want to thank the people who took the time and emotional energy to share their stories with me. Long conversations raking over the past are not easy but together we pieced together their stories and I hope I've done right by Caitlin, Francesca, Daniel, Gabrielle, Angela, Sandra, Nancy, Emma and Sarah. They are not the victims of this system; they are the experts in it. Their voices are important and their stories are precious.

The journalist Louise Tickle was the most generous colleague I could have had on this story. She has been looking into these issues for far longer than me, and has had a huge impact on the debate about transparency in the courts in particular. She introduced me to so many of the people I met for this book and offered guidance, support and very wise counsel. She also introduced me to Annie, a mother from Sunderland who is one of the most respected voices with lived experiences helping shape the national debate. I don't tell Annie's story, but her voice is in the book in the way I thought about this and approached it. Thank you, Annie.

I spoke to too many social workers to name everyone.

Alice, Kirsty, Daniel, James and Tim were pivotal to the story, but there were many more I met through the events we ran who shaped the complexity of this. They are heroes and being a hero is hard and imperfect. They know this. Frontline, which develops social work practice and leadership, was influential too, not least their former Chief Executive, Josh MacAlister, who is now running an independent review of the children's social system, to which this book will be submitted as evidence. Isabelle Trowler, the Chief Social Worker, contributed through her research and our conversations. She challenged simplistic thinking in a way that helped me understand more of the complexity about this.

The barrister Lucy Reed, Judge Wildblood, former president of the Family Division James Munby and Lisa Harker and Beverley Jones, both of the Family Justice Observatory, guided me through the legal processes, were candid in correcting me when I got things wrong and always operated with the utmost professionalism. Lisa Allera in the Judicial Office was thoughtful and accommodating in supporting interviews with Judges Keehan and Atkinson. I learnt a huge amount through those.

The alliances that have been built between the social work world, the legal profession, families and the academics contextualising and building the evidence is an amazing thing to see. Thank you to all the many academics I spoke to, and in particular Paul Bywaters, Anna Gupta, Elaine Farmer and Andy Bilson. Evidence is critical when the stakes are this high.

James Harding at Tortoise came up with the idea for the original story and asked me to investigate it. This book is the legacy of that commission and the unique and precious style of Tortoise reporting. It is so fundamentally important that there is space for thoughtful and curious reporting and James and Katie Vanneck-Smith have made that happen at Tortoise. Some of that reporting has morphed into this book and editors including Dave Taylor, Merope Mills and Ceri Thomas made those stories better. Katie Vanneck-Smith asked me to investigate the data that underpins all of this and Paul Caruana Galicia did the legwork on the methodology for that. Liv Leigh was my buddy as we went on the road holding ThinkIns on this subject in London, Sunderland and Newcastle. She felt the stories we heard as much as I did. Thank you to the whole Tortoise family.

Alice Lutyens at Curtis Brown read those pieces and saw the potential for this story. She is the most formidable and impressive agent I could want on my side. Rose Tomaszewska, my editor at Virago, is a superb, supportive and challenging editor. I've been an editor in journalism for much of my career. Rose is at a whole other level. Thank you for teaching me about writing and pushing me to own the arguments.

Finally, my family: my parents, grandmother, siblings, their partners and children. I wrote this book in lockdown missing you all. We know love, and we know how messy it can be. We are excellent at it.

And to my Martin, Ivy and Tam. Thank you. I can't believe how lucky I am.

Notes

Caitlin's story: 'They didn't give me a chance'

1 Caitlin and Adam are given pseudonyms to protect their identities.
2 'Children who are looked after in England (including adoption), year ending 31 March 2019', Department for Education, National Statistics, 5 December 2019; https://assets.publishing.service.gov.uk/government/uploads/system/uploads/attachment_data/file/850306/Children_looked_after_in_England_2019_Text.pdf
3 'The impact of the Baby Peter case on applications for care orders' (LGA Research Report), Macleod, S., Hart, R., Jeffes, J. and Wilkin, A. (2010). Slough: NFER; https://www.nfer.ac.uk/media/1630/bpi01.pdf
4 'The Child Welfare Inequalities Project: Final Report', Paul Bywaters and the Child Welfare Inequalities Project Team, July 2020, Nuffield Foundation; https://mk0nuffieldfounpg9ee.kinstacdn.com/wp-content/uploads/2019/11/CWIP-Overview-Final-V4.pdf
5 UK Poverty Statistics, Joseph Rowntree Foundation; https://www.jrf.org.uk/data?f[]=field_taxonomy_poverty_indicator:867&f[]=field_taxonomy_region:6
6 'More parents accused of child abuse than ever before', Andy Bilson, The Conversation, 6 August 2018; https://theconversation.com/more-parents-accused-of-child-abuse-than-ever-before-100477
7 'Care proceedings in England: The case for clear blue water', Isabelle Trowler, supported by: Professor Sue White, Calum Webb and Jadwiga T. Leigh, University of Sheffield; https://www.sheffield.ac.uk/polopoly_fs/1.812158!/file/Sheffield_Solutions_Clear_Blue_Water_Full_Report.pdf
8 'Vulnerable children and social care in England: A review of the evidence', Whitney Crenna-Jennings, Education Policy Institute, April 2018; https://epi.org.uk/wp-content/uploads/2018/05/Vulnerable-children-and-social-care-in-England_EPI_.pdf
9 'Pressure on children's social care', Department for Education, National

Audit Office, 23 January 2019; https://www.nao.org.uk/report/pressures-on-childrens-social-care/

10 Sir Martin Narey was interviewed in the author's research for Tortoise; https://www.tortoisemedia.com

11 'The Science of Neglect: The Persistent Absence of Responsive Care Disrupts the Developing Brain: Working Paper 12', National Scientific Council on the Developing Child (2012), Harvard University; https://46y5eh11fhgw3ve3ytpwxt9r-wpengine.netdna-ssl.com/wp-content/uploads/2012/05/The-Science-of-Neglect-The-Persistent-Absence-of-Responsive-Care-Disrupts-the-Developing-Brain.pdf

12 Quoted in *Our Kids: The American Dream in Crisis*, Robert D. Putnam (Simon and Schuster: 2015)

13 'Decision-making within a child's timeframe: An overview of current research evidence for family justice professionals concerning child development and the impact of maltreatment', Working Paper 16, Second Edition, Rebecca Brown and Harriet Ward, Childhood Wellbeing Research Centre, Institute of Education, Loughborough University and Kent University, February 2013; https://assets.publishing.service.gov.uk/government/uploads/system/uploads/attachment_data/file/200471/Decision-making_within_a_child_s_timeframe.pdf

14 'Re X (A child: care order) [2017] EWFC B8', 3 October 2017, Casemine; https://www.casemine.com/judgement/uk/5b516dad2c94e010ef2bae7f

15 'Assessing Parental Capacity to Change when Children are on the Edge of Care: an overview of current research evidence', Research report, June 2014, Harriet Ward, Rebecca Brown and Georgia Hyde-Dryden, Centre for Child and Family Research, Loughborough University, Department for Education; https://assets.publishing.service.gov.uk/government/uploads/system/uploads/attachment_data/file/330332/RR369_Assessing_parental_capacity_to_change_Final.pdf

Alice's story: 'It's a battle to stay in control'

1 Alice and Jemima are both pseudonyms to allow Alice to speak freely and to protect Jemima's identity.

2 'Pressure on children's social care', Department for Education, National Audit Office, 23 January 2019; https://www.nao.org.uk/wp-content/uploads/2019/01/Pressures-on-Childrens-Social-Care.pdf

3 'Care proceedings in England: The case for clear blue water', Isabelle Trowler; https://www.sheffield.ac.uk/polopoly_fs/1.808960!/file/Clear_Blue_Water_Policy_Briefing.pdf

4 'Pressures on children's social care', Department for Education; https://www.nao.org.uk/wp-content/uploads/2019/01/Pressures-on-Childrens-Social-Care.pdf

5 'Serious Case Review: "Child A", March 2009', Haringey Local Safeguarding Children Board, Department for Education, 26 October

2010; https://assets.publishing.service.gov.uk/government/uploads/
system/uploads/attachment_data/file/595135/second_serious_case_
overview_report_relating_to_peter_connelly_dated_march_2009.pdf

6 'A short life of misery and pain', John Murphy, *BBC News at Six*, 11
November 2008; http://news.bbc.co.uk/1/hi/uk/7708398.stm

7 Sharon Shoesmith and Ed Balls were both interviewed in the author's
research for Tortoise; https://www.tortoisemedia.com

8 'Child Welfare Inequalities in a Time of Rising Numbers of Children
Entering Out of Home Care', Martin Elliott, *The British Journal of Social
Work*, Volume 50, Issue 2, March 2020, pp. 581–597; https://academic.oup.
com/bjsw/article/50/2/581/5681458?searchresult=1

9 'UK Social workers: Working Conditions and Wellbeing', Dr Jermaine
M. Ravalier, Bath Spa University; https://www.basw.co.uk/system/files/
resources/basw_42443-3_1.pdf

10 Eileen Munro was interviewed in the author's research for Tortoise;
https://www.tortoisemedia.com

11 'Measuring burnout among UK social workers: A Community Care
Study', Dr Paula McFadden, Queen's University Belfast; https://www.
qub.ac.uk/sites/media/Media,514081,en.pdf

12 'Signs of Safety, What Works for Children's Social Care', Sheehan,
L., O'Donnell, C., Brand, S. L., Forrester, D., Addiss, S., El-Banna, A.,
Kemp, A., Nurmatov, U, 2018; https://whatworks-csc.org.uk/evidence/
evidence-store/intervention/signs-of-safety/

13 'Care proceedings in England: The case for clear blue water', Isabelle
Trowler; https://www.sheffield.ac.uk/polopoly_fs/1.808960!/file/Clear_
Blue_Water_Policy_Briefing.pdf

Judge Wildblood's story: 'We've got to do something'

1 'Recommendations to achieve best practice in the child protection and
family justice systems: Interim Report', Public Law Working Group, 2019,
https://www.judiciary.uk/wp-content/uploads/2019/07/Public-Law-
Working-Group-Child-Protection-and-Family-Justice-2019-1.pdf

2 'Adoption should be the last port of call – even in the storm of local
authority funding', Louise Tickle, *Guardian*, 25 September 2014;
https://www.theguardian.com/social-care-network/2014/sep/25/
adoption-last-resort-local-authority

3 Munby is a supporter of greater transparency in the family courts, a
cause taken up by his successor as President of the Family Division,
Sir Andrew McFarlane, who announced reforms to improve
transparency in October 2021, https://www.judiciary.uk/publications/
transparency-in-the-family-courts-report/

Francesca's story: 'It's always the ones you don't suspect'

1   Francesca, Jacob and Rufus are pseudonyms and other details have been changed to protect their identities.

2   'Children looked after in England including adoption: 2018 to 2019', Department for Education, National Statistics, 5 December 2019; https://www.gov.uk/government/statistics/children-looked-after-in-england-including-adoption-2018-to-2019

3   'The Child Welfare Inequalities Project: Final Report – Executive Summary', Paul Bywaters and the Child Welfare Inequalities Project Team, July 2020, Nuffield Foundation; https://research.hud.ac.uk/media/assets/document/research/cacyfr/CWIP-Executive-Summary-Final-V3.pdf

4   'Huge survey reveals seven social classes in UK', 3 April 2013, BBC; https://www.bbc.co.uk/news/uk-22007058

5   'Intimate personal violence and partner abuse', Office for National Statistics, 11 February 2016; https://www.ons.gov.uk/peoplepopulationandcommunity/crimeandjustice/compendium/focusonviolentcrimeandsexualoffences/yearendingmarch2015/chapter4intimatepersonalviolenceandpartnerabuse

6   'The Child Welfare Inequalities Project: Final Report – Executive Summary', Paul Bywaters and the Child Welfare Inequalities Project Team; https://research.hud.ac.uk/media/assets/document/research/cacyfr/CWIP-Executive-Summary-Final-V3.pdf

7   *Love, Money, and Parenting: How Economics Explains the Way We Raise Our Kids*, Matthias Doepke and Fabrizio Zilibotti (Princeton University Press: 2019)

8   '"Good enough" parenting is good enough, study finds', Lehigh University, *Science Daily*, 8 May 2019; https://www.sciencedaily.com/releases/2019/05/190508134511.htm

Daniel's story: 'Dad is not in the picture'

1   Daniel is a pseudonym used to protect his and his child's anonymity.

2   'Manufacturing ghost fathers: The paradox of father presence and absence in child welfare', Leslie Brown, Marilyn Callahan, Susan Strega, Christopher Walmsley, 7 January 2009; https://www.researchgate.net/publication/229938320_Manufacturing_ghost_fathers_The_paradox_of_father_presence_and_absence_in_child_welfare

3   'A Systematic Review of Research on Social Work Practice with Single Fathers', Simon Haworth, pp. 329–347, 1 March 2019; https://www.tandfonline.com/doi/abs/10.1080/09503153.2019.1575955

Kim's story: 'You don't know what you're sending them home to'

1 'Covid-19 and the family justice system', Nuffield Family Justice
Observatory, 2021, Nuffield Foundation; https://www.nuffieldfjo.org.uk/
coronavirus-family-justice-system/family-courts

Lucy's story: 'The whole thing gets really toxic'

1 Lucy's work with her clients is confidential but this is a typical scenario
based on real events; Mia is a pseudonym.
2 Ian Josephs was interviewed in the author's research for Tortoise; https://
www.tortoisemedia.com
3 'From cradle to court: The troubling surge in English children
being taken from their parents', Luca D'Urbino, *Economist*, 24
March 2018; https://www.economist.com/britain/2018/03/22/
the-troubling-surge-in-english-children-being-taken-from-their-parents
4 British and Irish Legal Information Institute, https://www.bailii.org

Gabrielle's story: 'We could have done it – with support'

1 All names in this chapter are pseudonyms in order to explore their
experiences in detail while providing the vulnerable adults and children
anonymity.
2 'Section 20 Children Act 1989: Consent, Not Coercion – Issue or be
Damned', Jacqui Gilliatt and Amy Slingo, 2015 archive, *Family Law Week*;
https://www.familylawweek.co.uk/site.aspx?i=ed151539
3 'The Child Welfare Inequalities Project: Final Report – Executive
Summary', Paul Bywaters and the Child Welfare Inequalities Project
Team; https://research.hud.ac.uk/media/assets/document/research/
cacyfr/CWIP-Executive-Summary-Final-V3.pdf
4 'Paradoxical evidence on ethnic inequities in child welfare: Towards
a research agenda', Paul Bywaters, Jonathan Scourfield, Calum Webb,
Kate Morris, Brid Featherstone, Geraldine Brady, Chantel Jones, Tim
Sparks, *Children and Youth Services Review*, January 2019, Volume 96,
pp. 145–154; https://www.sciencedirect.com/sdfe/pdf/download/
eid/1-s2.0-S019074091830728X/first-page-pdf
5 'Racism in the foster care system is depriving kids of support – and I've
seen it up close', Shadim Hussain, *Independent*, 23 January 2020; https://
www.independent.co.uk/voices/foster-care-racism-adoption-ethnicity-
bame-sandeep-reena-mander-a9298391.html
6 'Parents with learning disabilities', Ailsa Stewart and Gillian MacIntyre,
Iriss, 25 April 2017; https://www.iriss.org.uk/resources/insights/
parents-learning-disabilities
7 'Findings from a court study of care proceedings involving parents
with intellectual disabilities', Tim Booth and Wendy Booth, *Journal
of Policy and Practice in Intellectual Disabilities*, September 2004,

Volume 1, Issue 3–4, pp. 179–181; https://onlinelibrary.wiley.com/doi/10.1111/j.1741-1130.2004.04032.x

8　'A qualitative exploration of the views and experiences of family court magistrates making decisions in care proceedings involving parents with learning disabilities', Laura Kollinsky, Laura M. Simonds and Julie Nixon, *British Journal of Learning Disabilities*, June 2013, Volume 41, Issue 2, pp. 86–93; https://onlinelibrary.wiley.com/doi/10.1111/j.1468-3156.2012.00726.x

9　'Temporal Discrimination and Parents with Learning Difficulties in the Child Protection System', Tim Booth, David McConnell and Wendy Booth, *The British Journal of Social Work*, September 2006, Volume 36, Issue 6, pp. 997–1015; https://doi.org/10.1093/bjsw/bch401

10　'Good practice guidance on working with parents with learning difficulties', Working Together with Parents Network (WTPN) update of the DoH/DfES, University of Bristol; http://www.bristol.ac.uk/media-library/sites/sps/documents/wtpn/2016%20WTPN%20UPDATE%20OF%20THE%20GPG%20-%20finalised%20with%20cover.pdf

11　'Councils withholding advocacy from parents with learning disabilities in child protection process', Alice Blackwell, *Children*, 10 December 2020; https://www.communitycare.co.uk/2020/12/10/councils-withholding-advocacy-support-parents-learning-disabilities-involved-child-protection-process/

12　'Statistics: looked-after children: Statistics on children under local authority care at national and local authority level', Department for Education, 2019; https://www.gov.uk/government/collections/statistics-looked-after-children

13　'Policies on bruises in premobile children: Why we need improved standards for policymaking', Andy Bilson, *Child and Family Social Work*, November 2018, Volume 23, Issue 4, pp. 676–683; https://onlinelibrary.wiley.com/doi/abs/10.1111/cfs.12463

Angela's story: 'We are blaming mums who don't have anything'

1　'Children looked after in England (including adoption), year ending 31 March 2019', 5 December 2019, Department for Education, National Statistics; https://assets.publishing.service.gov.uk/government/uploads/system/uploads/attachment_data/file/850306/Children_looked_after_in_England_2019_Text.pdf

2　'Kent County Council v R&M', England and Wales Family Court Decisions; https://www.bailii.org/cgi-bin/format.cgi?doc=/ew/cases/EWFC/OJ/2016/B86.html&query=(Toxic)+AND+(trio)

3　'Domestic abuse in England and Wales: year ending March 2018', Office for National Statistics; https://www.ons.gov.uk/peoplepopulationandcommunity/crimeandjustice/bulletins/domesticabuseinenglandandwales/yearendingmarch2018#:~:text=still%20under%20development.-,An%20

estimated%202.0%20million%20adults%20aged%2016%20to%2059%20
years,7.9%25%20compared%20with%204.2%25)

4 'Coronavirus: Domestic abuse an "epidemic beneath a pandemic"',
June Kelly, *BBC News*, 23 March 2021; https://www.bbc.co.uk/news/
uk-56491643

5 'Statistics: looked-after children: Statistics on children under local
authority care at national and local authority level', Department
for Education, 2019; https://www.gov.uk/government/collections/
statistics-looked-after-children

6 'Britain's Everyday Drug Problem', Paul Caruana Galizia and Tom
Goulding, Tortoise Media, 14 January 2019; https://www.tortoisemedia.
com/2019/01/14/britains-everyday-drug-problem/

7 'Double Dealing', Louise Tickle, Tortoise Media, 19 December 2019;
https://members.tortoisemedia.com/2019/12/19/domestic-violence/
content.html?sig=n7KRrTZ5Mqq5wMKht-SguoQV_l7dn5wvEETE48-
DXi8&utm_source=Twitter&utm_medium=Social&utm_
campaign=18Dec2019&utm_content=double_dealing

8 'Left behind: Can anyone save the towns the economy forgot?', Sarah
O'Connor, *Financial Times*, 16 November 2017; https://www.ft.com/
blackpool

9 'New learning from serious case reviews: a two year report for 2009–2011',
Marian Brandon, Peter Sidebotham, Sue Bailey, Pippa Belderson, Carol
Hawley, Catherine Ellis & Matthew Megson, Centre for Research on the
Child and Family in the School of Social Work and Psychology, University
of East Anglia Health Sciences Research Institute, Warwick Medical
School, University of Warwick, Department for Education; https://
assets.publishing.service.gov.uk/government/uploads/system/uploads/
attachment_data/file/184053/DFE-RR226_Report.pdf

10 'Action on Loneliness: You can join us to help put a stop to loneliness',
British Red Cross; https://www.redcross.org.uk/about-us/what-we-do/
action-on-loneliness#Red%20Cross%20research%20into%20loneliness

11 'Bowling Alone: America's Declining Social Capital', Robert D. Putnam,
interview in *Journal of Democracy*, January 1995, 6:1, pp. 65–78; https://web.
archive.org/web/20100201190211/http://xroads.virginia.edu/~hyper/
DETOC/assoc/bowling.html

12 'The quality of group childcare settings used by 3–4 year old children
in Sure Start Local Programme areas and the relationship with child
outcomes', Edward Melhuish, Jay Belsky, Kristen MacPherson, Andrew
Cullis, Institute for the Study of Children, Families & Social Issues,
Birkbeck, University of London, Department for Education; https://
assets.publishing.service.gov.uk/government/uploads/system/uploads/
attachment_data/file/182027/DFE-RR068.pdf

My story: 'What is good enough parenting?'

1 'Working together to safeguard children: Statutory guidance on inter-agency working to safeguard and promote the welfare of children', Department for Education; https://www.gov.uk/government/publications/working-together-to-safeguard-children--2

2 'Re A (A Child) [2015] EWFC 11: The President reminds practitioners of the importance of three fundamental principles within s.31 applications', 2015 archive, *Family Law Week*; https://www.familylawweek.co.uk/site.aspx?i=ed143260

3 Ibid

Nancy's story: 'As normal as it can be'

1 Nancy and Sandra are pseudonyms used to protect the foster child's identity.

2 'Homeless young people: Over 30% of homeless people have a care background and too many children find themselves homeless and unsupported by children's services', Coram; https://www.coram.org.uk/supporting-young-people/our-supported-housing

3 'Almost a quarter of girls in care become teen mothers', Judith Burns, *BBC News*, 19 January 2015; https://www.bbc.co.uk/news/education-30882105

4 'Offending behaviour programmes and interventions: Offending behaviour programmes and interventions currently available for offenders in England and Wales', Ministry of Justice and Her Majesty's Prison and Probation Service, 23 November 2018; https://www.gov.uk/guidance/offending-behaviour-programmes-and-interventions

5 'Care leavers transition to adulthood', Department for Education, 17 July 2015, National Audit Office; https://www.nao.org.uk/wp-content/uploads/2015/07/Care-leavers-transition-to-adulthood.pdf

6 'Statistics: looked-after children: Statistics on children under local authority care at national and local authority level', Department for Education Statistics; https://www.gov.uk/government/collections/statistics-looked-after-children

7 Ibid

8 'The fostering system in England: Evidence review', Mary Baginsky, Sarah Gorin and Claire Sands, King's College London and Quest Research and Evaluation Ltd, Department for Education, July 2017; https://assets.publishing.service.gov.uk/government/uploads/system/uploads/attachment_data/file/629384/Evidence_review_-_Executive_summary.pdf

9 'Bright Spots Programme', Coram Voice; https://coramvoice.org.uk/for-professionals/bright-spots-2/

10 'Mental health and well-being of looked-after children: Fourth Report of Session 2015–16', House of Commons Education Committee, 20

April 2016; https://publications.parliament.uk/pa/cm201516/cmselect/
cmeduc/481/481.pdf

11 'The Educational Progress of Looked After Children in England:
    Linking Care and Educational Data', Judy Sebba, David Berridge,
    Nikki Luke, John Fletcher, Karen Bell, Steve Strand, Sally Thomas,
    Ian Sinclair, Aoife O'Higgins, University of Oxford, University
    of Bristol and Nuffield Foundation; https://ora.ox.ac.uk/objects/
    uuid:49b64928-4808-4898-911c-30e8981b2ffb/download_file?safe_
    filename=EducationalProgressLookedAfterChildrenOverviewReport_
    Nov2015.pdf&file_format=application%2Fpdf&type_of_work=Report

12 Lemn Sissay was speaking during a public ThinkIn for Tortoise; https://
    www.tortoisemedia.com

13 *So this is permanence: Joy Division lyrics and notebooks*, Ian Curtis (Faber and
    Faber: 2014)

    Emma and Sarah's story: 'There are no fairy-tale endings'

1   All the names of this family have been changed to protect the children's
    anonymity.

2   'Are we unusual in permitting non-consensual adoption?',
    Full Fact, 2 November 2015; https://fullfact.org/law/
    are-we-unusual-permitting-non-consensual-adoption/

3   'European Approaches to Adoption Without Parental Consent, Policy
    Department, Citizens' Rights and Constitutional Affairs, European
    Parliament; https://www.europarl.europa.eu/RegData/etudes/
    STUD/2015/519236/IPOL_STU(2015)519236_EN.pdf#page=29

4   'Children in care: a personal view from Andrew Adonis', Institute For
    Government, 19 April 2011; https://www.instituteforgovernment.org.uk/
    news/latest/children-care-personal-view-andrew-adonis

5   'An action plan for adoption: Tackling Delay', Department for Education,
    2011; https://assets.publishing.service.gov.uk/government/uploads/
    system/uploads/attachment_data/file/180250/action_plan_for_adoption.
    pdf

6   'Saved by the love of strangers: Michael Gove describes how adoption
    transformed his life', Michael Gove, *Daily Mail*, 5 November 2011; https://
    www.dailymail.co.uk/news/article-2057850/Michael-Gove-describes-
    adoption-transformed-life.html

7   'Re B-S (Children) [2013] EWCA Civ 1146', 2013 archive, *Family Law Week*;
    https://www.familylawweek.co.uk/site.aspx?i=ed117048

8   'The long-term consequences of domestic infant adoption',
    Barbara Maughan, Alan Rushton, Margaret Grant, Nuffield
    Foundation; https://www.nuffieldfoundation.org/project/
    the-long-term-consequences-of-domestic-infant-adoption

9   'A systematic review of the school performance and behavioural and
    emotional adjustments of children adopted from care', Andrew Brown,

Cerith S. Waters and Katherine H. Shelton, *Adoption and Fostering*, 24 November 2017, Volume 41, Issue 4; https://journals.sagepub.com/doi/abs/10.1177/0308575917731064

10 'Adverse childhood experiences of children adopted from care: The importance of adoptive parental warmth for future child adjustment', Rebecca E. Anthony, Amy L. Paine, Katherine H. Shelton, *International Journal of Environmental Research and Public Health*, 22 June 2019, Volume 16, Issue 12 , 2212; https://www.ncbi.nlm.nih.gov/pmc/articles/PMC6617038/

11 'Adoption breakdown: "No support" for violent children', *BBC News*, 28 October 2019; https://www.bbc.co.uk/news/uk-england-50083910

12 Ibid

'To love is to act'

1 'Sector-led Review of the "care crisis" launches today', Nuffield Foundation, 13 June 2018; https://www.nuffieldfoundation.org/news/sector-led-review-of-the-care-crisis-launches-today

2 'Leeds Family Valued Programme: Report on the Family Valued programme, which looked to improve practice across children's services and the social work service', Department for Education, 6 July 2017; https://www.gov.uk/government/publications/leeds-family-valued-programme

3 FGCs and Contextual Safeguarding briefing, https://frg.org.uk/news-blogs-and-vlogs/news/family-group-conferences-and-contextual-safeguarding-briefing/

4 The interviews in the US were made during the author's research for Tortoise.

5 This is in 2019, Donald Trump is the US president.